CONTENTS

P9-DCZ-617

www.primagames.com

INTRODUCTION

Thank you for purchasing Prima's Official Game Guide to *Dead Rising 2*. We've braved countless horrors to bring you the most comprehensive *DR2* guide imaginable. Owning this tome means you'll never have to worry about becoming stuck or lost, or missing out on a single second of awesomeness as you mercilessly slaughter the undead denizens of Fortune City.

HOW TO USE THIS BOOK

The information in this guide is presented in several chapters.

BRAIN FOOD

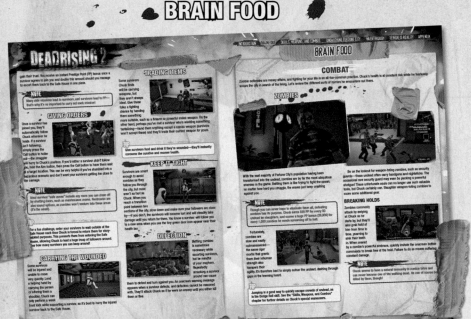

Satisfy your craving for knowledge in the "Brain Food" chapter, where we cover all vital aspects of gameplay. Tips abound in this informative chapter, so be sure to fully digest your Brain Food.

SKILLS, WEAPONS, AND COMBOS

Chuck unlocks a host of helpful skills as he levels up, and this chapter discloses all of these mighty moves. In addition, everything that Chuck can pick up and wield as a weapon is listed here, with complete damage, durability, and ammo values, along with informative descriptions of each weapon's unique function. A complete list of combo weapons and cards rounds it all off, giving you all the knowledge you need to cause unimaginable amounts of mayhem.

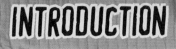

INTRODUCTION

UNEARTHING FORTUNE CITY

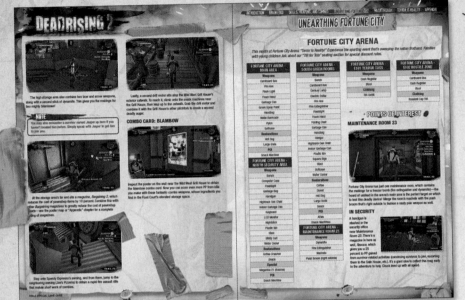

There's much more to Fortune City than meets the eye. Take an in-depth tour of "America's Playground" by perusing this informative chapter, where we list all of the weapons, clothing, food items, and various points of interest found in each section of the city.

WALKTHROUGH

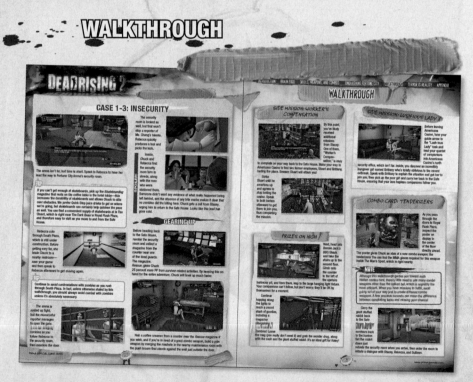

Chuck faces countless horrors on his path to uncovering the secret behind the Fortune City outbreak. Give him every advantage by following our step-by-step walkthrough, which guides you toward completing every vital Case File and optional side mission in one hurried yet productive run through the game.

"TERROR IS REALITY"

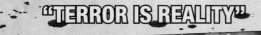

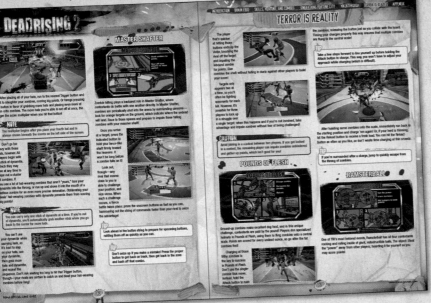

It's the gameshow that's sweeping the nation— it's "Terror Is Reality"! Flip to this chapter to discover a wealth of invaluable tips that will have you slaughtering the online competition in *DR2*'s hilariously brutal multiplayer mode.

APPENDIX

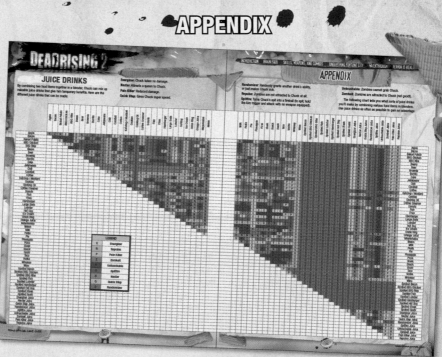

When fast answers are all you're after, flip to these final tables. Here we hand out quick-reference solutions and availability time frames for every Case File and side mission—there's no need to wade through that walkthrough. A complete list of Achievements and Trophies is also provided, with insightful tips to ensure you attain each one. The Appendix concludes with a complete location listing for every item in the game, along with a valuable juice drink chart that shows how to mix up every beneficial beverage blend.

BRAIN FOOD

Satisfy your insatiable craving for knowledge here, in the Brain Food chapter. This portion of the guide regurgitates all major aspects of gameplay in gratuitous detail, giving you the insight you need to survive and thrive in one of the most horrific zombie outbreaks in American history. Topics include combat, methods of saving time, ways to make money, the importance of completing missions, and much more.

TIME TO KILL

Time is always against you in *Dead Rising 2*. The military is set to arrive in just a handful of days, and anyone who is not present within the confines of the Safe House will be lost at that time—including Chuck, the overburdened hero. The clock is always ticking, forcing you to plan your actions carefully if you wish to rescue all of the city's stranded survivors.

These are the only instances in which time does not pass:

- During cinematics.
- While you view the map.
- While you view the Pause menu and its submenus.

NOTE

For conversion enthusiasts, one minute of game time passes every four seconds.

All missions have a certain "shelf life" in *DR2*—a brief window during which they can be completed. The amount of time remaining in any given mission is denoted by a white bar that runs beneath the mission's title. As time dwindles away, the bar begins to shrink, eventually becoming yellow and then red when it's almost gone. Completing missions is the primary way to level Chuck up, so it's important to complete as many as possible. Follow our walkthrough to discover the ideal mission path through the game.

First Floor

MESSAGES
Find Katey Zombrex

CASE 1-2: Alive on Location

Lost...

GOAL: Help the trigger happy lady
DESTINATION: Platinum Strip
A young woman is armed and taking out
some zombies near the Arena entrance.

One Man's Trash

B BACK | GUIDE ARROW | FLOOR | MESSAGES

Missions are listed in order of priority at the map screen's message list. Even if all timer bars are full, tasks at the top of the list will have less time remaining than those farther down.

When a mission's time is running out, its title and timer bar appear on the upper-right side of the game screen to alert you. The exceptions are

Case Files; these mandatory missions always appear at the top of the message list and are always present on the game screen while playing.

TIME-SAVERS

Running around Fortune City gets you where you're going, but it isn't the fastest way to travel. With time being a constant factor, you must find ways to reduce your travel time. There are several ways to do so.

PUSHABLE OBJECTS

Anything Chuck can push makes him move faster than normal. This includes wheelchairs, dollies, lawn mowers, utility carts, and more. Stand behind such

an object to receive the "push" command option. Chuck plows right through zombies while pushing objects!

TIP

Pushable objects are often found near the transition points between different sections of Fortune City. Exploit them whenever it's convenient to do so!

If a pushable object has been knocked over, pick it up and then set it down as if you were dropping the object to set it upright.

SKATEBOARDS

Skateboards help Chuck move quickly and they can be conveniently stored in his inventory for use at any time. Find skateboards at the In the Closet store, located in

Royal Flush Plaza. You'll also find skateboards in sporting goods shops, such as Palisades Mall's KokoNutz Sports Town.

CAUTION

Skateboards are extremely fragile and will shatter after just a few collisions with zombies or objects. Use them wisely and nab the *Skateboarding* magazine from the Fortune City Hotel's lobby area to improve their durability.

VEHICLES

Vehicles such as cars, motorbikes, and 4x4s are among the fastest methods of travel. Chuck can drive any 4x4 he finds, but he needs to locate special keys to start up

most cars and bikes. The following table lists where you'll find them.

VEHICLE KEY LOCATIONS		
Key	**Description**	**Location**
Bike Key	Starts Chuck's motorbike.	Encounter Leon (psychopath) during "Meet the Contestants" side mission.
Sports Car Key	Starts the sports car located at the Royal Flush Plaza.	Purchase from Royal Flush Plaza's second-floor pawnshop for $500,000.
Chopper Key	Starts the chopper motorcycle located at the Yucatan Casino.	Purchase from Palisades Mall's second-floor pawnshop for $1,000,000.
SUV Key	Starts the SUV located at the Silver Strip's Shamrock Casino.	Purchase from the Silver Strip's pawnshop for $2,000,000.

BRAIN FOOD

> **NOTE**
>
> All vehicles are labeled on the poster map to help you quickly find a ride.

SHORTCUTS

Shortcuts exist in Fortune City as well, but these welcome time-savers can't be accessed until you unlock them. Some shortcuts are better than others; Linette's is one of the best. Here's a list of every shortcut in the city:

Shortcut 1: Linette's Passage—Complete the "Wilted Flower" and subsequent "Linette's Passage" side missions to unlock this most useful shortcut, which allows you to move from the Royal Flush Plaza's first-floor restroom to Palisades Mall's second-floor clothing shop, "Brand New U."

Shortcut 2: Bank Job—After completing Case 3-2, a large hole remains in the wall of the Atlantica Casino where the mercenaries' getaway van was parked. You may exploit this opening to travel between the Atlantica Casino and Fortune Park a bit faster than normal.

Shortcut 3: Naughty Hallway—This is the only shortcut that's available from the start of the adventure. Explore the back room of the Silver Strip's Hot Excitorama shop to locate a passage that leads to Palisades Mall's first floor.

Shortcut 4: Car Tunnel—This shortcut becomes available after Case 6-1. Motor to the Silver Strip's north alley to access the Underground tunnels through the now-opened gate.

THE QUICK STEP

Increase Chuck's normal pace by consuming Quick Steps—special juice drinks concocted by using blenders. These handy drinks restore six units of Chuck's health and greatly increase his movement speed for about 30 seconds. Chuck can carry several Quick Steps, so these are ideal for fast travel.

The blender at Americana Casino's central bar, Shots & Awe, is the one that's closest to the Safe House. Get in the habit of mixing up Quick Steps here by blending two bottles of wine together. Conveniently, there's an endless supply of wine at the bar.

After you unlock Linette's shortcut, you can easily create Quick Steps at Palisades Mall's grotto bar, which is sometimes more convenient. Swipe coffees and coffee creamers from The Dark Bean on your way to the Royal Flush Plaza's restroom, bringing these beverages to the grotto bar's blender to mix up Quick Steps after you emerge from the passage.

> **NOTE**
>
> Blenders allow you to create all sorts of beneficial juice drinks. See the "Appendix" chapter for a full listing.

ZOMBREX

Miracle drug Zombrex has made it possible for the wealthy to avoid the horrors of zombification. Even if a person has been infected by a zombie, they can prevent themselves from "turning" by taking a prescribed dose of Zombrex once every 24 hours. Chuck's loving daughter, Katey, must be given a shot of Zombrex every day between 7:00 AM and 8:00 AM. Failure means a tragic end to Chuck's tale.

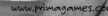

Zombrex is priceless to those in need, and is therefore extremely expensive and hard to come by. Chuck can acquire Zombrex by completing certain tasks or by finding hidden stashes of the drug. In a pinch, Zombrex can be purchased at a pawnshop for a tidy sum. When the clock nears 7:00 AM, drop everything and start looking for Katey's medicine.

FREE ZOMBREX

Location	How to Get
Roy's Mart (Royal Flush Plaza)	Acquired during the normal progression of the story.
Americana Casino	Go to the second floor of Bennie Jack's BBQ Shack, then leap along the casino's light fixtures.
Slot Ranch Casino	Climb onto the crates behind the north stage, then leap to the Zombrex.
Yucatan Casino	Climb to the top of the Lucky Marble minigame, then leap to the Zombrex.
Underground	Search the rise in the tunnel near Maintenance Room 32.

NOTE

Zombrex can also be obtained for no charge by completing the "Code Blue," "Mail Order Zombrex," "Hunger Pains," and "Demand and Supply" side missions. See the walkthrough for details.

GIFTS FOR KATEY

Taking shots of Zombrex every day is such a bummer. Bring a smile to little Katey's face by giving her special gifts as well! Each of the following gifts will please the sweet girl—and also net Chuck some valuable PP.

KATEY'S GIFTS

Gift	Location
Giant stuffed elephant	Stylin' Toddlers on Royal Flush Plaza's first floor.
Robot bear	Astonishing Illusions on Royal Flush Plaza's first floor.
Bag of marbles	Ye Olde Toybox on Royal Flush Plaza's first floor.
Beach ball	Ye Olde Toybox on Royal Flush Plaza's first floor.
Stick Pony	Ye Olde Toybox on Royal Flush Plaza's first floor.
Water gun	The watery areas of Fortune Park; also found in Moe's Maginations on the Platinum Strip.
Giant stuffed bull	Children's Castle on Royal Flush Plaza's second floor.
Giant stuffed donkey	Children's Castle on Royal Flush Plaza's second floor.
Giant stuffed rabbit	The hidden upper platforms of Americana Casino's and Royal Flush Plaza's second floors; also found in Moe's Maginations on the Platinum Strip.
Snowflake	Tame this ferocious tiger by feeding her three steaks after dispatching her master, Ted, at Yucatan Casino.
Funny painting	Can only be obtained at The Cleroux Collection in Palisades Mall during the "Art Appreciation" side mission. Costs $3,000.

NOTE

If you're not certain which gifts you've given to Katey, simply look around the Safe House's security room to find them all on display.

PAWNSHOPS

Wily looters have capitalized on the Fortune City tragedy by setting up pawnshops in various locations around the quarantine zone. All pawnshops are shown on your in-game map; complete the "One Man's Trash" side mission to gain access to them, then stop by and browse the special items each one offers. Though everything's sold at an absurd markup, pawnshops are a reliable source of obtaining Zombrex for little Katey. The first dose will cost you $25,000, and the price increases by that same amount for each subsequent purchase.

BRAIN FOOD

MAKING MONEY

As you might expect, earning cash isn't very difficult at Fortune City. Rarely will Chuck find himself in desperate need of dollars, but with so many expensive items for sale at pawnshops, it pays to know how to stockpile some serious scratch.

Casinos are a good start. Here you'll find countless slot machines, which Chuck can bash apart for bucks. Casinos also host some of the more profitable minigames; see the poster map for their locations, and check the "Unearthing Fortune City" chapter for details on every game.

ATMs are excellent money sources as well. Smash one to have it cough up $2,500—not too shabby, but you can withdraw even more with the use of a hacker. Build one of these combo weapons by merging a flashlight with a computer case, and carry it with you so you may zap any ATMs you see to score $10,000 from them instead.

TIP

Build hackers easily by visiting Maintenance Room 8 on Palisades Mall's first floor. You can find the necessary components there.

Karma equals cash in Fortune City, and completing certain side missions can make Chuck rich beyond his wildest dreams. Earn piles of moola by completing the following side missions, especially "High Rollers," which has Chuck walking away from the poker table with a cool million!

- Janus Survivor
- Secret of Charlie's Gold
- High Rollers
- Bank Run
- Bent Wood

NOTE

Slaughtering the competition in *Dead Rising 2*'s white-knuckle multiplayer mode, Terror Is Reality, is another excellent way to earn lots of cash that carries over into the single-player/co-op adventure. See the "Terror Is Reality" chapter of this guide for all the gory details.

SURVIVORS

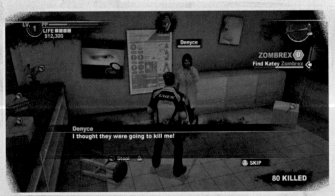

Not everyone has perished in Fortune City's terrible outbreak. Dozens of living, breathing survivors are still out there, in desperate need of help. These poor souls won't last long unless Chuck manages to find and rescue them, fearlessly escorting them back to the Safe House to ensure their survival. Remember: Anyone not secured within the Safe House by the time the military arrives will be lost!

Once you've located a survivor, speak with them to hear their story. You may need to beat back some zombies as you listen to their tale. Some survivors will be eager to join you; others will require you to complete a certain task for them to

www.primagames.com

gain their trust. You receive an instant Prestige Point (PP) bonus once a survivor agrees to join you and double this amount should you manage to escort them back to the Safe House in one piece.

> **NOTE**
>
> Many side missions lead to survivors, and survivors lead to PP—that's why it's so important to carry out each mission!

GIVING ORDERS

Once a survivor has joined you, they'll automatically follow Chuck wherever he leads. If a survivor isn't following, simply press the Call button to holler out—the straggler will hurry to Chuck's position. If you'd rather a survivor *didn't* follow you, hold the Aim button, then press the Call button to have them wait at a target location. This can be very helpful if you've stumbled into a hazardous scenario and don't want your survivors getting too close to the carnage.

> **NOTE**
>
> Ideal survivor "safe zones" include any room you can close off by shutting doors, such as maintenance rooms. Restrooms are also sound options, as zombies won't venture into these areas (it's the smell).

> **TIP**
>
> For a fun challenge, order your survivors to wait outside of the Safe House each time Chuck is forced to return there for story-related purposes. This prevents them from entering the Safe House, allowing Chuck to lead a huge troop of followers around. See how many survivors you can keep around!

CARRYING THE WOUNDED

Some survivors will be injured and unable to move very quickly. Lend a helping hand by carrying the person or offering them a shoulder. Chuck can only perform a weak front kick while supporting a survivor, so it's best to hurry the injured survivor back to the Safe House.

TRADING ITEMS

Some survivors Chuck finds will be carrying weapons, but they aren't always ideal. Give these folks a fighting chance by handing them something more suitable, such as a firearm or powerful melee weapon. On the other hand, perhaps you've met a survivor who's wielding something tantalizing—hand them anything except a combo weapon (survivors won't accept these) and they'll trade their current weapon for yours.

> **TIP**
>
> Give survivors food and drink if they're wounded—they'll instantly consume the curative and recover health.

KEEP IT TIGHT

Survivors are smart enough to avoid zombies as they follow you through the city, but most aren't as fast as Chuck. When you reach a transition point between two sections of the city, slow down and make sure your followers are close by—if you don't, the survivors will become lost and will steadily take damage until you return for them. You know a survivor will follow you to a new area when you see the tiny green door icon appear near their health bar.

DEFECTION

Battling zombies is sometimes necessary while escorting survivors, but be mindful of your mayhem. Repeatedly smacking a survivor around can cause them to defect and turn against you. An onscreen warning message appears when a survivor defects, and defectors cannot be reasoned with. They'll attack Chuck as if he were an enemy until you either kill them or flee.

BRAIN FOOD

COMBAT

Zombie outbreaks are messy affairs, and fighting for your life is an all-too-common practice. Chuck's health is at constant risk while he fearlessly scours the city in search of the living. Let's review the different sorts of horrors he encounters out there.

ZOMBIES

With the vast majority of Fortune City's population having been transformed into the undead, zombies are by far the most ubiquitous enemies in the game. Battling them is like trying to fight the ocean; no matter how hard you struggle, the waves just keep crashing against you.

> **NOTE**
>
> Though you can never hope to eliminate them all, defeating zombies has its purpose. Chuck earns 500 PP for every 50 undead he slaughters, and scores a huge PP bonus (20,000) for every 1,000 zombies he sends screaming off to hell.

Fortunately, zombies are slow and easily outmaneuvered— the same rigor mortis that grants them their inhuman strength also hampers their agility. It's therefore best to simply outrun the undead, dashing through gaps in the teeming hoard.

> **TIP**
>
> Jumping is a good way to quickly escape crowds of undead, as is the Dodge Roll skill. See the "Skills, Weapons, and Combos" chapter for further details on Chuck's special maneuvers.

Be on the lookout for weapon-toting zombies, such as security guards—these undead often carry handguns and nightsticks. The occasional rare security guard may even be packing a powerful shotgun! These unfortunate souls can no longer use such valuable tools, but Chuck certainly can. Slaughter weapon-toting zombies to score some additional gear.

BREAKING HOLDS

Zombies commonly attack by swiping at Chuck as he darts by, but they'll also grab hold of him from time to time, yearning to sink their teeth in. When snared

by a zombie's powerful embrace, quickly imitate the onscreen button commands to break free of the hold. Failure to do so means suffering constant damage.

> **NOTE**
>
> Chuck seems to have a natural immunity to zombie bites and can never become one of the walking dead. He can of course be killed by them, though!

DEADRISING 2

LOOTERS

The dead aren't Chuck's only adversaries in Fortune City. Immoral men are also present in the quarantine zone, seeking to plunder whatever they can get their hands on. Some of these looters will help Chuck by offering to sell him their ill-gotten goods from various pawnshops—others will attack our hero on sight with whatever weaponry they've gotten their greedy little paws on. Looters always travel in groups, but aside from their speed and aggression, they aren't much more challenging than zombies. Each looter you defeat earns Chuck 500 PP.

CAUTION

If a looter manages to cover Chuck's face in spray paint, Chuck will be knocked unconscious by the next hit while blinded, no matter how much health he may have. Our hero will then awake in the nearest restroom, having been relieved of all his belongings—including his clothes and dignity!

MERCENARIES

There's more to the outbreak in Fortune City than meets the eye, and Chuck encounters trained killers at various points throughout the adventure. These hired henchmen travel in squads and wield rapid-fire assault rifles, which they fire in short bursts to conserve ammo. Fortunately, mercenaries aren't very good shots, and Chuck suffers relatively little damage each time he's hit by their gunfire. Limit your exposure and close in fast to batter these villains, earning 1,000 PP for each one you kill.

PSYCHOPATHS

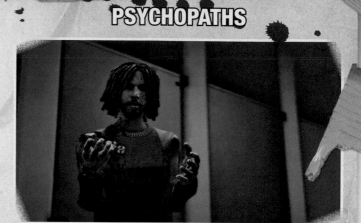

By far the most dangerous adversaries Chuck faces, psychopaths are deranged individuals who have been sent over the edge by the countless horrors of the zombie outbreak. Psychos come in all different varieties, each with their own unique reasons for being totally insane. One thing all psychos share is the ability to bring Chuck's heroics to a swift end, so treat these villains with respect.

Psychos serve as boss enemies in *Dead Rising 2*. Each encounter is unique, and you'd do well to have plenty of potent curatives on hand before taking them on. Of course, you never quite know when or where you'll encounter a psycho (unless you follow our walkthrough, of course), so it's best to keep Chuck loaded with food.

NOTE

Most psycho encounters allow you to flee the immediate area in search of additional weapons or curatives. Always keep this in mind and never feel forced to fight a psycho with only whatever Chuck has on hand.

Defeating psychos is worthwhile because many have taken survivor hostages—rescuing these poor souls equates to PP. The act of killing a psycho nets you significant PP as well, and can also earn you special bonuses, such as hidden combo cards. Follow side missions to seek out psychos and show them how dangerous a motivated sane man can be.

BRAIN FOOD

HEALTH AND DAMAGE

As Chuck confronts looters, psychos, mercenaries, and the legions of undead, he's certain to suffer damage. Chuck's health is measured by a number of yellow squares beneath the PP gauge at the upper left corner. The squares darken as Chuck suffers harm, and it's game over if they all disappear. Prevent this from happening by fleeing to safety when the going gets rough, consuming foods and drinks to restore Chuck's health.

Zombies, looters, and mercenaries all have a small amount of health that isn't visually represented in the game—just keep hitting them until they've had enough. Named characters, such as psychos and survivors, have a green health bar that appears above their name while they're within view—these characters have significantly more health than the aforementioned lot and, like Chuck, their health can be restored through consuming curatives. "(Only one psychopath, Chef Antoine, is able to consume food.)

WEAPONS

With so many hostiles out to get you, it's fortunate that practically everything you see in the environment can be used as a weapon. Chairs, tables, potted plants ... *massagers* ... You name it. All of these can be picked up and wielded against those who would do Chuck harm.

Anything that can be hoisted and used as a tool of mayhem is hallmarked by a tiny orange handgun icon when Chuck steps close. Simply press the Interact button to grab these items, then use the Attack button to swing or fire away. Press the Attack button rapidly to unleash normal attack combos, or press and hold the Attack button to perform a weapon's heavy attack (if applicable).

CAUTION

All weapons have a certain durability and will shatter after prolonged use. Some weapons are sturdier than others, which makes them more valuable.

Sometimes, it's best to keep your distance. To hurl objects at enemies, press and hold the Aim button, followed by the Attack button. Some weapons are deadlier when thrown, such as the long stick, which acts like a javelin.

NOTE

Some weapons, such as cardboard boxes and various trash receptacles, can be thrown to reveal additional items. Toss a cash register or money case to loose wads of bills!

The Aim button also allows you to sight targets when wielding a ranged weapon or firearm. Chuck can continue to move while aiming certain firearms, such as shotguns and handguns—use this to your advantage by remaining mobile while aiming to present a challenging target.

COMBO WEAPONS

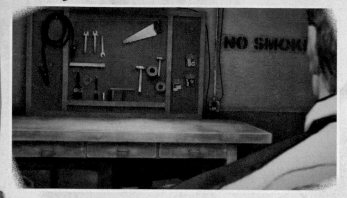

Chuck gains access to special maintenance rooms early in the adventure. Each of these rooms provides Chuck with the basic tools he needs (mostly duct tape) to mesh nearly any two items together, forming mighty combo weapons! Weapons forged in this fashion are usually far more powerful than standard killing tools, and—best of all—they give Chuck bonus amounts of PP when used. Wield combo weapons as often as possible to help Chuck level up much faster.

Once maintenance rooms become accessible, all items that can be combined into combo weapons will sport blue wrench icons when examined. When you see that wrench icon, you know that the item can be combined with another one somehow—experiment and see what sorts of devious devices you can develop!

> ### NOTE
> All maintenance rooms contain items that can be combined into one or more combo weapons. Fiddle with the items inside of maintenance rooms to see what you can build.

COMBO CARDS

After concocting a new combo weapon for the first time, you acquire that combo weapon's scratch card. These cards are stored under the "Combo Cards" section of the Pause menu, allowing you to review them in case you forget what it took to build something. Scratch cards are handy, but they aren't as valuable as combo cards!

As Chuck levels up, he'll regularly receive special combo cards in addition to new skills and stat enhancements. Combo cards are much the same as scratch cards, except that it's possible to receive them *before* combining a new weapon. Therefore, combo cards tell you exactly what is needed to make combo weapons, edging out the guesswork. In addition, owning a combo card means you'll earn even more PP when using the associated combo weapon—scratch cards only give you half!

But wait, there's more! Combo cards also allow you to unleash a combo weapon's heavy attack (if it has one)—you can't use a combo weapon's heavy attack if you only own its scratch card. Heavy attacks are just brutal, and they often give you even more PP than a combo weapon's normal attack. You're just not getting the full effect of combo weapons without those combo cards.

Some combo cards can only be acquired through special means, such as completing certain tasks. Others are scattered about Fortune City and must be discovered. There are 50 combo cards to collect in all, and owning them means Chuck will level up much faster through the use of combo weapons. See the "Skills, Weapons, and Combos" section of the guide for complete details!

> ### NOTE
> The poster map included with this guide reveals the locations of all hidden combo cards that can be found through exploring the city. All maintenance rooms are listed on the poster map as well, along with the items you'll find inside (or right near) each room.

BRAIN FOOD

FOOD AND DRINK

When Chuck's health begins to wane, consuming food and beverages is the way to reanimate him. Like weapons, there's an incredible variety of nourishment that will restore Chuck's health—you'll find food all over the place. Some tasty treats will replenish large amounts of health; others will restore only one or two squares. Check the "Appendix" chapter at the end of this guide to discover the potency of every type of food.

TIP

Life in Fortune City is hazardous in the extreme, so make sure to carry plenty of potent curatives around at all times. The Dark Bean coffee shop is close enough to the Safe House to make it a practical source—try the coffee creamer!

GETTING SICK

Be careful: Not everything Chuck swallows is easy to keep down. Spoiled foods may replenish a bit of health, but they also cause Chuck to periodically double over and vomit—not good when you're surrounded by mobs of zombies! Chuck spews three times after eating something icky. Each time he does, he drops his current weapon, thereby becoming extremely vulnerable. Thankfully, it's no secret what will make Chuck ill—anything with "spoiled" in its name will have this undesirable effect.

CAUTION

Chuck also becomes sick if he consumes three alcoholic beverages in rapid succession, including beer (what a light-weight). Space out those drinks!

BLENDERS

Certain restaurants and bars feature blenders—special objects that Chuck can use to combine any two foodstuffs into a single, powerful restorative. Blended drinks not only replenish a significant amount of Chuck's health, but also grant him short-term benefits. Blenders can be found at the following locations (refer to the "Appendix" chapter for a complete list of blends and their special effects):

- Shots & Awe (Americana Casino)
- Slot Ranch Casino (at the bar)
- Rojo Diablo Mexican Restaurant (Food Court)
- Baron Von Brathaus (Yucatan Casino)
- Palisades Mall (first-floor grotto bar)
- Sipparellos (Atlantica Casino)
- Pub O' Gold (Silver Strip)
- Juggz Bar & Grill (Platinum Strip)

MAGAZINES

Knowledge is power, especially when it comes in the form of trendy magazines. Find these special items sprinkled all about Fortune City and collect them to bestow special advantages to Chuck for as long as he carries them around. Press the Attack button while holding a magazine to read its effects, and see the poster map and "Appendix" chapter for a complete list of magazines, including their effects and locations.

TIP

Avoid carrying magazines around until Chuck has leveled up and gained a few extra inventory slots. The four precious slots he begins with are better filled with weapons and restoratives.

NOTE

The effects of magazines "stack," so carrying multiple copies of similar issues has exponentially greater benefits!

DEADRISING 2

INVENTORY MANAGEMENT

124 KILLED

Chuck begins with just four inventory slots, but he gains many more as he levels up. Still, it's vital to exercise sound judgement when deciding what to carry along, particularly in the early goings. If you're careful to avoid conflicts with zombies, you can usually make do with just one or two reliable weapons—the spiked bat combo weapon is always a fantastic choice because it's easy to construct whenever you're moving to or from the Safe House and it strikes a perfect balance between attack speed, damage, and durability.

All remaining inventory slots should be filled with potent healing items—you can never have too much food on hand. Once Chuck has gained several additional inventory

1369 KILLED

slots, start trading restoratives for useful magazines, and perhaps even a skateboard for faster travel.

RESTARTING

CASE FILE

CASE 4	SEPTEMBER 26 11:00 PM
Zombrex 3	SEPTEMBER 27 7:00 AM
CASE 5	SEPTEM 7:00 PM
Zombrex 4	SEPTEMBER 28 7:00 AM

THE TRUTH HAS VANISHED

CONTINUE

Dead Rising 2 puts Chuck through the meat grinder. It's easy to become stuck on some of the more challenging scenarios. Mercifully, you're able to restart the adventure at any point while still retaining all of the skills, stats, and combo cards you've unlocked. If you're finding the game too difficult, simply pause and choose "Quit," then select the "Restart" option. You'll have to replay the adventure from the very beginning, but at least Chuck will be better prepared to handle the horrors of Fortune City.

> **NOTE**
>
> While challenging, *Dead Rising 2* is entirely beatable without restarting. The secret lies in completing side missions—these lead to survivors and psychopath showdowns, both of which equate to huge PP bonuses for Chuck.

SAVING YOUR PROGRESS

Everyone needs a break now and then, and Chuck's no exception. Visit any restroom and examine a stall or urinal to give Chuck a chance to relieve himself of his burdens and record his current progress. You only get three save slots, however, so use them wisely. We recommend cycling through the slots so you can easily go back to a previous save without losing much ground (if need be).

0 KILLED

BRAIN FOOD

CO-OP ACTION

Why brave the horrors of Fortune City alone when you can kill twice as much stuff with a friend? *Dead Rising 2* features a fun co-op system that allows one player to join up with another at any time. Just choose "Co-op" from the Main menu to join another player's game.

★ CO-OP ★

The transceiver will let you receive co-op calls! Press ◯ to answer co-op calls.

People can drop in for a co-op game at any time. You can restrict who joins in the Gameplay Options menu.

Explore Fortune City with a friend and slaughter even more undead!

Ⓐ CONTINUE

NOTE

Ensure your game is open to others through the Options menu, or disable the option to receive co-op transmissions if you'd rather not be bothered.

To play co-op with another player, both players must have advanced far enough through the story to receive the transceiver from Stacy Forsythe at the Safe House. This means you must simply complete the brief introductory segment in which Chuck competes in "Terror Is Reality," then ferries his daughter away from the arena and into the Safe House for the first time.

CONNECTING

Once a player has invited you to join their game, your transceiver will ring and the player's name will appear next to it. Simply answer the transceiver to have that player join you as a co-op buddy.

While playing co-op, the "main" Chuck will be the only one to advance their story. The "buddy" Chuck will not advance their story, but they will retain all money and PP they acquire while assisting their pal. Co-op is therefore a great way for two friends to share in the adventure and level up with less difficulty.

CO-OP ADVANTAGES

There are a few things to know about playing co-op. First, all PP you acquire through escorts and missions is doled out to both players. The PP is not halved; both players simply receive an equal share. Nice!

Second, co-op players can resuscitate one another. Should one Chuck fall in battle, a message is sent to the surviving player. Simply hand the fallen Chuck any food item to bring him back to life. The reanimated player always rises with two units of health, unless the food item given would heal Chuck for an even greater amount.

The only limitation to playing with a buddy is that you must both be in close proximity to one another to move from one area of the city to another. Both players must also be nearby to initiate a Case File task as well. Still, this isn't much of a limitation when you consider the great advantages of having a second Chuck at your side!

MENUS AND INTERFACE

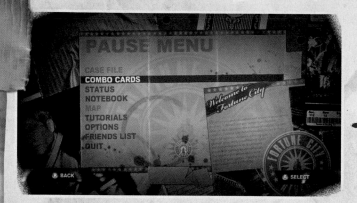

Is your brain feeling fed? Good. Let's wrap things up with a look at the Pause menu options.

CASE FILE

Much more is going on in Fortune City than meets the eye, and Chuck Greene is determined to get to the bottom of the horrendous outbreak. The Case File lists all mandatory missions that Chuck must complete to discover the truth. Failing to meet any of these objectives does not end the game—you're free to keep playing to explore, destroy, and level Chuck up if you wish. But you'll never uncover the truth of what's happened in Fortune City unless you meet these vital objectives.

COMBO CARDS

All of the scratch and combo cards that Chuck has acquired are listed under this section of the Pause menu. Here you may review the

cards at any time to see what you need to build the ultimate tools of zombie destruction. Refer to the next chapter, "Skills, Weapons, and Combos," for a complete list of combo cards that includes informative descriptions of their weapons and where to find them.

NOTEBOOK

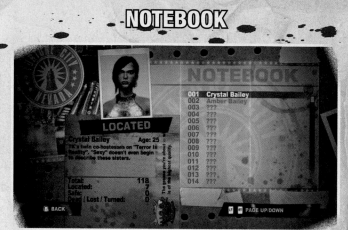

Chuck's a surprisingly detail-oriented guy—he keeps a faithful record of every named character he encounters during his time in Fortune City. Review this list of characters at any time by calling up the Notebook. Here you can see who Chuck has met, who's safe at the Safe House, and who has been tragically killed in the outbreak. Not every name on the list is someone that can be saved, mind you—psychopaths count as named characters as well!

STATUS

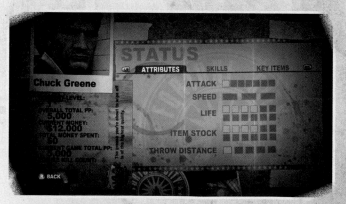

Call up the Status menu whenever you'd like a look at how far Chuck has progressed through leveling up. Here, all of Chuck's current stats, skills, and key items are displayed—flip through the menus to review all of this important info.

PRIMA OFFICIAL GAME GUIDE

18

BRAIN FOOD

LEVELING UP

Chuck steadily gains Prestige Points (PP) as he performs heroic deeds, and levels up after accumulating set amounts. Here are the most common actions that cause Chuck to gain PP:

- Convincing survivors to join you.
- Escorting survivors to the Safe House.
- Defeating looters, mercenaries, and psychopaths.
- Obliterating zombies with skills and combo weapons.

Rewards are bestowed at random each time Chuck levels up—you never know just what he'll get. It could be a new skill, combo card, or perhaps one of Chuck's stats will increase—any or all of these can happen when a new level is reached. Rest assured that everything will have unlocked by the time Chuck hits level 50 (the maximum). At that point, he'll be all the zombie slayer he can be.

> **NOTE**
>
> Peruse the next chapter, "Skills, Weapons, and Combos," for details on the various skills that Chuck can acquire.

CHUCK'S LEVELING CHART

Level	PP Required
1	0
2	20,000
3	40,000
4	60,000
5	80,000
6	110,000
7	140,000
8	170,000
9	200,000
10	230,000
11	280,000
12	330,000
13	380,000
14	430,000
15	480,000
16	550,000
17	620,000
18	690,000
19	760,000
20	830,000
21	920,000
22	1,010,000
23	1,100,000
24	1,190,000
25	1,280,000

Level	PP Required
26	1,380,000
27	1,480,000
28	1,580,000
29	1,680,000
30	1,780,000
31	1,910,000
32	2,040,000
33	2,170,000
34	2,300,000
35	2,430,000
36	2,580,000
37	2,730,000
38	2,880,000
39	3,030,000
40	3,180,000
41	3,350,000
42	3,520,000
43	3,690,000
44	3,860,000
45	4,030,000
46	4,210,000
47	4,390,000
48	4,570,000
49	4,750,000
50	5,000,000

The following table lists the likelihood of Chuck's skills increasing when he levels up. For example, through levels 1 to 10, Chuck is twice as likely to gain health or inventory slots as he is to increase his attack power or throwing distance. Speed increases are the rarest of all; Chuck is unable to improve this stat during levels 11 to 20, but it'll be maxed by the time he hits level 40.

STAT INCREASE PROBABILITY

Level Range	Health	Inventory	Attack	Throw	Speed
1–10	x2	x2	x1	x1	x1
11–20	x2	x1	x1	x1	—
21–30	x1	x2	x1	x1	x1
31–40	x2	x1	x2	x1	x1
41–50	x1	x2	x1	—	—

DEADRISING 2

MAP

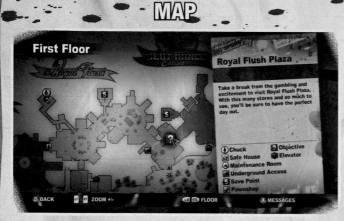

First Floor
Royal Flush Plaza

You'll spend plenty of time viewing Chuck's map of Fortune City, which provides a complete view of the entire game world. Pass your cursor over the various shops and locales to call up their names and descriptions. The map is extremely useful; consult it and plan your moves before you make them.

First Floor
MESSAGES

While viewing the map, you can call up your current list of messages—all of the side missions that Stacey has lined up for Chuck. Cycle through these tasks to view details about them, including where you must go to carry them out. Remember, tasks up top will expire before those at the bottom—the colored bars beneath their titles measures how much time remains.

TIP

View your messages and missions at the map screen rather than by examining Chuck's watch. The action is paused while you view the map, but zombies can still rip Chuck's head off while the watch is displayed!

TUTORIALS

★ GUIDE ARROW ★

Chuck needs to find his way to Katey in the green room.

Use the Guide Arrow to find the way to Katey.

The guide arrow will always point towards Chuck's current objective.

As you encounter new elements of gameplay, handy tutorial screens appear to give you the gist of each one. You can review these tutorial screens at any time by pausing the game and selecting "Tutorials." If you're ever unsure of a certain game mechanic, check through the tutorials to see if there's something in there that clears things up.

OPTIONS

Pause the game and choose "Options" to fine-tune your survival horror experience. Here you may adjust various control, audio, and gameplay options, each one being very straightforward.

FRIENDS LIST

The Pause menu gives you fast access to friends who are playing *Dead Rising 2*. This makes it easy to jump into a friend's game or ask them to join yours. Remember, two Chucks means twice the destruction!

QUIT

When you've had enough awesomeness for the day, go ahead and choose the "Quit" option from the Pause menu. This allows you to exit out to the Main menu—but make sure you've saved your progress at a restroom first! You can also choose to load a previous save from the Quit menu, or to restart the adventure from the very beginning. When you choose to restart, the story is reset, but Chuck retains all of the PP, cash, and combo cards you've earned for him thus far.

KATEY HAS TURNED

LOAD
RESTART STORY
CONTINUE PLAYING

Restarting the story will keep your current character level and unlockables, but story progress will be reset.

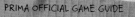

SKILLS, WEAPONS, AND COMBOS

Now that you've digested your "Brain Food," let's move on to dessert. Here we expose the many manly skill moves Chuck learns as he levels up, along with the vast array of lethal weapons he's able to wield, including all combo weapons Chuck constructs at maintenance rooms. A complete list of combo cards and their locations is also provided to ensure you get the most out of each deadly device.

SKILL MOVES

▶▶ Winch the helicopter and throw objects to damage its rotor.

Struggling for survival brings out the best in Chuck. Though Fortune City's foremost stuntman starts off green (pun intended, sorry), he soon develops a variety of combat-oriented skills that improve his odds of overcoming the endless ordeals he must face.

Like stats, Chuck's skills unlock as he levels up—and similarly, you never know exactly when he'll gain a new one. One thing remains constant, however: Chuck's skills always unlock in sequence, as detailed in the following table. (The first skill Chuck will learn is the Backdrop, and the last will be the Pick Up.) By the time Chuck hits level 50 (the maximum), all skills will have unlocked.

A few of Chuck's skills are passive, such as the DDT and Backdrop—Chuck automatically employs these skill when breaking away from a zombie's grasp, provided he escapes quickly. The majority of skills require your input, however. Pause and review their individual button commands under the "Skills" portion of the Status menu.

21

DEADRISING 2

CHUCK'S SKILLS

1. **Backdrop** Chuck automatically slams zombies that have grabbed him from behind, killing them. Chuck must escape quickly to perform this move.
2. **Jump Kick**: A fast, jumping kick that knocks enemies away. Useful when no suitable weapons can be found.
3. **DDT**: Chuck automatically slams zombies that have grabbed him from the front, killing them. Chuck must escape quickly to perform this move.
4. **Curbstomp**: A heavy ground stomp. Very useful against enemies that are down but not out.
5. **Front Kick**: A fast, frontal kick that knocks enemies away. Useful when no suitable weapons can be found.
6. **Dodge Roll**: A quick-diving somersault. Extremely useful, helping Chuck avoid attacks and close in on foes.
7. **Double Leg Drop Kick**: A powerful, diving kick with both legs. Knocks enemies away but leaves Chuck vulnerable while he regains his feet.
8. **Foot Sweep**: An area attack that knocks surrounding zombies away. Useful when being swarmed by undead.
9. **Elbow Drop**: A heavy, diving elbow strike to grounded enemies. Try it from great heights!
10. **Haymaker**: A slow but devastating punch that smashes zombies, knocking them back and killing them. As effective as any weapon, but the long wind up leaves Chuck vulnerable.
11. **Field Goal**: A mighty kick to a downed zombie's head that sends it flying off in a shower of gore. Kiss that Curbstomp good-bye!
12. **Smash**: A forceful shove that knocks zombies away from Chuck, bouncing them off nearby objects. Very effective and very deadly.
13. **Hands Off**: A special move that makes Chuck impossible for zombies to grab. Very useful when rushing through a teeming throng.
14. **Power Bomb**: A devastating finishing move initiated by standing near a downed zombie's feet. Awesomely fatal.
15. **Pick Up**: Allows Chuck to lift zombies overhead, hurling them into objects or other zombies. As manly as it gets.

WEAPONS

When the armies of darkness threaten to overwhelm, anything and everything becomes a weapon of survival. From fire axes to sledge hammers, potted plants to ketchup, you'll find each and every weapon that Chuck can wield listed here, with complete damage and durability values, and informative descriptions of each weapon's use.

NOTE

The durability/ammo rating tells you how many times a melee weapon can strike an enemy before breaking, and how many times a ranged weapon can be fired.

Turn to the "Appendix" at the back of this guide to discover the most convenient locations of all weapons.

NORMAL WEAPONS				
Name	Durability/Ammo	Damage	Category	Description
2x4	15	2	Melee	Impact swing attack.
Acetylene Tank	30	2	Explosive	Explosive weapon with propulsion.
Acoustic Guitar	10	2	Melee	3 swing attacks, can also be slammed onto zombies, blinding them.
Ad Board	15	1	Melee	2 swing attacks.
Amplifier	20	1	Melee	2 swing attacks and a heavy, push attack.
Assault Rifle	60	3	Firearm	Accurate rifle that can shoot in 3-round bursts.
Bag of Marbles	1	0	Novelty	Causes zombies that step on the marbles to slip.
Barstool	5	2	Melee	Push attack and a heavy, ground-slam attack.
Baseball Bat	30	3	Melee	2 swing attacks and a heavy, swing attack.
Basketball	15	2	Ranged	Thrown weapon that bounces at other nearby zombies.

SKILLS, WEAPONS, AND COMBOS

Name	Durability/Ammo	Damage	Category	Description
				NORMAL WEAPONS, CONT.
Bass Guitar	30	3	Melee	3 swing attacks and a heavy, ground attack.
Battery	25	2	Melee	2 swing attacks and a heavy, push attack.
Battleaxe	40	4	Melee	Slicing weapon with 3 swing attacks, a heavy, spinning attack and a jump attack.
Beach Ball	30	0	Novelty	Thrown weapon that bounces at other nearby zombies.
Bench	20	3	Melee	Has a big push attack that can clear out a large group of zombies in front of you. When it breaks it spawns a 2x4.
Bingo Ball Cage	10	2	Melee	Has a swing attack and a heavy, throw attack.
Blast Frequency Gun	50	0	Firearm	Special weapon engineered to be very effective versus gas zombies.
Bow and Arrow	30	2	Ranged	Projectile weapon; the arrows will stick into zombies.
Bowie Knife	35	2	Melee	Fast, slashing weapon with a brutal heavy attack.
Bowling Ball	15	3	Melee	Swing attack that can cause a zombie's head to explode when hit just right. In ranged mode you can charge up a unique bowling attack. The longer you charge, the more power in the throw.
Box of Nails	20	1	Ranged	It's possible for the nails to impale a zombie for a moment, causing it to suffer more damage.
Boxing Gloves	25	1	Melee	4 swing attacks and 2 heavy, swing attacks. Blocks attacks in ranged mode.
Brick	10	3	Melee	Swing attack and a heavy, throw attack.
Broadsword	40	4	Melee	Slicing weapon with 3 swings a heavy, overhead attack and a jump attack.
Broom Handle	20	3	Melee	Thrust weapon with 2 thrust attacks and a heavy, push attack.
Bucket	20	0	Novelty	Put on a zombie's head to blind it.
Bull Skull	40	3	Melee	Worn on Chuck's head. Has a headbutt attack and a heavy, charging attack.
Cactus Plant	8	2	Melee	2 swing attacks.
Cardboard Box	5	1	Melee	2 swing attacks; break it open to try to find something useful.
Cardboard Cutout	10	1	Novelty	Basic swing attack.
Cash Register	10	3	Melee	3 swing attacks; break it open for some cash.
Casino Chips	30	1	Novelty	Tosses a handful of chips per throw.
Cement Saw	40	4	Melee	Mechanical weapon with 2 thrust attacks.
Centurion Bust	20	3	Melee	2 swing attacks.
Chain Saw	30	4	Melee	Slicing weapon with 2 swing attacks and a heavy, spin attack.
Chef Knife	40	2	Melee	Fast, slashing weapon with a unique and brutal heavy attack.
Coffee Pot	1	2	Melee	Impact swing attack; causes coffee to splash on environment.
Comedy Trophy	20	2	Melee	Impact swing attack.
Computer Case	15	2	Melee	3 attacks: 2 swings then a push attack.
Construction Hat	7	1	Novelty	Impact swing attack.
Cooking Oil	6	1	Melee	Impact swing attack. When it's broken, the oil on the floor will cause zombies to slip.
Cooking Pot	15	2	Melee	2 swing attacks.
Croupier Stick	5	1	Melee	Impact swing attack and a unique and brutal heavy attack.
Crowbar	30	3	Melee	Impact swing attack.
Cushioned Tall Chair	5	3	Melee	Melee weapon with a push attack and a heavy, ground-slam attack.
Dolly	30	2	Melee	Pushable weapon that has a swing attack if picked up.
Donkey Lamp	10	1	Melee	Impact swing attack.
Drill Motor	40	3	Melee	2 swing attacks and a heavy, push attack.

DEADRISING 2

Name	Durability/Ammo	Damage	Category	Description
Drink Cart	40	2	Melee	Pushable weapon that can be found with wine and beer on it. It has a swing attack if picked up.
Drum	10	1	Melee	2 swing attacks and a heavy attack that slams the drum onto a zombie's head, blinding it.
Dumbbell	20	3	Melee	Impact swing attack.
Dynamite	10	5	Explosive	Explosive weapon that can be stuck in a zombie's mouth.
Electric Guitar	30	3	Melee	3 swing attacks and a heavy, spin attack.
Fancy Bench	20	2	Melee	Has a big push attack that can clear out a large group of zombies in front of you.
Fancy Painting	2	0	Novelty	Slam this over a zombie to pin its hands at its side, preventing it from attacking you.
Fancy Small Chair	5	3	Melee	Melee weapon with 1 push attack and a heavy, ground-slam attack.
Fancy Tall Chair	5	3	Melee	Melee weapon with 1 push attack and a heavy, ground-slam attack.
Fire Axe	35	3	Melee	Limb-slicing weapon with 2 swings and a heavy, overhead-chop attack.
Fire Extinguisher	20	0	N/A	Spray zombies long enough to freeze them. You'll gain some PP when they're shattered.
Firecrackers	20	0	N/A	Stackable weapon that acts as a lure. Can be thrown to areas where you want zombies to gather.
Flashlight	15	2	Melee	Impact swing attack. The flashlight turns on while it's being held
Flower Pot	1	1	Melee	Impact swing attack.
Foam Hand	10	0	Melee	Swing attack.
Folding Chair	5	2	Melee	Melee weapon with 1 push attack and a heavy, ground-slam attack.
Football	10	1	Ranged	Thrown weapon that bounces at other nearby zombies.
Fountain Firework	10	0	N/A	Slam into a zombie's mouth; the glowing light and sparks lure nearby zombies.
Funny Painting	5	0	Novelty	Slam over a zombie to pin its hands at its side, preventing it from attacking you.
Garbage Bag	10	1	Melee	2 swing attacks. Break it open to try to find something useful.
Garbage Can	20	3	Melee	3 swing attacks. Break it open to try to find something useful.
Gas Barrel	20	3	N/A	2 swing attacks. Mission-specific weapon.
Gas Can	30	2	N/A	Single swing attack. Mission-specific weapon. Can be shot to release green gas.
Gasoline Canister	10	4	Explosive	Impact swing attack and a heavy attack that slams the gas can into a zombie's mouth. Try shooting it afterward.
Gems	20	1	Ranged	Tosses a handful of gems per throw.
Generator	30	3	N/A	2 swing attacks. Mission-specific weapon.
Giant Die	40	2	Novelty	Swing attack and a heavy, throw attack.
Giant Pink Chain Saw	80	4	Melee	2 swing attacks followed by a pelvic thrust attack and a heavy, spinning attack.
Giant Stuffed Bull	12	0	Novelty	2 swing attacks and a heavy, slam attack. The slam attack puts the stuffed animal over the top of the targeted zombie, blinding it.
Giant Stuffed Donkey	12	0	Novelty	2 swing attacks and a heavy, slam attack. The slam attack puts the stuffed animal over the top of the targeted zombie, blinding it.
Giant Stuffed Elephant	12	0	Novelty	2 swing attacks and a heavy, slam attack. The slam attack puts the stuffed animal over the top of the targeted zombie, blinding it.
Giant Stuffed Rabbit	12	0	Novelty	2 swing attacks and a heavy, slam attack. The slam attack puts the stuffed animal over the top of the targeted zombie, blinding it.
Gift Shop Lamp	10	1	Melee	Impact swing attack.
Goblin Mask	20	0	Novelty	Put on a zombie's head to blind it.
Golf Club	20	3	Ranged	Projectile launching weapon. Unique charging attack when in ranged mode, increasing the damage and throw force.

SKILLS, WEAPONS, AND COMBOS

Name	Durability/ Ammo	Damage	Category	Description
NORMAL WEAPONS, CONT.				
Grenade	10	5	Explosive	Thrown explosive.
Gumball Machine	15	2	Melee	3 swing attacks. When it breaks, the gumballs will cause zombies to slip if they step on them.
Handbag	7	1	Melee	Simple swing attack.
Handgun	30	2	Firearm	Basic hand gun.
Hanger	5	1	Melee	Slam into a zombie's mouth.
Highback Oak Chair	5	3	Melee	Melee weapon with 1 push attack and a heavy, ground-slam attack.
Hockey Stick	30	2	Melee	2 swing attacks with a heavy, cross-check attack.
Hunk of Meat	10	0	Novelty	A lure weapon that can be slammed in a zombie's mouth.
Indoor Garbage Can	20	2	Melee	3 swing attacks. Break it open to try to find something useful.
Katana Sword	40	4	Melee	4 slicing swing attacks and a jump attack.
Keg	20	2	Melee	Simple swing attack. If shot it will spin around spewing beer, which zombies can slip on.
Ketchup	3	0	N/A	Spray a zombie to color it red.
Keyboard	10	1	Melee	Impact swing attack.
Lamp	3	1	Melee	Impact swing attack.
Lance	30	3	Melee	2 thrust attacks and a heavy impact that tosses zombies over Chuck's shoulder.
Large Barrel	10	2	Melee	Swing attack and a heavy attack that slams the barrel over the top of a zombie, incapacitating it.
Large Fern Tree	6	1	Melee	Swing attack.
Large Planter	6	2	Melee	Swing attack.
Large Potted Plant	6	1	Melee	Swing attack.
Large Vase	15	2	Melee	2 swing attacks.
Large Wrench	25	4	Melee	Impact attack animation with a unique heavy attack.
Lawn Dart	10	2	Ranged	Thrown weapon that aims for a zombie's head.
Lawn Mower	80	2	Melee	Pushable weapon that knocks zombies over and grinds them up.
LCD Monitor	10	1	Melee	2 swing attacks.
Lead Pipe	20	3	Melee	Impact swing attack and a heavy, impact swing attack.
Leaf Blower		0	N/A	Blows a zombie back lightly, keeping it at bay. It's inevitable; they will get you.
Leaf Rake	25	1	Melee	2 swing attacks.
Liberty Torch	25	2	Novelty	2 swing attacks.
Lizard Mask	20	0	Novelty	Put on a zombie's head to blind it.
LMG	200	4	Firearm	Heavy machine gun.
Long Stick	5	2	Melee	2 thrust attacks and a heavy, throw attack.
Machete	35	2	Melee	Fast, limb-slicing swing attacks.
Magician Sword	35	3	Melee	Fast, limb-slicing swing attacks.
Mailbox	30	3	Melee	3 swing attacks.
Mannequin Female	15	2	Melee	2 swing attacks. Breaks apart into multiple parts that are also weapons.
Mannequin Male	15	2	Melee	2 swing attacks. Breaks apart into multiple parts that are also weapons.
Massager	15	1	Novelty	Impact swing attack.
Mayonnaise	3	0	N/A	Spray a zombie to color it white.
Meat Cleaver	30	2	Melee	Fast, slashing swing attacks.

www.primagames.com

NORMAL WEAPONS, CONT.

Name	Durability/Ammo	Damage	Category	Description
Medicine Ball	25	2	Melee	2 swing attacks.
Merc Assault Rifle	30	4	Firearm	High rate of fire with powerful shots.
Metal Barricade	40	3	Melee	2 swing attacks with a heavy, charging push attack.
Metal Baseball Bat	40	3	Ranged	Projectile weapon that hits baseballs.
Metal Garbage Can	20	2	Melee	3 swing attacks. Break it open to try to find something useful.
Mic Stand	20	2	Melee	Thrust attack and a heavy, push attack.
Military Case	20	2	Melee	2 swing attacks.
Mining Pick	30	3	Melee	2 swing attacks.
MMA Gloves	20	1	Melee	4 swing attacks and 2 heavy, swing attacks. Blocks attacks in ranged mode.
Money Case	15	2	N/A	2 swing attacks. Breaks apart and rewards money. Mission-only weapon.
Moosehead	40	4	Melee	2 head-swinging attacks with a heavy, charging attack.
Motor Oil	15	1	Melee	Impact swing attack. Breaking the bottle will cause an oil slick on the ground that can cause zombies to slip.
Music Discs	10	1	Ranged	Tosses 1 disc per attack.
Mustard	3	0	N/A	Spray a zombie to color it yellow.
Newspaper Box	25	3	Melee	2 swing attacks and a heavy, ground attack.
Nightstick	20	3	Melee	Impact swing attack.
Novelty Beer Mug	20	2	Novelty	Push attack and a heavy, ground-slam attack.
Novelty Cell Phone	10	2	Novelty	2 swing attacks and a heavy, spin attack.
Novelty Liquor Bottle	10	2	Novelty	2 swing attacks and a heavy, ground attack. When the item breaks it creates liquid on the ground that can cause zombies to slip.
Novelty Perfume Bottle	10	2	Novelty	Swing attack.
Novelty Poker Chip		2	Novelty	2 swing attacks.
Padded Blue Chair	5	2	Melee	Melee weapon with 1 push attack and a heavy, ground-slam attack.
Paddle	25	1	Melee	2 swing attacks with a heavy, cross-check attack.
Paint Can	5	2	Melee	Impact swing attack; when it breaks it splashes green on zombies and the environment.
Painting	5	0	Novelty	Slam over a zombie to pin its hands at its side, preventing it from attacking you.
Pallet	15	2	Melee	2 swing attacks. When it breaks apart it spawns a 2x4.
Pan	15	2	Melee	Impact swing attack. Can be heated up on a stove to add a heavy, burning-face attack.
Parasol	30	2	Melee	Thrust attack with a heavy, running-charge attack.
Patio Chair	5	2	Melee	Melee weapon with 1 push attack and a heavy, ground-slam attack.
Patio Table	30	2	Melee	2 swing attacks with a heavy, charge push attack.
Peace Art	6	1	N/A	Impact swing attack.
Pitchfork	30	2	Melee	2 thrust attacks and a heavy impact attack that tosses zombies over Chuck's shoulder.
Plastic Bin	15	2	Melee	Swing attack and a heavy, ground-slam attack.
Plastic Garbage Can	15	2	Melee	Swing attack. Break it open to try to find something useful.
Plates	20	1	Ranged	Tosses 1 plate per attack.
Playing Cards	30	0	Novelty	Tosses a handful of cards per throw.
Plywood	15	3	Melee	4 swing attacks.

SKILLS, WEAPONS, AND COMBOS

				NORMAL WEAPONS, CONT.
Name	**Durability/ Ammo**	**Damage**	**Category**	**Description**
Power Drill	50	2	Melee	4 stabbing attacks.
Propane Tank	25	5	Explosive	Explosive weapon that has 2 swing attacks.
Protestor Sign	15	1	Melee	Thrust attack with a heavy, impale attack. The weapon can be impaled into a zombie's front or back.
Push Broom	15	1	Melee	Thrust attack with a heavy, cross-check attack. When it breaks it spawns the broom handle.
Pylon	30	0	Novelty	Put on a zombie's head to blind it.
Queen	10	5	N/A	Smash to instantly kill all nearby zombies.
Robot Bear	18	0	Novelty	2 swing attacks and a heavy slam onto zombie attack. The slam attack puts the stuffed animal over the top of the targeted zombie, blinding it.
Rocket Fireworks	5	0	Explosive	Slam-in-mouth attack and a heavy, lob throw attack in which Chuck tosses the firework rockets out in front of himself.
Rocket Launcher	50	4	N/A	Mechanical explosive projectile-launching weapon. The rockets will also stick into zombies if they hit. Boss reward version (Reed).
Rotating Display	30	2	Melee	3 swing attacks.
Roulette Wheel	20	3	Melee	Slam attack.
Round Potted Plant	10	2	Melee	2 swing attacks.
Sandwich Board	15	2	Melee	2 swing attacks.
Saw Blade	10	4	Ranged	Thrown, slicing weapon that can go through multiple zombies as Chuck improves his Throw stat.
Scissors	3	1	Melee	Slam into a zombie's eyes to blind it.
Servbot Mask	20	0	Novelty	Put on a zombie's head to blind it.
Serving Tray	30	1	Melee	Impact swing attack.
Shampoo	1	1	N/A	Thrown weapon attack. When it breaks it leaves shampoo on the ground that causes zombies to slip.
Shopping Boxes	10	1	Melee	2 swing attacks. Break it open to try to find something useful.
Shopping Valuables	30	1	N/A	2 swing attacks. Mission-specific weapon.
Shotgun	20		Firearm	Powerful, close-range gun.
Shower Head	8	2	Melee	Slam into a zombie's head to cause it to bleed to death.
Six Shooter	60	4	Firearm	Powerful handgun with a special heavy, hip-shooting attack. Boss weapon (Seymour).
Skateboard	4	1	N/A	Get on it to take a ride. Get the Skateboarding magazine to ollie.
Sledge Hammer	35	4	Melee	2 swing attacks and a heavy, ground-slam attack.
Small Fern Tree	10	1	Melee	2 swing attacks.
Small Painting	5	0	Novelty	Slam over a zombie's head.
Small Potted Plant	2	1	Melee	Impact swing attack.
Small Suitcase	10	2	Melee	2 swing attacks.
Small Vase	1	3	Melee	Impact swing attack.
Sniper Rifle	20	5	Firearm	Extremely powerful gun that can pierce multiple targets with each shot. In ranged mode, the scope can zoom in and out.
Soccer Ball	20	1	Ranged	Kick at nearby zombies. Bounces at other nearby zombies.
Speaker	15	2	Melee	2 swing attacks.
Spear	35	3	Melee	2 thrust attacks and a heavy, throw attack.
Spool of Wire	40	2	N/A	2 swing attacks. Mission-specific weapon.
Spot Light	10	2	Melee	Impact swing attack.

DEADRISING 2

				NORMAL WEAPONS, CONT.
Name	**Durability/ Ammo**	**Damage**	**Category**	**Description**
Spray Paint	10	0	N/A	Spray attack that colors zombies the color of the spray paint.
Square Sign	15	2	Melee	4 swing attacks.
Stand	30	3	Melee	3 swing attacks and a heavy, ground attack.
Steel Shelving	30	2	Melee	2 swing attacks and a heavy, charging push attack.
Step Ladder	20	2	Melee	3 swing attacks and a heavy, ground attack.
Stick Pony	10	1	Novelty	Thrust attack with a heavy, impale attack. The weapon can be impaled into a zombie's front or back.
Stone Statue	30	2	Melee	3 swing attacks.
Stool	5	2	Melee	Melee weapon with 1 push attack and a heavy, ground-slam attack.
Suitcase	10	2	Melee	2 swing attacks.
Swordfish	25	3	Melee	2 thrust attacks with a heavy, impale attack.
Table Lamp	5	1	Melee	Impact swing attack.
Tennis Racquet	40	1	Ranged	Projectile weapon that hits tennis balls at zombies. The balls will bounce toward other nearby zombies as well.
Tiki Mask	15	2	Novelty	2 swing attacks.
Tiki Torch	15	2	Melee	Thrust attack weapon with a heavy, swiping attack that lights zombies on fire.
Tire	20	0	Novelty	Put on a zombie's head to blind it.
Tomahawk	35	2	Melee	Fast, limb-slicing swing attacks.
Toy Helicopter	25	2	Novelty	2 swing attacks and a heavy, launch attack that causes the helicopter to hover in place, luring nearby zombies.
Toy Spitball Gun	20	0	Novelty	Toy gun that shoots harmless plastic balls.
Training Sword	20	2	Melee	4 swing attacks. Blocks attacks in ranged mode.
Treasure Chest	10	3	Novelty	2 swing attacks.
Utility Cart	60	2	Melee	Pushable weapon that has no swing attack if picked up, as it's too awkward to swing. A push broom may be attached.
Vacuum Cleaner	20	2	Melee	2 thrust attacks and a heavy, cross-check attack.
Velvet Bar	15	2	Melee	2 thrust attacks and a heavy, cross-check attack.
Vinyl Records	10	0	Ranged	Tosses 1 vinyl record per attack.
Wacky Hammer	20	0	Novelty	Impact swing attack.
Water Bottle	15	1	N/A	Impact swing attack. Spawned by water coolers when they break.
Water Cooler	15	2	Melee	3 swing attacks. The water bottle breaks off after a few attacks, becoming a weapon.
Water Gun	30	0	Novelty	Novelty gun that shoots harmless water.
Wheelchair	40	2	Melee	Pushable weapon that has a swing attack if picked up. Zombies can be knocked into the chair if you hit them from behind. Dump them out afterward by pressing the Jump button.
Whipped Cream	30	0	Novelty	Spray weapon that colors zombies white. The weapon can be sprayed on the ground to create a splotch that causes zombies to slip.
Yellow Tall Chair	5	2	Melee	Melee weapon with 1 push attack and a heavy, ground-slam attack.
Zombie Mask	20	0	Novelty	Put it on a zombie's head to blind it.

SKILLS, WEAPONS, AND COMBOS

COMBO WEAPONS AND CARDS

By combining two ordinary weapons, Chuck can form deviously lethal combo weapons—creative and formidable tools of mass destruction. Not only are combo weapons a thrill to use, they also give Chuck bonus PP with each kill, helping him level up fast. Use combo weapons at every opportunity to maximize your mayhem, along with Chuck's ability to grow and improve. The following table reveals everything there is to know about each deadly combo weapon that Chuck can forge.

NOTE

All PP values in the table are doubled when the weapon's combo card is owned.

Every maintenance room contains weapons that Chuck can use to build combo weapons, right there on the spot. See the poster map to discover the contents of each maintenance room.

COMBO WEAPONS (LISTED IN UNLOCK ORDER.)								
Display Name	Component 1	Component 2	Normal Attack PP	Heavy Attack PP	Ammo/ Durability	Damage	Description	Combo Card
Drill Bucket	Power Drill	Bucket	250 PP	N/A	10	5	Put on a zombie's head and watch it lose its head in the end.	Acquired by leveling.
I.E.D.	Box of Nails	Propane Tank	150 PP	N/A	40	5	Largest explosive weapon in the game. Also has 3 swing attacks and a heavy attack that sticks the weapon into a zombie, making it easier to detonate in a crowd.	Acquired by leveling.
Molotov	Whiskey	Newspaper	175 PP	N/A	20	4	Thrown explosive weapon that lights zombies on fire.	Acquired by leveling.
Pole Weapon	Push Broom	Machete	50 PP	75 PP	50	4	Slicing swing attack and a heavy slicing, spinning attack.	Acquired by leveling.
Air Horn	Pylon	Spray Paint	250 PP	N/A	10	0	Use to lure zombies; they don't like the high-pitched sound.	Acquired by leveling.
Gem Blower	Gems	Leaf Blower	75 PP	N/A	50	4	Projectile weapon that shoots multiple gems capable of slicing limbs off zombies.	Acquired by leveling.
Fountain Lizard	Lizard Mask	Fountain Firework	50 PP	N/A	3	0	Put on a zombie's head to lure all nearby zombies for a long period of time.	Acquired by leveling.
Hacker	Flashlight	Computer Case	50 PP	N/A	40	3	Electrocutes a zombie. Use on ATMs, slot machines, and vending machines to gain large amounts of money.	Acquired by leveling.
Ripper	Cement Saw	Saw Blade	50 PP	75 PP	50	4	2 limb-slicing attacks and a heavy, slice attack.	Acquired by leveling.

DEADRISING 2

COMBO WEAPONS, CONT.

Display Name	Component 1	Component 2	Normal Attack PP	Heavy Attack PP	Ammo/ Durability	Damage	Description	Combo Card
Electric Chair	Wheelchair	Battery	100 PP	N/A	60	5	Pushable weapon that electrocutes zombies. Knock a zombie into it then launch it at other zombies by pressing the Jump button; the electrified zombie zaps others. Has a swing attack if it is picked up.	Acquired by leveling.
Flaming Gloves	Boxing Gloves	Motor Oil	100 PP	150 PP	20	5	4 swing attacks and 2 heavy, swing attacks. A good way to knock zombies away while setting them on fire. Block attacks in ranged mode.	Acquired by leveling.
Heliblade	Toy Helicopter	Machete	125 PP	N/A	50	4	Lure weapon that cuts off zombies' limbs as they get too close to the blades.	Acquired by leveling.
Fire Spitter	Toy Spitball Gun	Tiki Torch	200 PP	N/A	40	4	Shoots small balls of fire at zombies to light them up.	Acquired by leveling.
Beer Hat	Construction Hat	Beer	50 PP	N/A	10	0	Wearable item that lets Chuck drink to gain health. Be careful not to drink too fast.	Acquired by leveling.
Sticky Bomb	Lawn Dart	Dynamite	200 PP	N/A	5	5	Thrown explosive that targets a zombie's head. Mimics the lawn dart's throw attack.	Acquired by leveling.
Driller	Power Drill	Spear	100 PP	150 PP	40	4	4 stabbing attacks and a unique, heavy attack.	Acquired by leveling.
Defiler	Sledge Hammer	Fire Axe	125 PP	175 PP	60	5	3 swing attacks, a heavy, spinning attack, and a jump attack	Acquired by leveling.
Hail Mary	Football	Grenade	250 PP	N/A	10	5	Thrown explosive.	Acquired by leveling.
Freezer Bomb	Fire Extinguisher	Dynamite	250 PP	N/A	20	0	Throw this into a group of zombies. Any zombies not killed by the initial blast will be frozen.	Acquired by leveling.
Knife Gloves	Bowie Knife	Boxing Gloves	150 PP	150 PP	30	4	4 swing attacks with 2 heavy swings, all capable of cutting off a zombie's limbs. Blocks attacks in ranged mode.	Acquired by leveling.
Roaring Thunder	Battery	Goblin Mask	150 PP	N/A	60	4	Put on a zombie's head to electrocute it and shoot electrical arcs at other nearby zombies.	Acquired by leveling.
Super Slicer	Servbot Mask	Lawn Mower	100 PP	150 PP	80	5	Slicing-head weapon that has a headbutt attack and a heavy, charging attack.	Acquired by leveling.
Handy Chipper	Wheelchair	Lawn Mower	125 PP	N/A	60	4	Pushable weapon that grinds up zombies that fall into it.	Acquired by leveling.
Dynameat	Hunk of Meat	Dynamite	500 PP	N/A	10	5	Lure weapon that explodes when a zombie picks it up. Can also be shoved into a zombie's mouth for more precise detonation.	Acquired by leveling.
Electric Rake	Battery	Leaf Rake	250 PP	N/A	50	5	Thrust attack that zaps a zombie with a powerful charge of electricity. The attack can arc to other nearby zombies.	Acquired by leveling.

SKILLS, WEAPONS, AND COMBOS

							COMBO WEAPONS, CONT.		
Display Name	Component 1	Component 2	Normal Attack PP	Heavy Attack PP	Ammo/ Durability	Damage	Description	Combo Card
Parablower	Leaf Blower	Parasol	150 PP	225 PP	50	4	Mechanical thrust weapon with a unique, heavy attack.	Acquired by leveling.
Boomstick	Pitchfork	Shotgun	100 PP	1,250 PP	30	5	Basic attack can clear out multiple zombies when they are lined up. The heavy attack lifts a zombie into the air, shooting it until it is blown off the pitchfork.	Acquired by leveling.
Auger	Drill Motor	Pitchfork	150 PP	250 PP	50	4	Heavy, "clear out" swipe attack. Can also impale a zombie, then use it to bash other zombies.	Acquired by leveling.
Infernal Arms	Training Sword	Motor Oil	225 PP	N/A	60	4	4 swing attacks that light zombies on fire, as well as a heavy, shield-charge attack. Blocks attacks in ranged mode.	Acquired by leveling.
Porta Mower	2x4	Lawn Mower	250 PP	500 PP	35	4	Thrust attack with a unique, heavy attack.	Acquired by leveling.
Super B.F.G.	Blast Frequency Gun	Amplifier	50 PP	N/A	15	5	Most powerful gun in the game. Shoots a large shock wave that can take out a massive amount of zombies in one shot.	Acquired by leveling.
Tesla Ball	Bingo Ball Cage	Battery	175 PP	N/A	80	5	Swing attack and a heavy, throw attack that electrocutes nearby zombies for a short period of time.	Acquired by leveling.
Spear Launcher	Leaf Blower	Spear	150 PP	500 PP	50	4	Mechanical projectile weapon that shoots spears and has a unique, impact attack.	Acquired by leveling.
Blitzkrieg	Merc Assault Rifle	Electric Chair	50 PP	N/A	250	5	Drivable wheelchair with mounted guns. High damage output with low mobility.	Acquired by leveling.
Flamethrower	Water Gun	Gasoline Canister	25 PP	N/A	30	5	Effective spray weapon that quickly lights zombies on fire.	Acquired by defeating the psychopath Slappy (Brent Ernst).
Rocket Launcher	Rocket Fireworks	Lead Pipe	50 PP	N/A	50	4	Mechanical explosive projectile weapon. The rockets can stick into zombies prior to detonation.	Acquired from defeating the magician psychopaths (Reed Wallbeck and Roger Withers).
Plate Launcher	Plates	Cement Saw	100 PP	N/A	50	3	Mechanical projectile weapon that shoots plates that slice zombies in half.	Reward from the side mission "Tape It Or Die 1."
Blazing Aces	Tennis Racquet	Tiki Torch	250 PP	N/A	40	3	Hits flaming tennis balls into zombies, lighting them on fire and bouncing off to ignite other nearby zombies.	Reward for rescuing Left Hand Lance during the side mission "Tape It Or Die 2."

www.primagames.com

DEADRISING 2

Display Name	Component 1	Component 2	Normal Attack PP	Heavy Attack PP	Ammo/ Durability	Damage	Description	Combo Card
Exsanguinator	Vacuum Cleaner	Saw Blade	125 PP	250 PP	40	5	2 thrust attacks and a unique heavy attack.	Reward for rescuing Wallace Hertzog during the side mission "Tape It Or Die 2."
Power Guitar	Electric Guitar	Amplifier	150 PP	150 PP	40	3	Knock down attack and a unique heavy attack that causes a zombie's head to explode from the heavy metal.	Reward for rescuing Floyd Stone during the side mission "Rock Heroes."
Burning Skull	Bull Skull	Motor Oil	333 PP	N/A	50	4	Worn on your head. Has 3 head-swing attacks and a heavy charge attack that can light zombies on fire.	Hidden in Fortune City (see poster map).
Laser Sword	Gems	Flashlight	75 PP	150 PP	40	5	3 slicing swing attacks with a heavy, spin attack, also has a jump attack.	Hidden in Fortune City (see poster map).
Blambow	Bow and Arrow	Dynamite	50 PP	N/A	10	5	Explosive projectile weapon.	Hidden in Fortune City (see poster map).
Holy Arms	Training Sword	Box of Nails	150 PP	225 PP	60	4	4 swing attacks and a unique, heavy attack. Blocks attacks in ranged mode.	Hidden in Fortune City (see poster map).
Freedom Bear	Robot Bear	LMG	150 PP	N/A	400	5	A sentry gun that guns down anything that moves into its area of coverage.	Hidden in Fortune City (see poster map).
Paddlesaw	Paddle	Chain Saw	125 PP	N/A	60	5	2 swinging attacks.	Hidden in Fortune City (see poster map).
Snowball Cannon	Fire Extinguisher	Water Gun	200 PP	N/A	40	0	Gun-like weapon that freezes zombies hit by the icy snowballs.	Hidden in Fortune City (see poster map).
Tenderizers	MMA Gloves	Box of Nails	50 PP	125 PP	25	4	4 punch attacks followed by a kick and a unique, heavy attack. Blocks attacks in ranged mode.	Hidden in Fortune City (see poster map).
Spiked Bat	Baseball Bat	Box of Nails	25 PP	100 PP	60	4	2 swing attacks and a unique, heavy attack.	Hidden in Fortune City (see poster map).

UNEARTHING FORTUNE CITY

It's pure fun & game!

FORTUNE CITY NEVADA

Whether you seek relaxation and luxury or an exquisite location, it doesn't get any better than Fortune City. Step inside to discover the essence of indulgence and comfort. Fortune City defines modern luxury in the midst of timeless elegance, offering guests glorious amenities, breathtaking views, and pampering service.

Experience the thrill of gaming excitement with the latest in slot action and a wide variety of table games. Feel the exhilaration with a roll of the dice. Try to resist spending all of those winnings at one of our many fine stores. Fortune City, where the good times never know when to end!

Indulge yourself

FORTUNE CITY

POINTS OF INTEREST

◆ MAINTENANCE ROOMS

Chuck acquires the Maintenance Room Key early in the adventure, which grants him access to the many maintenance rooms scattered across Fortune City. Each of these rooms provides Chuck with the basic tools he needs to combine items into hilariously lethal combo weapons. See the "Skills, Weapons and Combos" or "Appendix" chapters of this guide for a complete list of the many different combo weapons Chuck can build.

> **NOTE**
>
> Any combo weapon can be built at any maintenance room, but each maintenance room contains a few items that help you easily construct one or two specific combo weapons there. Refer to the poster map or the tables in this chapter to quickly discover each maintenance room's contents.

S RESTROOMS (SAVE POINTS)

In a city filled with zombies and rampant psychopaths, dying can be an all-too-common occurrence. Make sure to save your progress regularly by visiting one of Fortune City's many restrooms. Here, Chuck may unload himself of his heavy burdens, marking his progress to ensure that an unexpected death or missed opportunity doesn't become a major setback.

▥ ELEVATORS

Elevators go up and down, allowing for travel between floors. Call one by interacting with the controls outside the elevator doors, then step inside and use the inner controls to put the lift in motion. Most elevators lead to the city's few rooftop areas and remain locked until you progress to a certain point in the adventure.

> **NOTE**
>
> The elevator icon is also used to denote ladders on the map.

▯ DOORS

Most doors Chuck encounters can be opened by simply approaching them and pressing the Interact button. Some doors lead to small security offices or maintenance halls—these can be closed behind Chuck after he passes through to stem the tide of zombie followers.

UNEARTHING FORTUNE CITY

Other doors are used to separate different sections of the city—these are all marked by special icons on the map. Chuck automatically closes these doors behind him after he moves through, preventing zombies from following.

TIP

Leave a section of Fortune City and then return to reset all items and objects in that area. This allows you to claim multiple items from the same place!

CAUTION

Make sure that any survivors following Chuck are close by before moving through a door that leads to a different section of the city. Survivors suffer steady damage when left behind.

UNDERGROUND ACCESS

At a certain point in the adventure, Chuck gains the ability to access the city's Underground. These dank, subsurface tunnels are accessed via special service doors, which are clearly marked with orange signage. Underground access doors are also marked on the maps for easy reference. Beware: The Underground is not a place for the faint of heart!

VEHICLES

Chuck is able to drive a variety of motorized vehicles around Fortune City to help him get where he's going with more speed and less hassle. The locations of these special vehicles area marked on this guide's poster map for your reference. Here's a look at the different vehicles Chuck can drive.

CAUTION

All vehicles can be destroyed if they suffer enough damage. This includes collisions with objects and zombies. If you don't want to lose your ride, play it safe and resist the urge to run over undead.

4X4S

4x4s are small utility trucks, and the most common vehicles in Fortune City. Driving one won't make you feel very glamorous and they're not particularly fast, but it beats having to trudge through endless waves of zombies. Chuck needs no special item to use 4x4s—he can simply get in and go. This, combined with their abundance, makes 4x4s very useful.

CARS

Have you drooled over that sports car on display inside Royal Flush Plaza? How about the SUV inside the Silver Strip's Shamrock Casino? Chuck can drive both of these vehicles, but he first needs to acquire the keys.

DEADRISING 2

Visit the pawnshop on Royal Flush Plaza's second floor to find the keys to the sports car on sale for the low, low price of only $500,000. Pop into Tinkerbox on the Silver Strip to purchase the SUV's keys for a cool $2,000,000. Save up enough moola to buy these keys and you'll be able to ride in style!

NOTE

There are plenty of ways to amass cash in Fortune City. See the previous "Brain Food" chapter for a list of the best money-making schemes.

CHOPPERS

Perhaps you've noticed the studly motorcycle that's parked atop the slots at Yucatan Casino. Chuck can drive this bad boy around after he drops down $1,000,000 to purchase its keys from the Army Surplus Gift Store on Palisades Mall's second floor. Busting up a casino has never been so easy!

Another chopper can be found in the city's Underground at Warehouse E. You don't need to spend a dime to take this beauty out for a spin, so check it out!

BIKES AND THE COMBO BAY

The chopper is great fun, but nothing beats Chuck's motorbike. Defeat the psychopath Leon Bell during the "Meet the Contestants" side mission to acquire the keys to Chuck's bike without spending a dime. Beating Leon also gives you access to the Combo Bay, located at the Silver Strip's north end.

The motorbike is the only vehicle that Chuck can customize with new paint jobs, and he can even affix certain weapons to the bike to make it far more deadly and fun. The following table lists everything that you can combine with Chuck's motorbike to transform it into a high-octane death machine.

CAUTION

Ram into all the zombies you want, but avoid collisions with objects while riding on motorbikes—crashing harms Chuck.

UNEARTHING FORTUNE CITY

COMBO BAY BIKE MODIFICATIONS			
Bike Name	**Item Required**	**Best Source**	**Notes**
Bazooka Bike	Rocket launcher (combo weapon)	Unlimited rocket fireworks at Rockets Red Glare (Silver Strip); lead pipes in alley south of Hot Excitorama (Silver Strip)	Bike with fireworks rocket launcher attached. Beware of splash damage! Ammo: 150.
Chain Saw Bike	Chain saw	Atop the Angel Lust stage's steel girders (Silver Strip)	Bike with chain saws mounted to the sides.
Machine Gun Bike	LMG	Atop the Yucatan Casino's Lucky Marble minigame.	Bike with twin machine guns attached. Ammo: 250.
Rabbit Bike	Giant stuffed rabbit	Moe's Maginations (Platinum Strip)	Bike with a stuffed rabbit attached. Zombies bounce off.
Wheelchair Bike	Wheelchair	Slot Ranch Casino or south end of Platinum Strip	Bike with an attached wheelchair. Survivors and co-op partners can ride in it!
Red Rocket	Red spray paint	American Historium (Americana Casino)	Paints the bike red.
Blue Thunder	Blue spray paint	American Historium (Americana Casino)	Paints the bike blue.
Green Machine	Green spray paint	American Historium (Americana Casino)	Paints the bike green.
Purple Punisher	Purple spray paint	Food Court (near central platform)	Paints the bike purple.
Great American	USA spray paint	American Historium (Americana Casino)	Paints the bike with a USA theme (red, white, and blue).

NOTE

The Safe House appears first in this chapter because it's the most commonly visited area; the Underground is covered last because you'll rarely venture there. All other sections of Fortune City are listed alphabetically for easy reference.

SAFE HOUSE

Only for use during citywide emergencies such as natural disasters or the unlikely event of a zombie outbreak.

SAFE HOUSE - MAIN AREA
Weapons
2x4
Bricks
Bucket
Cardboard Box
Coffee Pot
Fire Axe
Fire Extinguisher
Folding Chair
Garbage Bag
Ketchup

Weapons, cont.
Metal Trash Can
Mustard
Pallet
Pickup Dolly
Plastic Bin
Propane Tank
Push Broom
Pylon
Scissors
Serving Tray
Shower Head
Small Fern Tree

Weapons, cont.
Small Suitcase
Steel Shelving
Vacuum Cleaner
Water Cooler
Curatives
Coffee
Coffee Creamer
Melon
Milk
Orange Juice

POI
Chuck's Locker
Slot Machines
SAFE HOUSE - ROOFTOP
Weapons
Garbage Bag
Leaf Rake
Metal Barricade
Pylon
Spot Light

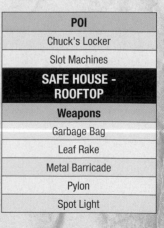

www.primagames.com

POINTS OF INTEREST

SECURITY ROOM

Chuck makes multiple visits to the Safe House's security room, where his friend Stacey Forsythe and his beloved daughter, Katey, linger, awaiting rescue. Visit Katey to bring her special gifts, along with her daily doses of Zombrex. Stacey keeps a vigilant watch over the security monitors, feeding Chuck valuable intel over a transceiver as he braves the horrors of Fortune City.

> **NOTE**
>
> See the "Appendix" chapter of this guide for a complete list of the various gifts Chuck can give to Katey for PP bonuses.

RESTROOM

The Safe House restroom provides Chuck a convenient place to break and save his progress. Chuck's locker is also located here, where all of his unlockable attire is stored.

CAFETERIA

Plenty of nutritious foods are found within the Safe House's cafeteria, although the supply does dwindle as hungry survivors help themselves. Check the cafeteria often to speak with survivors you've saved and see if they have any special tasks that need doing.

CLINIC

Chuck finds some survivors badly wounded, and these poor souls must wait it out at the clinic. Stop by often to see if Chuck can lend any of these unfortunate victims a hand.

UNEARTHING FORTUNE CITY

AMERICANA CASINO

Catch the winning fever with Americana Casino's nonstop gaming action. Whether you are a one-armed bandit or the king of poker, this casino's lively, rocking atmosphere will leave you in awe. At Americana Casino, winning is all of the fun.

AMERICANA CASINO - MAIN AREA

Weapons
Broadsword
Casino Chips
Croupier Stick
Cushioned Tall Chair
Electric Guitar
Handbag
Indoor Garbage Can
Metal Garbage Can
Novelty Poker Chip
Playing Cards
Pylon
Roulette Wheel
Spear
Square Sign
Stand
Stool
Velvet Bar
Water Cooler
Wheelchair
Yellow Tall Chair

Restoratives
Beer
Whisky

POI
Minigame 13 (Cash Me If You Can)
Minigame 14 (Ride the Thunder)
Minigame 15 (Wild West Poker Draw!)
Slot Machines

AMERICANA CASINO - UPPER PLATFORMS

Weapons
Broadsword
Giant Stuffed Rabbit
Handgun

Special
Magazine 24 (Bargaining 1)
Zombrex

AMERICANA CASINO - WEST RESTROOM AREA

Weapons
2x4
Bowie Knife
Cardboard Box
Lead Pipe
Pylon

AMERICANA CASINO - EAST CASHIER/VAULT AREA

Weapons
Battery
Casino Chips
Computer Case
Construction Hat
Drill Motor
Handgun
Keyboard
LCD Monitor
Merc Assault Rifle
Propane Tank
Sledge Hammer
Stool

Restoratives
Coffee
Coffee Creamer

AMERICANA CASINO - NORTH SECURITY OFFICE

Weapons
Computer Case
Fire Extinguisher
Handgun
Indoor Garbage Can
Keyboard
LCD Monitor
Metal Garbage Can
Nightstick
Small Potted Plant
Stool
Vacuum Cleaner
Water Cooler

Restoratives
Coffee

Clothing
Dealer Visor

AMERICANA CASINO - MAINTENANCE ROOM 28

Weapons
Battery
Fountain Firework
Lizard Mask
Wheelchair (right outside)

AMERICANA CASINO - A101 BENNIE JACK'S BBQ SHACK

Weapons
Bowie Knife
Boxing Gloves
Bucket
Cash Register
Chain Saw
Chef Knife
Cooking Oil
Drink Cart
Giant Stuffed Rabbit
Handbag (upstairs)
Handgun
Highback Oak Chair
Ketchup
Lizard Mask
Metal Garbage Can
Mustard
Pan
Plates
Push Broom
Serving Tray
Spear (upstairs)
Stool (upstairs)

Restoratives
Baked Potato
BBQ Ribs
Beer
Hamburger
Whiskey

Special
Magazine 25 (*Driving*)

POI
Stove
ATMs (right outside)

AMERICANA CASINO - A102 SHOTS & AWE	AMERICANA CASINO - A103 THE AMERICAN HISTORIUM
Weapons	**Weapons**
Cash Register	Blue Spray Paint
Cushioned Tall Chair	Cash Register
Gasoline Canister	Fountain Firework
Restoratives	Green Spray Paint
Beer	Power Drill
Vodka	Red Spray Paint
Wine	Small Suitcase
Clothing	USA Spray Paint
Casual Beach Wear	**Clothing**
POI	American Showman Helmet
Blender	American Showman Jumpsuit
	Fortune City Red Shirt
	White Leisure Suit

POINTS OF INTEREST

MAINTENANCE ROOM 28

Have a look at the poster map and you'll notice that Americana Casino is home to the 28th maintenance room. Combine the lizard mask and fountain firework you discover inside the room to form the fountain lizard combo weapon, and merge the battery with the wheelchair that's right outside the room to build the electric chair.

SWORD FIGHT

Sure, you noticed all of those electric guitars on Americana Casino's walls, but did you spot the *broadswords*? Three of them adorn the walls: One is near the small north security office, and another is on the opposite wall, just to the south. The third wall-mounted broadsword is found near the door to Platinum Strip. Broadswords are awesome, but don't take our word for it—grab one and slay for yourself.

UP IN ARMS

Swords are great, but you might prefer a bit more range. Find two handguns in Americana Casino's small, north security room—these are always accessible. After you complete Case 3-1, you'll also gain access to the northwest cashier/vault area; here you can always find a rapid-fire assault rifle.

WILD WEST POKER DRAW!

Inspect Americana Casino's east wall to discover a special video poker minigame. Pay the game's low buy-in to draw your hand of five cards, which light up on the wall. After drawing your hand, choose which cards you wish to keep by standing in front of them and pressing the Interact button when the "hold" command appears. Hit the draw button on the far left a second time to swap out any cards you didn't hold onto for new ones. The goal is to make your best five-card poker hand.

UNEARTHING FORTUNE CITY

647 KILLED

The higher the hand you make after your second draw, the more cash you'll win. If you're not familiar with poker, here are the best possible hands, from highest (most rare) to lowest (most common). Keep in mind that the highest hands are extremely difficult to make—keep it simple and try for pairs for the best odds of making money.

- Royal Flush (ace, king, queen, jack, 10, all of the same suit)
- Straight Flush (a five-card Straight, all of the same suit)
- Four of a Kind (four of any one card, such as four kings or four 4s)
- Full House (Three of a Kind, plus one Pair)
- Flush (any five cards, all of the same suit)
- Straight (five cards in consecutive order, such as 3, 4, 5, 6, 7.)
- Three of a Kind (three of any one card, such as three jacks or three 3s)
- Two Pair (two separate Pairs of cards, such as two 9s and two 5s)
- One Pair (one Pair of cards, such as two aces or two 2s)

NOTE

Finishing Wild West Poker Draw! with just a high card won't win you any prize money. Try again!

CASH ME IF YOU CAN

512 KILLED

Just north of the casino's central bar, Shots & Awe, stands a special minigame booth. Pay $100 to hop inside, then mash the indicated button as fast as you can to grab all the cash you can carry. The faster you hit that button, the more moola you'll pocket.

RIDE THE THUNDER

615 KILLED

Ready for more minigames? Mosey just west of Cash Me If You Can to locate Thunder, the mechanical bull. Hop on and hold on tight as you press the onscreen buttons before they vanish. Taming this raging bull isn't easy but doing so earns you significant PP—and the more times you win, the more PP you can earn.

PREMIUM BLEND

520 KILLED

The casino's central bar, Shots & Awe, sports a very special object: a blender. Chuck can throw any two food or drink items into blenders to create powerful mixed drinks that bestow special benefits! With unlimited amounts of wine and vodka at the Shots & Awe bar, it's easy to mix together two wine bottles to form Quick Steps that increase Chuck's speed, or two vodkas that create Pain Killers, which reduce the damage Chuck suffers from attacks.

NOTE

See the "Appendix" chapter of this guide for a complete list of juice blends and their effects.

HACK UP THE SHACK

Bennie Jack's BBQ Shack holds plenty of delicious foodstuffs that are certain to keep Chuck in good health. But check its kitchen to discover (gasp!)—a chain saw! Rip that ignition cord and start carving out your own sides of undead beef.

Make sure to check out the Shack's second story, where you'll discover a spear and handgun. If you're feeling adventurous, hop onto the counter to the left of the fire pit, then make a daring leap onto the casino's hanging light fixtures!

While slaughtering the BBQ Shack's undead patrons, search around to find a *Driving* magazine sitting on a table. When carried, this mag greatly increases the durability of all four-wheeled vehicles, such as 4x4s and cars.

Leap along the lights to locate a very special ledge. Another magazine awaits up here, *Bargaining*, which reduces the cost of items at pawnshops by 10 percent. You'll also find a broadsword, handgun, lots of cash, and—best of all—a dose of that most rare miracle medicine, Zombrex. As you can see, it pays to explore everything that Fortune City has to offer—so keep reading!

UNEARTHING FORTUNE CITY

ATLANTICA CASINO

The fabled riches of Atlantis have returned and await you in the tides of gold at Atlantica Casino! Try your hand at our signature Wheel of Destiny or watch Reed and Roger, the magical duo that are taking Fortune City by storm!

ATLANTICA CASINO - MAIN AREA

Weapons

Handbag
Square Sign
Large Fern Tree
Casino Chips
Croupier Stick
Indoor Garbage Can
Stand
Suitcase
Velvet Bar
Treasure Chest
Fancy Tall Chair
Beach Ball
Water Gun
Drink Cart
Swordfish
Machete
Newspaper
Flashlight
Spear
Lobster
Serving Tray
Amplifier
Acoustic Guitar
Training Sword
Whipped Cream

Restoratives

Beer
Fish
Drink Cocktail
Whiskey

Special

Combo Card 5 (Holy Arms)

POI

ATMs
Minigame 8 (Killer Blackjack)
Minigame 9 (Ride the Waves)
Minigame 10 (Wheel of Destiny)
Slot Machines
Snack Machines

ATLANTICA CASINO - UPPER PLATFORMS

Weapons

Battle Axe
Box of Nails
Cardboard Box
Gasoline Canister
Giant Stuffed Rabbit
Handbag
Handgun
Machete
Suitcase
Training Sword
Treasure Chest
Water Gun
Whipped Cream

Special

Magazine 14 (Drinking)

ATLANTICA CASINO - NORTH POKER ROOM

Weapons

Bucket
Casino Chips
Computer Case
Drink Cocktail
Flashlight
Green Spray Paint
Handbag
Handgun
Indoor Garbage Can
Keyboard
Large Fern Tree
LCD Monitor
Playing Cards
Push Broom
Serving Tray
Stand
Velvet Bar
Water Cooler

Restoratives

Beer
Drink Cocktail
Whiskey

Special

Magazine 15 (Games)

ATLANTICA CASINO - NORTH MAINTENANCE AREA

Weapons

Bucket
Crowbar
Garbage Bag
Newspaper
Power Drill
Push Broom

ATLANTICA CASINO - SOUTH SECURITY OFFICE

Weapons

Casino Chips
Computer Case
Fire Extinguisher
Green Spray Paint
Handgun
Keyboard
LCD Monitor
Merc Assault Rifle
Nightstick
Push Broom
Stool
Water Gun

Restoratives

Coffee Creamer

ATLANTICA CASINO - SOUTH MAGIC STAGE

Weapons

Box of Nails
Flashlight
Handbag
Large Fern Tree
Lizard Mask
Mic Stand
Newspaper
Padded Blue Chair
Power Drill
Push Broom

Restoratives

Beer
Drink Cocktail
Whiskey
Wine

ATLANTICA CASINO - MAINTENANCE ROOM 10

Weapons

Box of Nails
Construction Hat
Training Sword

ATLANTICA CASINO - T101 SIPPARELLOS

Weapons

Barstool
Cardboard Box
Cash Register
Chef Knife
Gift Shop Lamp
Handbag
Keg
Large Fern Tree
Square Sign
Treasure Chest

Restoratives

Beans
Beer
Drink Cocktail
Pineapple
Vodka
Whiskey

POI

Blender

POINTS OF INTEREST

MAINTENANCE ROOM 10

Atlantica Casino has just one maintenance room, located to the south beyond Reed and Roger's magic stage. Inside you find the makings for the holy arms combo weapon (a box of nails and a training sword), along with a construction hat that can be merged with one of the many beer bottles around stage to create a health-replenishing beer hat.

COMBO CARD: HOLY ARMS

Inspect Atlantica Casino's south wall (near the craps tables) to locate a poster that gives Chuck the notion to build the holy arms combo weapon. Now you can earn even more PP from the holy arms you build in the casino's maintenance room!

RIDE THE WAVES

Behind Atlantica Casino's west statue lies a challenging minigame called Ride the Waves. This one's similar to the bull-riding game at Americana Casino; hop onto the dolphin and press the onscreen buttons to hold tight as Chuck thrashes all about. Play to win cash and PP—the more times you win, the bigger the payouts!

KILLER BLACKJACK

Explore the east side of the casino to discover a video blackjack game affixed to the far wall. Place a bet to be dealt your two cards—the object is to approach a score of 21 without "busting" (scoring over 21). Aces are scored as either one point or 11, depending on which would be most beneficial to your hand. Kings, queens, and jacks are worth 10 points apiece. All other cards are scored at face value.

After placing your bet and being dealt your initial two cards, use the machine's buttons to either "hit" (take another card to increase your score), "stand" (stick with what you've got), or "double down" (double your bet and take another card, then automatically stand). If your first two cards don't put you close to 21, you've got to hit to have any chance of beating the dealer. If you've scored close to 21, such as a 19, stand to see if you've beaten the dealer's hand. Doubling down is risky—only do this when you're fairly certain that taking one more card will make your hand a winner.

TIP

The best time to double down is when you've drawn a hand worth 11 points. This is because there are several cards in the deck that are worth 10 points, which would give you 21, and nothing you could draw next could possibly cause you to bust.

WHEEL OF DESTINY

Ready to test the whims of fate? Then spin the Wheel of Destiny! Located aboard the large pirate ship, the Wheel of Destiny is a fun yet pricey minigame that can have you winning big—or burning through lots of your hard-earned scratch. Spin the wheel for a chance to win a huge cash payout or a significant amount of PP. The only other option is to win nothing, at which point you're out a whole lot of moola.

UNEARTHING FORTUNE CITY

SECURITY BREACH

Smash out a window and leap into Atlantica Casino's south security room to score a handgun, a coffee creamer, and a powerful assault rifle, among other goodies. Not a bad little cache, especially since you can claim these goodies during any visit to the casino.

ON THE JUICE

Swing by Atlantica Casino's central bar, Sipparellos, to score plenty of health-boosting booze. There's a blender here as well; use it to mix up potent juice drinks with special properties. See the "Appendix" chapter for a complete list of juice blends.

POKER ROOM

When the action on the casino floor gets a little too heavy, duck into the north poker room and close the door behind you to catch a breather. Here you'll discover a magazine, *Games*, which increases the durability of gaming weapons, such as croupier sticks. There's a handgun in here as well.

TIP

Two ATMs stand just outside the poker room—smash 'em for fast cash, or better yet, use a hacker combo weapon to withdraw even more dough! You can easily build a hacker at Maintenance Room 8, located in the nearby Palisades Mall.

HIDDEN HEIGHTS

Climb onto the standing poster display near the north poker room, and you can reach the high ledge above. Up here you find some of the Atlantica Casino's best weapons, including a machete and battle-axe.

NOTE

You can also reach the casino's upper platforms by climbing around the giant clamshell to the south, near the magic stage.

From the height of the ledge, leap to the decorative octopus arms that spiral high above the casino floor. Here you can score a training sword and box of nails, which combine to form the holy arms combo weapon. You also find a magazine up here, *Drinking*, which allows Chuck to overindulge in alcoholic beverages without fear of becoming ill.

TIP

Grab that *Drinking* mag, then build a beer hat at the nearby maintenance room. Now you can heal Chuck over and over without fear of making him ill!

FOOD COURT

Come over to the Food Court for hearty meals from all four corners of the globe. From burgers to pasta, cheesecake to tacos, we've got everything your empty stomach craves!

FOOD COURT - MAIN AREA

Weapons

Ad board
Cactus Plant
Green Spray Paint
Large Fern Tree
Patio Chair
Patio Table
Plastic Garbage Can
Shopping Boxes
Stone Statue

Restoratives

Coffee
Donut
Fries
Hamburger
Large Soda
Pasta
Pizza
Snack
Taco
Whiskey
Wine

Special

Combo Card 2 (Blambow)

POI

ATMs
Snack Machines

FOOD COURT - CENTRAL PLATFORM AND INFO BOOTH

Weapons

Acoustic Guitar
Bucket
Drum
Green Spray Paint
Keyboard
LCD Monitor
Mic Stand
Moosehead (atop south info booth)
Purple Spray Paint
Push Broom
Small Suitcase
Square Sign
Stool

Restoratives

Coffee

FOOD COURT - UPPER PLATFORMS

Weapons

2x4
Assault Rifle
Bow and Arrow
Drill Motor
Dynamite
Giant Stuffed Bull
Green Spray Paint
Large Barrel
Paint Can
Power Drill
Push Broom
Saw Blade
Step Ladder

Restoratives

Coffee
Snack

Special

Magazine 6 (Bargaining 2)

FOOD COURT - MAINTENANCE ROOM 5

Weapons

Dynamite
Green Spray Paint (just outside)
Lawn Dart
Newspaper
Pylon (just outside)

Restoratives

Whiskey (just outside)

FOOD COURT - F101 WILD WEST GRILL HOUSE

Weapons

Bull Head
Cooking Oil
Cooking Pot
Handbag
Keg
Ketchup
Large Barrel
Meat Cleaver
Mining Pick
Motor Oil
Mustard
Pitchfork
Plates
Round Potted Plant
Serving Tray
Small Painting
Tiki Torch

Restoratives

Bacon
BBQ Chicken
BBQ Ribs
Beer
Vodka

POI

Stoves

FOOD COURT - F102 CUCINA DONNACCI

Weapons

Cardboard Box
Chef Knife
Cooking Oil
Cooking Pot
Handbag
Large Potted Plant
Meat Cleaver
Padded Blue Chair
Pan
Plastic Garbage Can
Plates
Serving Tray
Small Fern Tree
Small Vase

FOOD COURT - F103 CHEESECAKE MANIA

Weapons

Cardboard Box
Cash Register
Handbag
Highback Oak Chair
Patio Table
Plates
Push Broom

UNEARTHING FORTUNE CITY

Restoratives
Brownie
Cake
Cookies
Donut
Ice Cream
Pie
Whiskey

FOOD COURT - F104 LOMBARDI'S

Weapons
Cardboard Box
Cash Register
Giant Stuffed Rabbit
Gumball Machine
Sandwich Board

Restoratives
Jellybeans

FOOD COURT - F105 HAMBURGER FIEFDOM

Weapons
Cash Register
Cooking Oil
Fire Extinguisher
Ketchup
Lance
Mustard
Pan
Plastic Garbage Can
Serving Tray

Restoratives
Fries
Hamburger
Large Soda
Onion Rings

POI
Stove

FOOD COURT - F106 ROJO DIABLO MEXICAN RESTAURANT

Weapons
Acoustic Guitar
Cactus Plant
Cardboard Box
Cash Register
Donkey Lamp
Fancy Painting
Highback Oak Chair
Metal Garbage Can
Pan
Plates
Serving Tray
Stool

Restoratives
Apple
Beans
Burrito
Chili
Taco

POI
Blender
Stoves

FOOD COURT - F107 HUNGRY JOE'S PIZZERIA

Weapons
Cardboard Box
Machete (atop kitchen vents)
Plastic Garbage Can
Serving Tray
Stool

Restoratives
Large Soda
Pizza

FOOD COURT - F108 SPEEDY EXPRESSO

Weapons
Cardboard Box
Cash Register
Coffee Pot
Metal Garbage Can
Patio Chair
Patio Table

Restoratives
Brownie
Coffee
Coffee Creamer
Donut
Milk

POINTS OF INTEREST

MAINTENANCE ROOM 5

Visit the Food Court's only maintenance room to score the makings for a sticky bomb (a lawn dart and dynamite), along with the components for a fiery molotov (a newspaper and bottle of whiskey, which lies just outside the room). Talk about explosive flavor!

GOOD EATS

There's obviously no shortage of health-restoring nourishment within the Food Court, but certain spots supply better foods than others. You'll find unlimited amounts of pie and cake at Cheesecake Mania if you smash the glass counter—these aren't the most powerful restoratives, but with an unlimited supply, it's a good spot to hit if you just want to heal Chuck.

Speedy Expresso sports two milks behind the counter, along with a potent coffee creamer. Very nutritious!

Of course, nothing beats a healthy juice blend, and the Rojo Diablo Mexican Restaurant has the blender you need to mix up all sorts of drinks. Juices bestow special benefits to Chuck; see the "Appendix" chapter for full disclosure.

COOK IT UP

Did you know that Chuck can score 1,000 PP by getting cheffy in the kitchen? Several of the Food Court's eateries have stoves in their kitchens that can be examined; do this with a pan in hand to have Chuck place the pan on the burner, heating it up for a tasty PP morsel.

> **NOTE**
>
> Chuck only receives the PP bonus from stoves when a fresh pan is set atop a burner that has not yet been used for this purpose.

The following stores have one or more stoves that can be used to score a bit of bonus PP:

- Hamburger Fiefdom
- Rojo Diablo Mexican Restaurant
- Wild West Grill House
- Cucina Donnacci

FOOD FIGHT

Health-restoring nourishment is everywhere in the Food Court, but there are some fine weapons to be had here as well. Most of the best are found within Hamburger Fiefdom; here you'll discover a training sword mounted to the wall, along with two lances held by suits of armor—all very deadly.

UNEARTHING FORTUNE CITY

Inside Hungry Joe's Pizzeria, make a leap from the back counter to reach the top of the kitchen vents. This is a jump for joy, for up here you discover a razor-sharp machete!

Then there's the pair of pitchforks you can't miss as you enter the Wild West Grill House. These aren't the best weapons around, but by combining them with the drill motors hidden atop the Food Court's upper platforms, you can create some exceptional augers. (More on the upper platforms in a bit.)

CASH DIET

Low on funds? Find an ATM just outside of Rojo Diablo Mexican Restaurant, and another on the wall between Cucina Donnacci and the Wild West Grill House. Bash these for fast cash, or zap 'em with a hacker combo weapon for even more bills.

DINE AND DASH

Climb to the top of the small, circular booth near the food court's south entrance to discover a very rare item: the mighty moosehead! Don this unique piece of headgear, then hold the Attack button to run around, ramming through zombies as you move at speed. The skulls affixed to the wall of the Wild West Grill House can be used in a similar fashion.

UP ALONG THE AWNINGS

Hop onto the snack machines near Lombardi's. From this height, you can jump onto Lombardi's awning to access a hidden storage space!

First things first: Circle around Lombardi's awning to discover a hidden stick of dynamite. Hang onto this for now.

The storage space contains a drill motor—this can be combined with one of the pitchforks at the Wild West Grill House to create the deadly auger combo weapon.

DEADRISING 2

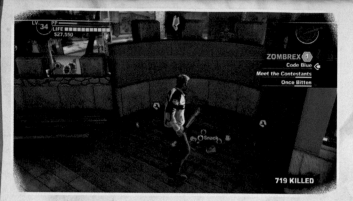

The high storage area also contains two bow and arrow weapons, along with a second stick of dynamite. This gives you the makings for two mighty blambows!

NOTE

You may also encounter a survivor named Jasper up here if you haven't located him before. Simply speak with Jasper to get him to join you.

At the storage area's far end sits a magazine, *Bargaining 2*, which reduces the cost of pawnshop items by 10 percent. Combine this with other *Bargaining* magazines to greatly reduce the cost of pawnshop goods—see the poster map or "Appendix" chapter for a complete listing of magazines.

Step onto Speedy Expresso's awning, and from there, jump to the neighboring awning (Joe's Pizzeria) to obtain a rapid-fire assault rifle that makes short work of zombies.

Lastly, a second drill motor sits atop the Wild West Grill House's exterior catwalk. To reach it, climb onto the snack machines near the Grill House, then leap up to the catwalk. Grab the drill motor and combine it with the Grill House's other pitchfork to create a second deadly auger.

COMBO CARD: BLAMBOW

Inspect the poster on the wall near the Wild West Grill House to obtain the blambow combo card. Now you can score even more PP from kills you make with these fantastic combo weapons, whose ingredients you find in the Food Court's elevated storage space.

UNEARTHING FORTUNE CITY

FORTUNE CITY ARENA

This month at Fortune City Arena: "Terror Is Reality!" Experience the sporting event that's sweeping the nation firsthand. Families with young children: Ask about our "TIR for Tots" seating section for special discount rates.

FORTUNE CITY ARENA - MAIN AREA
Weapons
Cardboard Box
Fire Axe
Flash Light
Foam Hand
Garbage Can
Green Spray Paint
Handbag
Metal Barricade
Pylon
Suitcase
Restoratives
Hot Dog
Large Soda
POI
Snack Machine

FORTUNE CITY ARENA - NORTH SECURITY AREA
Weapons
Bench
Computer Case
Flashlight
Garbage Bag
Handgun
Highback Oak Chair
Indoor Garbage Can
Keyboard
LCD Monitor
Nightstick
Plastic Bin
Stool
Utility Cart
Water Cooler
Restoratives
Coffee Creamer
Snack
Special
Magazine 21 (Rescue)
POI
Snack Machine

FORTUNE CITY ARENA - SOUTH GREEN ROOMS
Weapons
Bench
Cardboard Box
Donkey Lamp
Electric Guitar
Fire Axe
Fire Extinguisher
Flashlight
Foam Hand
Folding Chair
Garbage Can
Handbag
Hanger
Highback Oak Chair
Indoor Garbage Can
Plastic Bin
Square Sign
Stool
Suitcase
Water Cooler
Restoratives
Coffee
Donut
Hot Dog
Large Soda
Snack
POI
ATMs
Snack Machines

FORTUNE CITY ARENA - MAINTENANCE ROOM 23
Weapons
Dynamite
Fire Extinguisher
Machete
Push Broom (right outside)

FORTUNE CITY ARENA - E101 TERROR TOGS
Weapons
Cash Register
Stool
Clothing
TIR Outfit

FORTUNE CITY ARENA - E102 HOSTILE ZONE
Weapons
Cardboard Box
Cash Register
Stool
Clothing
Baseball Cap TIR

POINTS OF INTEREST

MAINTENANCE ROOM 23

Fortune City Arena has just one maintenance room, which contains the makings for a freezer bomb (fire extinguisher and dynamite)—the hoard of undead in the arena's main area is the perfect target on which to test this deadly device! Merge the room's machete with the push broom that's right outside to fashion a nasty pole weapon as well.

IN SECURITY

A handgun is stashed in the security office near Maintenance Room 23. There's a magazine in here as well, *Rescue*, which gives you a 25 percent to PP gained from survivor-related activities (convincing survivors to join, escorting them to the Safe House, etc.). It's a good idea to collect this mag early in the adventure to help Chuck level up with all speed.

MONEY AND GRUB

If you're in need of cash or healing, check the arena's south maintenance hall to locate several snack machines and a couple of ATMs. Smash or zap the ATMs with a hacker combo weapon to loose some bills, then insert some into the snack machines to score as many snacks as you desire.

> **TIP**
>
> Find a flashlight and computer case in the arena's security room, which combine to form the hacker.

FORTUNE CITY HOTEL

Stay a night in the lap of luxury at the five-star Fortune City Hotel! World-renowned for its fantastic views, this four-story "Good Fortune" suite is complete with four hot tubs, three saunas and the largest "mini"-bar in the continental USA.

FORTUNE CITY HOTEL - LOBBY
Weapons
Computer Case
Fancy Painting
Handbag
Handgun
Indoor Garbage Can
Keyboard
Large Fern Tree
Large Vase
LCD monitor
Long Stick
Protestor Sign
Round Potted Plant
Scissors
Small Suitcase
Small Vase
Square Sign
Stand
Table Lamp
Water Bottle
Water Cooler
Wheelchair
Restoratives
Coffee
Coffee Creamer
Fries
Hamburger
Large Soda
Special
Magazine 23 (Skateboarding)

FORTUNE CITY HOTEL - ROOFTOP
Weapons
Cardboard Box
Flashlight
Garbage Bag
Golf Club
Indoor Garbage Can
Metal Barricade
Military Case
Money Case
Patio Chair
Patio Table
Playing Cards
Pylon
Spot Light
Restoratives
Beer
Orange Juice
Vodka

POINTS OF INTEREST

COUNTER ATTACK

The hotel lobby is a small area with limited weapons and food, but the best of the bunch are found behind the south reception counter. Here you find a handgun and a coffee creamer.

The brass stands and velvet bars in front of the reception counter are some of the better melee weapons in the hotel lobby. Stands are particularly effective at beating back the undead, but they won't last long.

PRIMA OFFICIAL GAME GUIDE   52

UNEARTHING FORTUNE CITY

SKATE OR DIE

Find a magazine, *Skateboarding*, on the coffee table near the door to South Plaza. This mag greatly enhances the durability of those speedy skateboards, and it also allows Chuck to ollie (jump) while riding a skateboard, helping him clear obstacles. Just press the Jump button to perform this handy trick.

STICK IT TO 'EM

Chuck can obtain an endless supply of long stick weapons from the tall reed-filled vases near the hotel lobby's elevators and north entry doors. These fragile weapons break after just a few uses, but at least you won't run out of them. Try hurling them like spears.

FORTUNE PARK

Scenic Fortune Park, where the sun is always shining and the birds are always singing. A perfect centerpiece to fantastic Fortune City and a great place to take an afternoon stroll, see the sights, and breathe in the fresh desert air.

FORTUNE PARK - MAIN AREA
Weapons
Bench
Chain Saw
Construction Hat
Dynamite
Football
Garbage Bag
Garbage Can
Grenade
Handgun
Leaf Blower
Leaf Rake
Power Drill
Small Fern Tree
Soccer Ball
Speaker
Square Sign
Water Gun
Special
4x4
POI
Minigame 11 (Motion Madness)

FORTUNE PARK - CENTRAL GROTTO
Weapons
Football
Garbage Bag
Lawn Dart
Lawn Mower
Metal Baseball Bat
Pitchfork
Small Fern Tree
Water Gun
Clothing
Flower Head Piece

FORTUNE PARK - MAINTENANCE ROOM 11
Weapons
Bowie Knife
Boxing Gloves
Dynamite (right outside)
Hunk of Meat (right outside)

FORTUNE PARK - MAINTENANCE ROOM 12
Weapons
2x4
Battery
Lawn Mower (right outside)
Leaf Rake (right outside)
Special
Magazine 16 (Domestic)

FORTUNE PARK - MAINTENANCE ROOM 13
Weapons
Fire Extinguisher
Green Spray Paint (just outside)
Lawn Mower (just outside)
Pylon

POINTS OF INTEREST

MAINTENANCE ROOM 11

Fortune Park's south maintenance room contains a bowie knife and a pair of boxing gloves, allowing you to shred through zombies with an awesomely lethal set of knife gloves. A stick of dynamite and a hunk of meat lie on the ground just outside; combine these to form some dynameat.

> **TIP**
>
> For massive amounts of PP, charge into the hoard of zombies near the park's south gate, shove dynameat into a zombie's mouth and then split—the catastrophic explosion that follows is well worth the risk!

MAINTENANCE ROOM 12

Another lawn mower rests just outside of the central park's maintenance room, along with a leaf rake. Inside there's a battery and two 2x4s. Combine the battery with the leaf rake to form an electric rake, and rig the lawn mower and a 2x4 together to build an extremely nasty porta-mower. There's a magazine inside this maintenance room as well, *Domestic*, which increases the durability of furniture items.

MAINTENANCE ROOM 13

A can of spray paint and lies just outside of Fortune Park's north maintenance room; inside you find a fire extinguisher and a pylon. This allows you to build a head-bursting air horn (spray paint + pylon). Combine the fire extinguisher with one of the numerous water guns found in watery sections of the park to form a snowball cannon.

HAVING A BALL

A strange-looking wireframe ball stands on a platform just south of Maintenance Room 13. Use the nearby pedestal to play a unique minigame called Motion Madness, in which Chuck enters the ball and rolls around in place like a human hamster. Follow the onscreen commands to roll the ball in various directions until the game ends and Chuck exits the ball a winner, pocketing some easy PP.

Beat the Motion Madness minigame three times for a special treat: Chuck not only earns a boatload of PP, but also gets to remain inside the ball afterward, where  he's able to roll all around the park! Let the good times roll as you smash through zombies for as long as the ball lasts.

UNEARTHING FORTUNE CITY

GRASS STASHES

Many useful items are stashed in the grassy patches around Fortune Park. Examine the grassy ledge along the south wall to discover a football and two grenades—use these to make a hail mary that can score you big points around here.

Finally, explore the grass to the north of the grotto to locate another football, along with a rare leaf blower. Use the football to form another hail mary; the leaf blower can be combined with any parasol to construct a high-powered parablower.

Two fenced-off grassy areas lie to the south of the central grotto. There's a stick of dynamite hidden in the one to the east, and two grenades are found in the one to the west. You'll also find a deadly chain saw and a useful 4x4 near the west patch of fenced-off grass.

A lawn mower awaits in the grass that's just south of the central grotto, and four lawn darts are close by. Combine a lawn dart with the aforementioned dynamite to build a sticky bomb, and have as much fun with the lawn mower as you like, perhaps combining it with that other 2x4 inside of the central maintenance room for a second porta-mower.

PALISADES MALL

You've never seen a shopping mall like this, with marble statues and towering pillars, Palisades Mall brings classic style to a new age of consumerism. Two floors of shopping utopia are waiting for you!

PALISADES MALL 1F - MAIN AREA

Weapons

| Ad Board |
| Centurion Bust |
| Drill Motor |
| Fancy Tall Chair |
| Indoor Garbage Can |
| Large Fern Tree |
| Lawn Dart |
| Lead Pipe |
| Newspaper |
| Novelty Perfume Bottle |
| Pitchfork |
| Sandwich Board |
| Shopping Boxes |
| Soccer Ball |
| Square Sign |
| Tennis Racquet |

Restoratives

| Brownie |
| Coffee |
| Cookies |
| Jellybeans |
| Pineapple |

POI

| ATMs |
| Slot Machines |

PALISADES MALL 1F - GROTTO

Weapons

| Beach Ball |
| Casino Chips |
| Chain Saw |
| Hunk of Meat |
| Keg |
| LMG |
| Massager |
| Paddle |
| Parasol |
| Playing Cards |
| Speaker |
| Tiki Torch |
| Water Gun |
| Whipped Cream |

Restoratives

| Drink Cocktail |
| Melon |
| Vodka |

Special

| Magazine 8 (Playboy) |

POI

| Blender |

PALISADES MALL 1F - MAINTENANCE ROOM 7

Weapons

| Fire Extinguisher |
| Push Broom |
| Water Gun |

PALISADES MALL 1F - MAINTENANCE ROOM 8

Weapons

| Computer Case |
| Flashlight |
| Motor Oil |
| Boxing Gloves (right outside) |

PALISADES MALL 1F - P101 FINDERS PEEPERS

Weapons

| Cash Register |
| Large Fern Tree |
| Rotating Display |
| Small Potted Plant |

Clothing

| Black-Rimmed Glasses |
| Rocker Glasses |

PALISADES MALL 1F - P102 FAIRMOANS

Weapons

| Cardboard Box |
| Cash Register |
| Novelty Perfume Bottle |
| Shampoo |
| Shopping Boxes |

Restoratives

| Hot Dog |
| Large Soda |

Clothing

| Blue Hair |
| Pink Hair |

PALISADES MALL 1F - 103 ULTIMATE PLAYHOUSE

Weapons

| Bag of Marbles |
| Cash Register |
| Servbot Mask |
| Toy Helicopter |
| Toy Spitball Gun |
| Water Gun |

Restoratives

| Fries |
| Large Soda |

Clothing

| Funny Servbot Mask |
| Kid's Super Hero Costume |

Special

| Magazine 9 (Amusement) |

PALISADES MALL 1F - P104 FLEXIN'

Weapons

| Baseball Bat |
| Beach Ball |
| Boxing Gloves |
| Bucket |
| Cardboard Box |
| Cash Register |
| Dolly |
| Dumbbell |
| Medicine Ball |

Restoratives

| Snack |

POI

| Exercise Bikes |

PALISADES MALL 1F - P105 BEACH BODY SWIM HOUSE

Weapons

| Beach Ball |
| Cash Register |
| Computer Case |
| Hanger |
| Keyboard |
| Lamp |
| LCD Monitor |

Restoratives

| Coffee |
| Donut |

Clothing

| Banana Hammock |
| Sport Glasses |
| Surf Wetsuit |
| Tourist Boat Hat |

UNEARTHING FORTUNE CITY

PALISADES MALL 1F - P106 WALLINGTON'S

Weapons
Cardboard Box
Cash Register
Computer Case
Handbag
Hanger
LCD Monitor
Padded Blue Chair
Small Suitcase

Restoratives
Whiskey

Clothing
Highbrow Ensemble
Tuxedo

PALISADES MALL 1F - P107 SHANK'S

Weapons
Bow and Arrow
Bowie Knife
Broadsword
Cash Register
Machete
Meat Cleaver
Serving Tray

Restoratives
Large Soda
Melon

Clothing
Mohawk Hair
Shaved Head

PALISADES MALL 1F - P108 BAGGED!

Weapons
Cash Register
Handbag
Small Fern Tree
Small Suitcase
Suitcase

Restoratives
Large Soda

Clothing
Black Dress Shoes
Yellow Sneakers

PALISADES MALL 1F - P109 THE VENUS TOUCH

Weapons
Cushioned Tall Chair
Fancy Painting
Flower Pot
Handbag
Keyboard
Large Fern Tree
LCD Monitor
Massager
Shampoo
Small Vase
Stool

Restoratives
Coffee
Snack

Clothing
Grey Hair

PALISADES MALL 1F - P110 KOKONUTZ SPORTS TOWN

Weapons
Basketball
Cardboard Box
Cash Register
Hanger
Soccer Ball
Tennis Racquet

Clothing
Basketball Uniform
Cleats
Sporty Track Suit
Tennis Head Band
Tennis Outfit
White Tennis Shoes

PALISADES MALL 1F - P111 CHOCOLATE CONFESSION

Weapons
Cash Register
Giant Stuffed Rabbit
Gumball Machine
Robot Bear

Restoratives
Brownie
Cookies
Jellybeans

PALISADES MALL 1F - P112 FOR YOUR LEISURE

Weapons
Cardboard Box
Cash Register
Hanger

Restoratives
Chili
Coffee

Clothing
Business Casual
Polo Shirt Blue Jeans
Sandals

PALISADES MALL 1F - P113 TRENDY CINDY

Weapons
Cash Register
Handbag
Hanger
Shopping Boxes

Restoratives
Jellybeans

Clothing
Knotted Top Cutoffs
Summer Dress

PALISADES MALL 1F - P114 ENTERTAINMENT ISLE

Weapons
Acoustic Guitar
Amplifier
Bass Guitar
Cash Register
Electric Guitar
Music Discs
Vinyl Records

Restoratives
Apple
Milk

PALISADES MALL 2F - MAIN AREA

Weapons
Ad Board
Box of Nails
Dynamite
Indoor Garbage Can
Large Fern Tree
Sandwich Board
Square Sign

Restoratives
Jellybeans

Special
Combo Card 4 (Snowball Cannon)

PALISADES MALL 2F - MAINTENANCE ROOM 9

Weapons
Dynamite
Fire Extinguisher
Lawn Mower
Servbot Mask

PALISADES MALL 2F - P201 KICKS FOR HER

Weapons
Cash Register
Handbag
Potted Plant
Shopping Boxes

Restoratives
Whiskey

Clothing
Bunny Slippers
Go-Go Boots
White Low Heels

PALISADES MALL 2F - P202 QUE'S HATS

Weapons
Cash Register
Handbag
Stool

Clothing
Fedora
Knit Cap
Ladies Hat
Russian Hat

PALISADES MALL 2F - P203 BRAND NEW U

Weapons
Cardboard Box
Cash Register
Handbag
Hanger
Large Fern Tree
Robot Bear
Round Potted Plant

Restoratives
Hot Dog
Large Soda

Clothing
- Summer Dress
- Tube Top Mini Skirt
- White Low Heels

PALISADES MALL 2F - P204 NED'S KNICK-NACKERY
Weapons
- Battleaxe
- Bowie Knife
- Broadsword
- Cash Register
- Flashlight
- Gems
- Handbag
- Lamp
- Lance
- Large Vase
- Small Vase
- Spear

PALISADES MALL 2F - P205 SPACE
Weapons
- Cardboard Box
- Cash Register
- Hanger

Restoratives
- Coffee
- Onion Rings

Clothing
- Boardwalk Apparel
- Loud Summer Special
- Tourist Boat Hat
- Wild Frontier Hat
- Yellow Sneakers
- Yellow Track Suit

PALISADES MALL 2F - P206 STAN'S LARGE PRINT BOOKS & MAGAZINES
Weapons
- Cash Register
- Handbag
- Newspaper
- Newspaper Box
- Round Potted Plant
- Scissors
- Stool

Restoratives
- Coffee

Special
- Magazine 10 (Combat 1)
- Magazine 11 (Gambling 2)
- Magazine 12 (Horror 2)
- Magazine 13 (Sports)

PALISADES MALL 2F - P207 UNDER THE SEA TRAVELS
Weapons
- Beach Ball
- Computer Case
- Keyboard
- Lamp
- Large Potted Plant
- LCD Monitor
- Paddle
- Parasol
- Spear
- Swordfish
- Water Cooler

Restoratives
- Snack

Clothing
- Hula Dress

PALISADES MALL 2F - P208 ARMY SURPLUS GIFT STORE
Special
- Battleaxe ($15,000)
- Bowling Ball ($2,000)
- Chopper Key ($1,000,000)
- Fire Spitter ($25,000)
- Flaming Gloves ($25,000)
- Knife Gloves ($30,000)
- Plate Launcher ($35,000)
- Spear Launcher ($35,000)
- Super Slicer ($35,000)
- Zombrex ($25,000 or more)

PALISADES MALL 2F - P209 KID'S CHOICE CLOTHING
Weapons
- Bag of Marbles
- Cardboard Box
- Cash Register
- Chain Saw
- Dynamite
- Giant Stuffed Rabbit
- Water Gun

Clothing
- Funny Zombie Mask
- Kid's Super Hero Boots
- Toddler Outfit

PALISADES MALL 2F - P210 THE CLEROUX COLLECTION
Weapons
- Cardboard Box
- Fancy Painting
- Fire Extinguisher
- Large Potted Plant
- Painting
- Peace Art
- Small Painting
- Small Vase

Restoratives
- Wine

PALISADES MALL 2F - P211 LEIGH'S FINE LIQUOR
Weapons
- Cash Register
- Keg
- Novelty Liquor Bottle

Restoratives
- Vodka
- Whiskey
- Wine

PALISADES MALL 2F - P212 SEVERED TIES
Weapons
- Cardboard Box
- Computer Case
- Keyboard
- LCD Monitor
- Scissors
- Shotgun (atop stand)
- Stool
- Water Cooler

Restoratives
- Vodka

PALISADES MALL 2F - P213 ROBSAKA DIGITAL
Weapons
- Amplifier
- Cash Register
- LCD Monitor
- Music Discs
- Newspaper
- Speaker

Restoratives
- Large Soda
- Onion Rings

PALISADES MALL 2F - P110 KOKONUTZ SPORTS TOWN
Weapons
- Cardboard Box
- Cash Register
- Hockey Stick
- Metal Baseball Bat
- Skateboard
- Soccer Ball

Clothing
- Baseball Cap Sport
- Baseball High Tops
- Baseball Uniform
- Cleats
- Sporty Track Suit
- Tennis Head Band

PALISADES MALL 2F - P215 EVERYTHING DIAMOND
Weapons
- Cardboard Box
- Cash Register
- Gems
- Handbag

PALISADES MALL 2F - P216 CHRIS'S FINE FOODS
Weapons
- Bucket
- Cardboard Box
- Cash Register
- Cooking Oil
- Gasoline Canister
- Keg
- Ketchup
- Large Potted Plant
- Mayonnaise
- Mustard
- Pan
- Push Broom
- Water Gun

UNEARTHING FORTUNE CITY

Restoratives
Apple
Fish
Hamburger
Jellybeans
Melon
Milk
Orange Juice
Pineapple
Pizza
Steak
Wine

PALISADES MALL 2F - P217 ROBSAKA MOBILE
Weapons
Cash Register
LCD Monitor
Newspaper
Novelty Cell Phone
Padded Blue Chair
Small Fern Tree

PALISADES MALL 2F - P218 HIGH-NOON SHOOTING RANGE
Weapons
Cardboard Box
Cash Register
Green Spray Paint
Grenade
Handgun
Moosehead
Shotgun
Sniper Rifle
Square Sign
USA Spray Paint
Clothing
Army Jacket Pants
Black Military Boots
Swat Helmet
Swat Outfit

POINTS OF INTEREST—FIRST FLOOR

MAINTENANCE ROOM 7

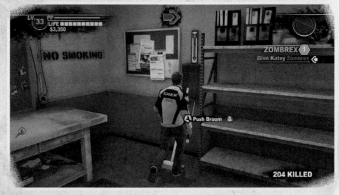

The northeast maintenance room on Palisades Mall's first floor contains a toy water gun and a push broom. Merge the toy water gun with the fire extinguisher that's just outside the room to form a fun snowball cannon that freezes and kills zombies. Grab a machete from within the nearby store, Shank's, and affix it to the push broom to form a nasty pole weapon.

MAINTENANCE ROOM 8

Duck into the southwest maintenance room on Palisades Mall's first floor to locate the makings for a hacker (flashlight + computer case)—this comes in handy when used against ATMs, causing them to cough up $10,000 when zapped. A pair of boxing gloves and a container of motor oil can be found just outside the room as well—everything you need to assemble some righteous flaming gloves!

ROCKIN' 'ROUND THE GROTTO

Palisades Mall's central grotto is a hub of awesomeness. Let's start with the interior bar: here you find a paddle on a ledge and a chain saw behind the counter—just the ingredients you need to construct the incredibly nasty paddlesaw.

There are two tiki torches in here as well; combine these with toy spitball guns, which can be found inside the nearby toy store, Ultimate Playhouse, to create a pair of long-range fire spitters.

The grotto bar also features a blender. Mix up some juice drinks to keep Chuck in good health and grant him special advantages. See this guide's "Appendix" chapter for complete details on juice drinks and their effects.

Scale the grotto's exterior steps to reach the lounge pool up top. A *Playboy* magazine is floating in the water up here, which gives you a 10 percent PP bonus whenever you earn PP from assisting a female survivor.

Snag one of the many parasols atop the grotto and locate a leaf blower in the grassy ledges that border the area. These two items can be combined to form a parablower that sends zombies flying.

When you're ready to return to the ground floor, don't take the stairs again—that's boring. Instead, approach the grotto's slide and press the Interact button to slide down, scoring 10,000 PP in the process!

MORE IN STORES

Palisades Mall has plenty of unique boutiques. Let's run down some of the cooler things you'll find in the first floor's stores.

Among all manner of exciting toys, the Ultimate Playhouse also has a magazine, *Amusement*, that increases the durability of toy-based weapons. Practical? Not really, but it's there!

Flexin' has a pushable dolly that can help Chuck motor through the mall. Don't leave the store until you've given Chuck a workout on each of its exercise bikes, though. Chuck can score 1,000 PP just by riding each bike for a brief period.

UNEARTHING FORTUNE CITY

Shank's is an excellent source of all things sharp and pointy. Swing by and smash those display cases to wrap your mitts around bowie knives, meat cleavers, machetes, and even a zombie-slaughtering broadsword. Bow and arrow weapons can also be acquired here, which combine with the dynamite you find upstairs to craft lethal blambows. (More on that in a bit.)

ODD COMBOS

A pitchfork is stuck in the dirt near the tall plants between Palisades Mall's south escalators. Grab it, then leap atop the nearby King's Crown slot machines (near the ATMs) to obtain a drill motor. Combine these two items to form an awesome auger! Or merge the pitchfork with a shotgun from the second floor's High-Noon Shooting Range to build an excellent boomstick.

More King's Crown slot machines stand at the first floor's north end. Leap onto them to locate a lead pipe, then combine this with the rocket fireworks found in Ultimate Playhouse to build a gloriously lethal rocket launcher.

POINTS OF INTEREST— SECOND FLOOR

MAINTENANCE ROOM 9

Palisades Mall's second floor has just one maintenance room, located along its west wall—but it's a doozy. Inside you find a lawn mower and a stick of dynamite, and there's a Servbot mask and fire extinguisher just outside the door. Combine the dynamite and fire extinguisher for a crowd-clearing freezer bomb, and merge the lawn mower with the Servbot mask for a hilariously lethal Super Slicer.

PAWNSHOP: ARMY SURPLUS GIFT STORE

Plenty of interesting wares are on sale at the Army Surplus Gift Store, including Zombrex, but the chopper key is of particular interest. Though pricey at $1,000,000, this  key lets you drive the chopper motorcycle that's parked on high at the Yucatan Casino. See the "Brain Food" chapter for tips on how to amass that kind of cash.

SHOTGUN DIVORCE

Climb onto the counter of the second floor's north kiosk, Severed Ties, then scamper up onto the kiosk's roof. Vault onto the circular sign up here to locate a hidden shotgun!

DEADRISING 2

NOT FOR KIDS

Pop into Kid's Choice Clothing to locate two very unexpected items. Near the far wall, a chain saw rests atop some boxes in the corner. There's a stick of dynamite in the nearby crib as well. If it weren't for the recent outbreak, this store would have quite the lawsuit on its hands.

Grab that chain saw from Kid's Choice Clothing and sprint to the nearby store, Under the Sea Travels, to discover a couple of paddles. Merge one with the chain saw to create the exceptionally deadly paddlesaw.

SPORTS AND SPARKLIES

The second floor of KokoNutz Sports Town features skateboards to help Chuck get around, along with an endless supply of hockey sticks that make ideal crowd-control weapons. Inside Everything Diamond you'll find lots of gems—combine some with the leaf blower that's found atop the first-floor grotto to assemble a lethal, long-range gem blower!

FINE DINING

For nutritional nourishment, you really can't beat Chris's Fine Foods. Here you'll find endless supplies of some of the best curatives in the game, such as steak, pizza, milk and orange juice. Find key components for potent juice drinks here and bring them down to the first-floor grotto's blender to whip them together.

FEEL THE HEAT

Leigh's Fine Liquor holds a bevy of alcoholic beverages, including plenty of whiskey. Combine these bottles with the many newspapers found in Robsaka Mobile and Stan's Large Print Books & Magazines to create a host of flaming-hot molotovs.

You'll also find several magazines inside Stan's, including *Sports* (increases the durability of sports-related weapons), *Horror 2* (25 percent more PP from zombies you kill), and *Gambling 2*, which significantly increases the chances of winning at the city's various slot machines and assorted gambling games.

UNEARTHING FORTUNE CITY

GUNS, GUNS, GUNS

High Noon Shooting Range is to firearms what Palisades Mall's first-floor store, Shank's, is to bladed weapons. Here you find an endless supply of handguns and grenades, along with two shotguns and two sniper rifles. All of these can be tucked away for later use, making High Noon Shooting Range your number 1 source of firearms in Fortune City!

BLADES FOR DAYS

Speaking of Shank's, you can find many other devious bladed devices in Ned's Knicknackery. Smash the display cases within Ned's to score spears, battleaxes, a broadsword and a lance—all thoroughly lethal weapons in their own unique ways.

LOOSE BOOMSTICKS

Peek at the plants on the second floor's far south end to discover two hidden sticks of dynamite. Merge these with the bow and arrow weapons found at Shank's on the first floor and enjoy some good times with blambows.

COMBO CARD: SNOWBALL CANNON

Inspect the poster on the wall to the left of Ned's Knicknackery to acquire the snowball cannon's combo card. Drop down to the first floor and visit Maintenance Room 7 to find the components for this bone-chilling combo weapon.

DEADRISING 2

PLATINUM STRIP

If you're looking for great food and wholesome fun, look no further! Platinum Strip's family-friendly environment will keep you coming back again and again. So come down, grab a bite and enjoy all that Fortune City has to offer!

PLATINUM STRIP - MAIN AREA

Weapons
- Bucket
- Cardboard Box
- Fancy Bench
- Foam Hand
- Fountain Firework
- Garbage Bag
- Garbage Can
- Green Spray Paint
- Handbag
- Handgun
- Indoor Garbage Can
- Large Potted Plant
- Lawn Dart
- Lizard Mask
- Mailbox
- Metal Barricade
- Newspaper Box
- Parasol
- Plastic Bin
- Plastic Garbage Can
- Power Drill
- Protester Sign
- Push Broom
- Sandwich Board
- Serving Tray
- Small Suitcase
- Speaker
- Spot Light
- Square Sign
- Utility Cart

Restoratives
- Fries
- Hot Dog

Special
- Motorbike

PLATINUM STRIP - NORTH UPPER PLATFORMS

Weapons
- Cardboard Box
- Flashlight
- Folding Chair
- Gems
- Giant Stuffed Elephant
- LMG

Special
- Magazine 20 (*Psychos*)

PLATINUM STRIP - SOUTH UPPER PLATFORMS

Weapons
- Cardboard Box
- Folding Chair
- Fountain Firework
- Giant Stuffed Bear
- Meat Cleaver
- Mining Pick
- Serving Tray
- Shotgun
- Step Ladder

Restoratives
- Beer
- Fries
- Hamburger
- Large Soda
- Milk
- Pie

PLATINUM STRIP - CINEMA ROOFTOP

Weapons
- 2x4
- Box of Nails
- Folding Chair
- Handgun
- Lead Pipe
- Plywood
- Power Drill
- Pylon

Restoratives
- Hamburger
- Snack

PLATINUM STRIP - MAINTENANCE ROOM 20

Weapons
- Baseball Bat (just north)
- Box of Nails
- Propane Tank

PLATINUM STRIP - MAINTENANCE ROOM 21

Weapons
- Bucket (right outside)
- Leaf Blower
- Parasol (right outside)
- Power Drill

POI
- Ladder to Cinema Rooftop (right nearby)

PLATINUM STRIP - MAINTENANCE ROOM 22

Weapons
- Lawn Mower
- Newspaper (right outside)
- Wheelchair (right outside)

Restoratives
- Whiskey

PLATINUM STRIP - SOUVENIR KIOSK

Weapons
- Protestor Sign (right nearby)

Clothing
- Baseball Cap TIR
- TIR Outfit

POI
- Standee (right nearby)

PLATINUM STRIP - CASH GORDON'S CASINO

Weapons
- Casino Chips
- Croupier Stick
- Cushioned Tall Chair
- Handgun
- Roulette Wheel
- Square Sign
- Stand
- Velvet Bar
- Wheelchair (right outside)

POI
- ATMs
- Slot Machines
- Snack Machine (right outside)
- Weapon Machine (right outside)

PLATINUM STRIP - JUGGZ BAR & GRILL

Weapons
- Barstool
- Cardboard Box
- Keg
- Metal Garbage Can
- Novelty Beer Mug (right outside)
- Padded Blue Chair

Restoratives
- Snack
- Whiskey

POI
- Blender

PLATINUM STRIP - PARADISE PLATINUM SCREENS

Weapons
- Cardboard Cutout
- Cash Register
- Coffee Pot
- Fire Extinguisher
- Gumball Machine
- Handbag
- Metal Garbage Can

Special
- Combo Card 7 (Laser Sword)

POI
- ATMs
- Snack Machines

UNEARTHING FORTUNE CITY

PLATINUM STRIP - MOE'S MAGINATIONS
Weapons
Bag of Marbles
Folding Chair
Giant Stuffed Rabbit
Kid's Bike
Lizard Mask
Wacky Hammer
Water Gun
Special
Assault Rifle ($20,000)
Defiler ($35,000)
Hail Mary ($15,000)
Knight Boots ($2,000,000)
Power Guitar ($35,000)
Robot Bear ($1,000)

PLATINUM STRIP - DINING AT DAVEY'S
Weapons
Ad Board (on patio)
Cardboard Box
Cash Register
Chef Knife
Coffee Pot
Cooking Oil
Cooking Pot
Highback Oak Chair (on patio)
Ketchup
Meat Cleaver
Mustard
Pan
Patio Table (on patio)
Plates
Serving Tray
POI
Stove

PLATINUM STRIP - FROM FORTUNE WITH LOVE
Weapons
Cash Register
Giant Poker Chip
Gift Shop Lamp
Hanger
Mannequin Female
Mannequin Male
Small Painting
Clothing
Flip Flops
Fortune City Gray Shirt
Hawaiian Holiday Gear

PLATINUM STRIP - SOUVENIR KIOSK
Weapons
Crowbar (atop kiosk)
Foam Hand
Protestor Sign (right nearby)
Clothing
TIR Outfit

POINTS OF INTEREST

MAINTENANCE ROOM 20

Platinum Strip's southeast maintenance room sports two boxes of nails and a propane tank. Several baseball bats are found on the cart just north of the room as well. This gives you the easy makings for two spiked bats (baseball bat + box of nails), or one spiked bat and a deadly I.E.D. (box of nails + propane tank).

MAINTENANCE ROOM 21

The north maintenance room contains a leaf blower and a power drill, and there's a bucket and parasol just outside. This gives you the ingredients for a parablower and drill bucket.

MAINTENANCE ROOM 22

Inside the strip's southwest maintenance room you find a lawn mower and two bottles of whiskey. There's a newspaper and a wheelchair right outside the room as well. With these items you can cobble together a molotov (newspaper + whiskey) and a handy chipper (wheelchair + lawn mower), and still have a bottle of whiskey left for after the show.

PAWNSHOP: MOE'S MAGINATIONS

All pawnshops offer Zombrex and other interesting wares, but only at Moe's Maginations will you find knight boots on sale for a cool two million. Buy these boots, which are stored in Chuck's locker at the Safe House, to compliment the knight armor that unlocks after you beat the game's special Overtime ending. See the "Brain Food" chapter for tips on how to stockpile funds quickly in Fortune City.

ELEVATED GOODIES

Chuck can elevate himself in a variety of ways here at Platinum Strip. For starters, vault onto the two large cement blocks near the steps leading up to Fortune Park, then climb onto the wooden ledge above. From here, you can run west along a series of shop awnings.

Several common items are stashed along the south awnings, including a carton of milk and other curatives. A hidden shotgun awaits at the end of the run.

To explore the strip's northern awnings, first climb onto the snack machine that's right outside of Cash Gordon's Casino. This leads you to a ledge with a powerful LMG firearm.

Continue leaping along the awnings past the LMG to discover some gems next to a flashlight. This gives you the makings for a powerful laser sword, and as luck would have it, there's a maintenance room just below.

Past the gems and flashlight lies a magazine, *Psychos*, which gives Chuck a 25 percent PP boost whenever he defeats a dangerous psychopath enemy. Psychos pay out huge amounts of PP when killed, so this mag's well worth keeping!

LONG LADDER

Locate a ladder in the alley near Maintenance Room 21 and use it to climb up to the small roof of the Paradise Platinum Screens cinema. There isn't a whole lot of interest up here, but this ladder comes in handy when Chuck faces off against some psychotic snipers.

UNEARTHING FORTUNE CITY

PLATINUM PLATES

Food is strangely scarce at Dining at Davey's, but there is a coffee creamer in the shop's far southwest corner. You can also grab pans and place them on the stove in

the kitchen to score a small amount of bonus PP. This trick only works when a fresh pan is placed on an as-yet unused burner, mind you.

Then there's Juggz Bar & Grill, where Chuck discovers a handy blender. Use this device to combine different foods into potent juice drinks that give Chuck special abilities! See this guide's "Appendix" chapter for a list of the various juices you can mix.

COMBO CARD: LASER SWORD

No visit to Platinum Strip is complete without a stroll through the Paradise Platinum Screens movie theater. Chuck finds a bit of junk food in here, and more importantly, a poster that can be examined to acquire the light sword combo card!

Don't leave the theater without checking out the latest blockbuster hit. Watching a flick on the big screen here is worth easy PP, and there's a new movie playing each day.

STRIP TEASERS

Last but not least, there's a handgun in the strip's northwest grassy ledge. This could come in handy!

There's also a special standee near the north TIR Souvenir Kiosk. Get behind the standee and examine it to have Chuck strike a silly pose worth a handful of PP.

DEADRISING 2

ROYAL FLUSH PLAZA

Take a break from the gambling and excitement to visit Royal Flush Plaza. With this many stores and so much to see, you'll be sure to have the perfect day out.

ROYAL FLUSH PLAZA 1F - MAIN AREA

Weapons

Ad Board
Bowie Knife
Bucket
Chef Knife
Fancy Bench
Flashlight
Garbage Can
Giant Die
Green Spray Paint
Handbag
Hunk of Meat
Indoor Garbage Can
Large Planter
Large Potted Plant
Lawn Dart
Leaf Rake
Metal Garbage Can
MMA Gloves
Newspaper
Newspaper Box
Nightstick
Push Broom
Round Potted Plant
Sandwich Board
Scissors
Square Sign
Tomahawk
Utility Cart
Wheelchair

Restoratives

Apple
Coffee
Coffee Creamer
Cookies
Melon
Pineapple
Snacks
Spoiled Hamburger

Special

Combo Card 1 (Tenderizers)

POI

Minigame 3 (Flaming Craps)
Slot Machines
Sports Car

ROYAL FLUSH PLAZA - NW MAINTENANCE AREA

Weapons

Baseball Bat
Box of Nails
Bucket
Cardboard Box
Fire Extinguisher
Folding Chair
Garbage Bag
Large Wrench
Power Drill
Propane Tank
Push Broom
Pylon
Saw Blade
Sledge Hammer

Restoratives

Snack

ROYAL FLUSH PLAZA - SE MAINTENANCE AREA

Weapons

Bucket
Cardboard Box
Large Wrench
Plastic Bin
Push Broom
Spear

ROYAL FLUSH PLAZA - MAINTENANCE ROOM 1

Weapons

Baseball Bat
Box of Nails

ROYAL FLUSH PLAZA - MAINTENANCE ROOM 2

Weapons

Battery
Wheelchair (right outside)

ROYAL FLUSH PLAZA - MAINTENANCE ROOM 3

Weapons

Bucket
Power Drill

ROYAL FLUSH PLAZA - CASUAL GALS

Weapons

Cash Register
Fancy Painting
Handbag
Hanger
Sandwich Board
Shopping Boxes

Restoratives

Brownie
Coffee
Coffee Creamer

Clothing

Knotted Top Cutoffs
Ladies Hat

ROYAL FLUSH PLAZA - IN THE CLOSET

Weapons

Brick
Cardboard Box
Cash Register
Foam Hand
Green Spray Paint
Handbag
Handgun
Red Spray Paint
Skateboard
Speaker
Vinyl Records

Restoratives

Hot Dog
Large Soda

Clothing

Hip Hop Outfit
Skater Outfit
Yellow Sneakers

ROYAL FLUSH PLAZA - THE MAN'S SPORT

Weapons

Boxing Gloves
Cardboard Box
Cash Register
Dumbbell
Hunk of Meat
Metal Baseball Bat
MMA Gloves
Stool

POI

Minigame 1 (Test Your Strength)

ROYAL FLUSH PLAZA - THE SHOEHORN

Weapons

Cardboard Box
Cash Register
Crowbar
Flower Pot
Handbag
Large Fern Tree
Painting
Stool

Restoratives

Orange Juice

Clothing

Black Canvas Sneakers
Yellow Sneakers

UNEARTHING FORTUNE CITY

ROYAL FLUSH PLAZA - TUNEMAKERS

Weapons

Acoustic Guitar
Amplifier
Bass Guitar
Cardboard Box
Cash Register
Drum
Electric Guitar
Square Sign
Stool
Wheelchair

Restoratives

Large Soda

ROYAL FLUSH PLAZA - WAVE OF STYLE

Weapons

Cash Register
Handbag
Nightstick
Red Spray Paint
Scissors
Shampoo
Water Bottle
Water Cooler

Restoratives

Cash Money
Coffee
Coffee Creamer
Large Soda

Clothing

Blue Hair
Full Beard Moustache

ROYAL FLUSH PLAZA - YE OLDE TOYBOX

Weapons

Bag of Marbles
Beach Ball
Cash Register
Stick Pony
Toy Helicopter
Toy Spitball Gun

Clothing

Funny Lizard Mask

ROYAL FLUSH PLAZA - MARRIAGE MAKERS

Weapons

Cash Register
Gems
Handbag
Large Vase
Padded Blue Chair
Shopping Boxes
Stool

Restoratives

Wine

ROYAL FLUSH PLAZA - ROY'S MART

Weapons

Cash Register
Computer Case
Crowbar
Fire Extinguisher
Handbag
Highback Oak Chair
Indoor Garbage Can
Keyboard
LCD Monitor
Novelty Perfume Bottle
Rotating Display
Serving Tray
Shampoo
Small Painting
Small Potted Plant
Small Suitcase
Stool
Utility Cart
Water Cooler

Restoratives

Burrito
Coffee Creamer
Orange Juice

Clothing

Hygiene Mask

Special

Zombrex

ROYAL FLUSH PLAZA - MODERN BUSINESSMAN

Weapons

Cardboard Box
Cash Register
Centurion Bust
Gems
Hangers
Large Fern Tree
Painting

Restoratives

Vodka

Clothing

Black Dress Shoes
Business Casual
Collegiate Ensemble
Tuxedo

ROYAL FLUSH PLAZA - STYLIN' TODDLERS

Weapons

Beach Ball
Cash Register
Giant Stuffed Elephant
handbag
Hanger
Highback Oak Chair
Shipping Boxes
Stool

Restoratives

Jellybeans

Clothing

Kids Super Hero Boots
One-Piece Pajama
Zombie Mask

ROYAL FLUSH PLAZA - SPORTRANCE

Weapons

Baseball Bat
Basketball
Bowling Ball
Cardboard Box
Cash Register
Football
Golf Club
Hanger

Weapons, cont.

Mannequin Female
Mannequin Male
Skateboard

Restoratives

Orange Juice

Clothing

Basketball High Tops
Football Helmet
Football Uniform
Sporty Track Suit
Yellow Sneakers

POI

Minigame 2 (Casino Cup)

ROYAL FLUSH PLAZA - THE CHIEFTAIN'S HUT

Weapons

Bow and Arrow
Cardboard Box
Cash Register
Fancy Painting
Playing Cards
Small Painting
Spear
Tomahawk

Restoratives

Chili
Taco

ROYAL FLUSH PLAZA - YESTERDAY, TODAY & TOMORROW

Weapons

Cash Register
Newspaper Box
Round Potted Plant
Scissors

Restoratives

Orange Juice
Snack

Special

Magazine 1 (Health 1)
Magazine 2 (Combat 2)

DEADRISING 2

ROYAL FLUSH PLAZA - HAT RACKS

Weapons
Cash Register
Computer Case
Hanger
Keyboard
LCD Monitor
Stool

Clothing
Tourist Boat Hat
Wild Frontier Hat

ROYAL FLUSH PLAZA - UNIVERSE OF OPTICS

Weapons
Cash Register
Crowbar
Metal Garbage Can
Rotating Display
Serving Tray

Pizza
Restoratives

Clothing
Aviator Glasses
Sport Glasses
Yellow Tinted Glasses

ROYAL FLUSH PLAZA - THREE CLUB MONTE

Weapons
Cardboard Box
Cash Register
Hanger
Round Potted Plant

Clothing
Black Dress Shoes
Fedora
Polo Shirt Blue Jeans

ROYAL FLUSH PLAZA - ASTONISHING ILLUSIONS

Weapons
Cash Register
Firecrackers
Fountain Firework
Giant Die
Gift Shop Lamp
Handbag
Robot Bear
Stool

Restoratives
Jellybeans

Clothing
Novelty Glasses

ROYAL FLUSH PLAZA - STURDY PACKAGE

Weapons
Box of Nails
Cash Register
Crowbar
Ketchup
Power Drill
Small Suitcase
Small Suitcase
Stool
Suitcase

Restoratives
Fries

ROYAL FLUSH PLAZA - THE DARK BEAN

Weapons
Barstool
Cash Register
Cash Register
Highback Oak Chair
Newspaper
Patio Table
Serving Tray

Restoratives
Brownie
Cake
Coffee
Coffee Creamer
Donut

ROYAL FLUSH PLAZA 2F - MAIN AREA

Weapons
Broadsword (atop triangular directory stand north of Rush Wireless kiosk)
Dynamite (atop large south palm tree near Children's Castle)
Fancy Bench
Garbage Can
Handbag
Indoor Garbage Can
Large Planter
Large Potted Plant
Leaf Rake
Newspaper
Newspaper Box
Sandwich Board
Serving Tray
Square Sign
Wheelchair

Restoratives
Apple
Coffee Creamer
Cookies
Snack

POI
ATMs

ROYAL FLUSH PLAZA 2F - UPPER PLATFORMS

Weapons
Cardboard Box
Dynamite
Dynamite
Giant Stuffed Rabbit
Highback Oak Chair
Patio Chair
Patio Table
Sniper Rifle
Speaker
Spear

Restoratives
Steak

ROYAL FLUSH PLAZA 2F - ALBERT'S APPAREL

Weapons
Cash Register
Centurion Bust
Gems
Hanger
Hunk of Meat
Machete
Small Suitcase

Clothing
Black Dress Shoes
Collegiate Ensemble
Plaid Suit

ROYAL FLUSH PLAZA 2F - WILY TRAVELS

Weapons
Computer Case
Fire Extinguisher
Flower Pot
Keyboard
Lamp
Large Potted Plant
LCD Monitor
Scissors
Water Cooler

Restoratives
Coffee Creamer

ROYAL FLUSH PLAZA 2F - ANTOINE'S

Weapons
Cardboard Box
Cash Register
Chef Knife
Cooking Oil
Cooking Pot
Fire Extinguisher
Lamp
Large Fern Tree
Pan
Plates
Round Potted Plant
Small Fern Tree

Restoratives
Pasta

UNEARTHING FORTUNE CITY

ROYAL FLUSH PLAZA 2F - ESTELLE'S FINE-LADY COSMETICS

Weapons
Cash Register
Handbag
Handgun
Novelty Perfume Bottle
Shampoo
Shopping Boxes
Stool

Clothing
Grey Hair
Pink Hair

ROYAL FLUSH PLAZA 2F - JUST IN TIME PAYDAY LOANS

Special
Assault Rifle ($20,000)
Beach Ball ($1,500)
Blambow ($40,000)
Gem Blower ($30,000)
Laser Sword ($25,000)
Pole Weapon ($30,000)
Roaring Thunder ($15,000)
Sports Car Key ($500,000)
Tenderizers ($25,000)
Zombrex ($25,000 or more)

ROYAL FLUSH PLAZA 2F - ETERNAL TIMEPIECES

Weapons
Cardboard Box
Cash Register
Gems
Keyboard
LCD Monitor
Speaker
Stool
Vinyl Records

Restoratives
Beer
Wine

ROYAL FLUSH PLAZA 2F - KATHY'S SPACE

Weapons
Cardboard Box
Flower Pot
Handbag
Hanger
Shopping Boxes
Shopping Valuables

Restoratives
Jellybeans
Large Soda
Pizza

Clothing
Knotted Top Cutoffs
Tube Top Mini Skirt

ROYAL FLUSH PLAZA 2F - EARMARK LEATHER

Weapons
Acoustic Guitar
Cactus Plant
Cash Register

Restoratives
BBQ Ribs
Large Soda

Clothing
Black Cowboy Boots
Black Cowboy Hat
Black Cowboy Outfit
White Cowboy Boots
White Cowboy Hat
White Cowboy Outfit

ROYAL FLUSH PLAZA 2F - CHILDREN'S CASTLE

Weapons
Bag of Marbles
Cardboard Box
Cash Register
Giant Stuffed Bull
Giant Stuffed Elephant
Goblin Mask
Gumball Machine
Kid's Bike
Stick Pony
Stool
Toy Helicopter

Restoratives
Orange Juice

Clothing
Funny Goblin Mask
Kid's Super Hero Eye Mask

ROYAL FLUSH PLAZA 2F - SMALL FRY DUDS

Weapons
Bag of Marbles
Cash Register
Giant Stuffed Donkey
Shopping Boxes

Clothing
Knit Cap
One-Piece Pajama

ROYAL FLUSH PLAZA 2F - RUSH WIRELESS

Weapons
Cash Register
Computer Case
Handbag
Keyboard
LCD Monitor
Newspaper
Novelty Cell Phone
Small Fern Tree

Restoratives
Apple
Hamburger
Orange Juice
Snack

ROYAL FLUSH PLAZA 2F - RAGAZINES

Weapons
Cardboard Box
Cash Register
Round Potted Plant

Special
Magazine 3 (Gambling 1)
Magazine 4 (Hand to Hand)
Magazine 5 (Horror 1)

ROYAL FLUSH PLAZA 2F - PLAYERS

Weapons
Cash Register
Music Discs
Shopping Boxes
Speaker

ROYAL FLUSH PLAZA 2F - SPORTRANCE

Weapons
Baseball Bat
Bowling Ball
Cardboard Box
Cash Register
Golf Club
Hanger
Mannequin Male
Skateboard

Restoratives
Orange Juice

Clothing
Baseball Cap Sport
Baseball Uniform
Basketball High Tops
Sporty Track Suit
Yellow Sneakers

DEADRISING 2

POINTS OF INTEREST— FIRST FLOOR

MAINTENANCE ROOM 1

Royal Flush Plaza's northwest maintenance room is the first one Chuck enters and the closest to the Safe House. Inside lies a box of nails and a baseball bat—the makings for the extremely effective spiked bat combo weapon. Grab the other baseball bat that lies at the foot of the nearby stairs and find a second box of nails in the nearby storage room to form a second spiked bat for double the crowd control!

> **TIP**
>
> Grab a fire axe from the Safe House and merge it with the sledge hammer near this maintenance room to form the mighty defiler. Chuck can't swing this combo weapon as quickly as the spiked bat, but the defiler yields greater amounts of PP with each kill.

MAINTENANCE ROOM 2

This maintenance room is located at the back of the Tunemakers store and contains several batteries. Merge these with the wheelchair found just outside to craft a lethal electric chair. Or combine one of Tunemakers' many electric guitars and amplifiers to assemble a rockin' power guitar.

MAINTENANCE ROOM 3

Swing by Royal Flush Plaza's southeast maintenance room to discover a power drill and bucket— these combine to form the drill bucket, the very first combo card Chuck receives through leveling up.

SUPPLY ON DEMAND

You must pass through Royal Flush Plaza on every trip to or from the Safe House, so it's important to know where healthy foods are stashed. The Dark Bean is a good source of coffee creamers, which are surprisingly effective curatives. Find a coffee creamer on the outer counter and two more on the central counter.

> **NOTE**
>
> The giant Flaming Craps table also sports a couple of coffee creamers, but you'll have to contend with the zombified security guards to get them.

Another good source of nourishment is Roy's Mart, located on the far east end of the mall's first floor. Here you can score a number of orange juices, found on the ground near the row of refrigerators. There's another orange juice and a coffee creamer inside the pharmacy's back room as well.

UNEARTHING FORTUNE CITY

READ ALL ABOUT IT

Yesterday, Today & Tomorrow   387 KILLED

Just west of The Dark Bean stands a small newspaper kiosk called Yesterday, Today and Tomorrow. Here you find a health-boosting orange juice on the counter, along with two magazines, *Health 1* and *Combat 2*. The former increases the potency all curatives by 50 percent, while the latter gives Chuck a 10 percent PP bonus from all weapon-related kills. Both are worth hanging onto once Chuck levels up and his inventory increases, particularly the *Health 1* mag.

LUCKY NUMBER 7

406 KILLED

You can't miss the giant Flaming Craps table as you dart through Royal Flush Plaza's first floor—it reeks of intrigue. Hop the fence and beat down a few security guard zombies to secure the table, then grab one of those giant dice and toss it to give it a roll. If both dice add up to make a seven, you win 10,000 PP! You can also find a couple of coffee creamers on the Flaming Craps table—useful restoratives that are easy to collect as you pass through.

STRENGTH AND SKILL

The Man's Sport   399 KILLED

Grab the sledge hammer in Royal Flush Plaza's northwest maintenance hall and bring it to a nearby store, The Man's Sport. There's a strongman challenge inside the store; simply hold the Attack button to perform a powerful downward blow with the sledge hammer, ringing the bell to pocket some easy PP.

For a greater challenge, cross the mall and enter SporTrance, Royal Flush Plaza's two-story sporting goods store. A minigame called Casino Cup is  located on the store's first floor; pay the modest fee to attempt this fun and challenging golf minigame.

The goal in Casino Cup is simple: Make a hole in one. You have three chances to make the shot, and it makes no difference if you sink one ball or all three—you won't earn more for sinking them all.

436 KILLED

Press the onscreen button to fill the meter on the right, quickly pressing the button a second time when the meter fills to the indicated zone. Success means a hole in one—and a fabulous cash and PP prize! Keep playing the Casino Cup to increase the challenge level, along with the potential rewards.

DEADRISING 2

COMBO CARD: TENDERIZERS

Examine the standing poster display near the doors to Americana Casino to obtain the combo card for the tenderizers. Grab some MMA gloves from the nearby store, The Man's Sport, and combine them with the box of nails in Maintenance Room 1 to form these satisfying close-range zombie-maulers.

POINTS OF INTEREST— SECOND FLOOR

PAWNSHOP: JUST IN TIME PAYDAY LOANS

There's no maintenance room to be found on Royal Flush Plaza's second floor, but there is a pawnshop. Zombrex can be purchased here—a convenient source, given its close proximity to the Safe House. Better still, the key to the sports car you've surely noticed downstairs is also on sale here for $500,000. That's quite a price tag; see the previous "Brain Food" chapter for tips on how to make that kind of moola here at Fortune City.

SECOND-FLOOR SLICER

Good weapons are hard to find on Royal Flush Plaza's second floor, but a very deadly machete can be found inside of Albert's Apparel. In addition, a broadsword sits atop the triangular directory that stands just north of the central Rush Wireless kiosk. Put these blades to good use against those vicious undead!

CONVENIENT HEALING

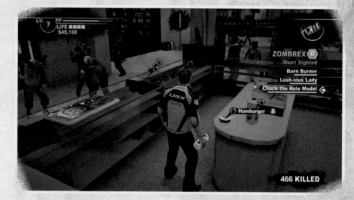

Speaking of the Rush Wireless kiosk, you'll find a coffee creamer north of the stand, close to the aforementioned broadsword. There's also an orange juice, apple, and a snack item at the kiosk itself. This makes this kiosk a good place to visit whenever Chuck's feeling peckish.

MORE MAGS

Enter the Ragazines shop to discover several performance-enhancing magazines worthy of perusal. *Hand to Hand* greatly increases the power of Chuck's bare-handed blows. *Gambling 1* increases Chuck's chances

UNEARTHING FORTUNE CITY

of winning when playing when playing gambling minigames. *Horror 1* grants Chuck a 25 percent increase to PP when defeating zombies.

MIGHT ON HIGH

Two ATMs stand just outside of Ragazines, but the nearby phone booth merits even more attention. Leap onto the phone booth, then jump up to the broken walkway above.

Don't follow the walkway around the floor—there's nothing of interest at its far end. Instead, turn around and jump up to an even higher platform (a flower box). From here, you can access the high loft of the Players store, where you discover a sniper rifle, spear, and steak, among other common items. Put that rifle to good use against those wicked zombies!

That's not all—exit the loft and make a daring leap over to the floating hot air balloon. Here you discover three sticks of dynamite and a giant stuffed rabbit. The former merges nicely with the bow and arrow weapons you find in The Chieftains Hut downstairs, creating blambows. The latter makes an ideal gift for little Katey.

TNT PALM TREE

While loitering near the Children's Castle shop, take a close look at the top of the tall palm tree that extends up from Royal Flush Plaza's first floor. Two sticks of dynamite rest atop the tree. Vault the railing and step onto the tree's solid palms to collect these volatile treats, then visit The Chieftains Hut and build more blambows.

SILVER STRIP

See all the sights and hear all the sounds that the heart of the city has to offer. When all shops are open 24 hours a day, the adventure never dies and the party never ends on Fortune City's Silver Strip!

SILVER STRIP - MAIN AREA

Weapons
2x4
Ad Board
Cardboard Box
Crowbar
Fancy Bench
Flashlight
Garbage Bag
Garbage Can
Handbag
Handgun
Kid's Bike
Machete
Mailbox
Newspaper Box
Plastic Bin
Red Spray Paint
Sandwich Board
Small Suitcase
Square Sign
Utility Cart

Restoratives
Beer
Hot Dog

Special
Combo Card 6 (Paddlesaw)

POI
ATMs

SILVER STRIP - NORTH ALLEY

Weapons
Cardboard Box
Cash Register
Cement Saw
Foam Hand
Garbage Bag
Garbage Can
Gasoline Canister
Metal Barricade
Pallet
Plastic Bin
Pylon
Servbot Mask
Small Suitcase
Square Sign
Stool
Tire

POI
Combo Bay

SILVER STRIP - STAGE AREA

Weapons
Acoustic Guitar
Bass Guitar
Cardboard Box
Chainsaw (on high steel girders)
Drum
Electric Guitar
Garbage Bag
Garbage Can
Green Spray Paint
Metal Barricade
Mic Stand
Plastic Bin
Shotgun (on high steel girders)
Toy Helicopter

SILVER STRIP - ROYAL FLUSH PLAZA ROOFTOP

Weapons
Beach Ball
Bowie Knife
Brick
Cardboard Box
Crowbar
Handgun
Large Wrench
Pylon
Toy Helicopter

Restoratives
Beer
Hamburger
Whiskey

SILVER STRIP - ATLANTICA CASINO ROOFTOP

Weapons
2x4
Box of Nails
Brick
Cardboard Boxes
Construction Hat
Garbage Bag
Highback Oak Chair
Large Barrel
Large Wrench
Paint Can
Playing Cards
Push Broom
Pylon
Sledge Hammer
Steel Shelving

Restoratives
Whiskey

SILVER STRIP - HOT EXCITORAMA MAINTENANCE HALL

Weapons
Cardboard Box
Garbage Bag
Large Wrench
Lead Pipe
Pallet
Plastic Bin

SILVER STRIP - SOUTH MAINTENANCE HALL

Weapons
Bucket
Cardboard Box
Fire Extinguishers
Garbage Bag
Indoor Garbage Can

POI
Ladder to Atlantica Casino Rooftop
Snack Machines

SILVER STRIP - MAINTENANCE ROOM 14

Weapons
Battery
Goblin Mask (right outside)
Lead Pipe
Rocket Fireworks

POI
Ladder to Royal Flush Plaza Rooftop (right outside)

SILVER STRIP - MAINTENANCE ROOM 15

Weapons
Box of Nails
Chainsaw
Lead Pipe (right outside)
Paddle (just outside)
Propane Tank

UNEARTHING FORTUNE CITY

SILVER STRIP - MAINTENANCE ROOM 16

Weapons

Bowie Knife
Boxing Gloves (right outside)
Flashlight (right outside)
Gems

SILVER STRIP - MAINTENANCE ROOM 17

Weapons

Amplifier (right outside)
Dynamite
Electric Guitar (right outside)
Fire Extinguisher

SILVER STRIP - MAINTENANCE ROOM 18

Weapons

Lead Pipe
Machete
Push Broom
Rocket Fireworks (right outside)

SILVER STRIP - MAINTENANCE ROOM 19

Weapons

2x4 (right outside)
Box of Nails
Cement Saw (right outside)
Saw Blade

SILVER STRIP - N101 SWEPT AWAY

Weapons

Indoor Garbage Can
Massager
Suitcase

Restoratives

Large Soda
Snack
Spoiled Hamburger

SILVER STRIP - N102 ONE LITTLE DUCK BINGO

Weapons

Bingo Ball Cage
Flashlight (right outside)
Gems
Handbag
Large Potted Plant
Large Vase
Speaker
Stool

Special

Magazine 17 (Leadership)

POI

Minigame 12 (Fortune Whisperer)

SILVER STRIP - N103 TINKERBOX

Weapons

2x4
Cardboard Box
Flashlight (right outside)
Golf Club
Music Discs
Vinyl Records

Special

Broadsword ($15,000)
Driller ($20,000)
Flamethrower ($40,000)
Hacker ($35,000)
Heliblade ($30,000)
Keg ($2,000)
Rocket Launcher ($40,000)
SUV Key ($2,000,000)
Tesla Ball ($35,000)

SILVER STRIP - N104 BARREL OF GOODS

Weapons

Baseball Bat
Boxing Gloves
Cardboard Box
Cash Register
Kid's Bike
Novelty Poker Chip
Water Gun

SILVER STRIP - N105 LUAII WAUWII

Weapons

Beer
Bowie Knife (outdoor patio)
Broadsword (outdoors, stuck in boulder)
Cardboard Box
Chef Knife
Cooking Oil
Cooking Pot
Handbag
Large Potted Plant
Lawnmower (outdoor patio)
Lizard Mask (outdoor patio)

Weapons, cont.

Meat Cleaver
Metal Garbage Can
Paddle
Pan
Patio Chair (outdoor patio)
Plates
Serving Tray
Stool
Swordfish
USA Spray Paint (right outside)

Restoratives

Beer
Fish
Sushi
Vodka

Special

Magazine M18 (Juice Boost)

POI

Stove

SILVER STRIP - N106 SHAMROCK CASINO

Weapons

Casino Chips
Croupier Stick
Drink Cart
Fancy Painting
Indoor Garbage Can
Roulette Wheel
Stand
Suitcase
Velvet Bar
Yellow Tall Chair

Restoratives

Beer

Special

Magazine 19 (Gambling 3)

POI

ATMs
Slot Machines
Snack Machines
SUV

SILVER STRIP - N107 PUB O' GOLD

Weapons

Barstool
Cash Register
Gems

Weapons, cont.

Handbag
Keg
Table Lamp

Restoratives

Beer
Orange Juice
Vodka
Whiskey

POI

Blender

SILVER STRIP - N108 ROCKETS RED GLARE

Weapons

Dynamite (atop kiosk)
Fire Extinguisher
Firecrackers
Fountain Firework
Rocket Fireworks

SILVER STRIP - N109 PEEP HOLE

POI

Peep Shows

SILVER STRIP - N110 HOT EXCITORAMA

Weapons

Cash Register
Gift Shop Lamp
Handbag
Hanger
Mannequin Female
Mannequin Male
Massager
Stool

Clothing

Blue Oyster Biker Outfit
Flip Flop
Go-Go Boots
Mesh Party Wear

SILVER STRIP - N111 JUGGZ BAR & GRILL KIOSK

Weapons

Cardboard Box
Flashlight
Keg
Novelty Beer Mug
Propane Tank

Restoratives

Beer

POINTS OF INTEREST

MAINTENANCE ROOM 14

The maintenance room to the left of the doors to Slot Ranch Casino contains a lead pipe, rocket fireworks, and a battery. Combine the lead pipe and rocket fireworks to assemble a rocket launcher, and merge the battery with the goblin mask that's right outside the room to form a roaring thunder.

MAINTENANCE ROOM 15

This one's our favorite. In the alley south of Hot Excitorama, you'll find a maintenance room that contains a chain saw, a box of nails, and a propane tank, and there's a paddle right outside atop a dumpster. Merge the box of nails with the propane tank to build a volatile I.E.D., and combine the paddle with the chain saw to form a death-dealing paddlesaw!

MAINTENANCE ROOM 16

Sprint through the back door of Hot Excitorama to reach a maintenance room that sports a lead pipe, a machete, and a push broom. Rocket fireworks lie on the ground just outside as well. This allows Chuck to build a pole weapon (machete + push broom), along with a rocket launcher (lead pipe + rocket fireworks) to help him slaughter zombies both near and far.

MAINTENANCE ROOM 17

Enter the maintenance room behind the Angel Lust stage to acquire the makings for a freezer bomb (dynamite + fire extinguisher). An electric guitar and an amplifier sit right outside as well; merge these to assemble a shock wave-spawning power guitar.

MAINTENANCE ROOM 18

The north maintenance room near Tinkerbox pawnshop contains two gems and a bowie knife. Just outside, you discover boxing gloves and a flashlight.  Make deadly knife gloves by combining the boxing gloves and bowie knife, and build a lethal laser sword by merging the flashlight with one of the piles of gems.

UNEARTHING FORTUNE CITY

MAINTENANCE ROOM 19

Last but not least, the maintenance room that's tucked back in the corner near the Luaii Wauwii restaurant contains a saw blade and two boxes of nails. Outside lies a cement saw and a 2x4. Merge the saw blade and cement saw to make a ripper. You can assemble a porta-mower by merging the 2x4 with the lawn mower found in the nearby grass near Luaii Wauwii.

CA-CA-COMBO!

The large trailer at the Silver Strip's far north end is known as the Combo Bay. Chuck must defeat a psychopath named Leon Bell during the "Meet the Contestants" side mission to access the Combo Bay, where he's free to modify motorbikes in a variety of ways. Reference the table at the beginning of this chapter to discover all of the devious devices Chuck can install onto his bike.

PRICEY GUIDANCE

Think strategy guides are expensive? Try paying for hints at the Fortune Whisperer, an automated advisor that stands just outside of One Little Duck Bingo. Doling out heaps of cash to this mechanical wise man has its purpose; you'll earn significant PP bonuses as you continue to feed the machine and eventually unlock the burning skull combo card when you at last deposit the final $500,000 fee!

TIP

See the "Brain Food" chapter for tips on how to pad Chuck's bankroll in Fortune City.

After toying with the Fortune Whisperer, enter One Little Duck Bingo to locate two unique items. First, there's the bingo ball cage; this can be combined with a battery (find one in the nearby Maintenance Room 14) to build the electrifying tesla ball combo weapon. There's also a magazine near the bingo ball cage called *Leadership*, which increases the effectiveness of all survivors that follow Chuck for as long as he's carrying the mag—helpful if you enjoy keeping followers around.

THE TINKERER'S KEY

Pop into Tinkerbox to visit the Silver Strip's pawnshop. Among Zombrex and other interesting wares, you'll find the SUV key on sale here that allows you to drive the SUV parked in the nearby Shamrock Casino. The price tag is steep at two million bucks, but trust us, it's worth the expense!

LAUII WOWIE

The restaurant at the north end of Silver Strip, Luaii Wauwii, is a great place to find lots of food and several functional weapons. First, there's a lawn mower on the outside grass to the east—it's deadly in its own right, but even more lethal when combined with one of the 2x4s found around the nearby Maintenance Room 19.

On the opposite side of the restaurant, you find a powerful broadsword lodged in a boulder. You don't need to be King Arthur to pulleth out this mighty blade!

Find a magazine called *Juice Boost* on the counter of the restaurant's outdoor bar. This handy mag doubles the duration of all juice drink benefits while held, making it extremely valuable and well worth keeping.

Inside Luaii Wauwii, you find multiple curatives, including sushi that restores significant amounts of health. There are also paddles and a swordfish inside the eatery that serve as comical yet functional weapons. Find a stove in the kitchen and place a pan upon it to claim an easy 1,000 PP before you leave.

WORLD'S MOST DANGEROUS RIDE

Swing into Shamrock Casino to drool over a burly SUV that's on display. You need to accumulate two million dollars to buy the key for this ultimate zombie-masher. The key can be purchased at the nearby Tinkerbox pawnshop.

Considering how much scratch it takes to buy that SUV, you might want to grab the *Gambling 3* magazine that's tucked away in Shamrock Casino's northeast corner. This mag enhances your chances of winning big when playing the many gambling minigames found around Fortune City.

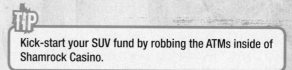

TIP

Kick-start your SUV fund by robbing the ATMs inside of Shamrock Casino.

STAGING AN ASSAULT

Rock gods Angel Lust have erected quite a stage along Silver Strip, and there's plenty of nasty weapons lying all around it.

You'll find all manner of zombie-rocking guitars around the stage, but the best treats are hidden up high. Climb up to the top of the steel girders to reach a chain saw and shotgun that are sure to knock 'em dead.

UNEARTHING FORTUNE CITY

DROWN YOUR SORROWS

Plenty of strong spirits can be swallowed within Pub O' Gold, but the blender behind the counter is the real find here. Mix up some delicious juice drinks,  referencing the "Appendix" chapter of this guide for a complete listing of blender concoctions.

PRESTIGIOUS PEEP SHOW

 There isn't much to see at the Silver Strip's Peep Show—in terms of items, that is. Chuck can take in quite the view here, however, just steer him into one of the shop's three doors to net him 1,000 PP, along with plenty of sexual frustration. Enter all three doors to really rev Chuck's motor and walk away with a satisfying 10,000 PP bonus!

SAUCY SHORTCUT

 After pillaging bills from the pair of ATMs that stand outside of Hot Excitorama, enter the shop and explore the back room to locate a maintenance hall that leads to Palisades Mall. This shortcut is always available, so take advantage.

GOING UP

Silver Strip sports two special ladders that lead to the roofs of the Royal Flush Plaza and the Atlantica Casino.

 One is located near Maintenance Room 14; the other is found at the far end of the alley to the south of Hot Excitorama.

There isn't a whole lot of interest atop these roofs—just an assortment of common items—but scaling these ladders becomes helpful when you're faced with a quartet  of psycho snipers at one point during the adventure. Climb the ladders to confront these snipers on even ground.

CRAZY KIOSKS

The Rockets Red Glare kiosk contains unlimited amounts of every firework. Of particular interest are the rocket fireworks—bring a few of these to Maintenance Room  15 and using the nearby lead pipes to assemble some spectacular rocket launchers.

> **TIP**
> Scale the Rockets Red Glare kiosk to discover dynamite atop its roof.

It's also worth noting that three baseball bats can be found at the Barrel of Goods kiosk. Carry two of these up to Maintenance Room 19 and build a couple of spiked  bats using the two boxes of nails found inside the room.

COMBO CARD: PADDLESAW

Examine the standing display at the Silver Strip's south end, close to the doors to Slot Ranch Casino. The poster on one side of the display inspires Chuck with  the paddlesaw combo card—one of the coolest combo weapons in the game.

> **TIP**
> Climb onto the poster display to locate a hidden handgun on top.

DEADRISING 2

SLOT RANCH CASINO

Slots as far as the eye can see—you're sure to strike it rich in the Slot Ranch Casino! And this month only, Slot Ranch Casino hosts the first stop of famed pop star Bibi Love's epic comeback tour!

SLOT RANCH CASINO - MAIN FLOOR	SLOT RANCH CASINO - NORTH STAGE AREA	SLOT RANCH CASINO - NE CASHIER/VAULT AREA	SLOT RANCH CASINO - WEST BAR AREA
Weapons	**Weapons**	**Weapons**	**Weapons**
Barstool	Acoustic Guitar	Battery	Barstool
Casino Chips	Cardboard Box	Casino Chips	Bucket
Croupier Stick	Casino Chips	Crowbar	Cardboard Box
Drink Cart	Drum	Drill Motor	Cash Register
Fancy Tall Chair	Gems	Fire Extinguisher	Casino Chips
Flashlight	Handbag	Flashlight	Handbag
Gems	Leaf Blower	Gems	Handgun
Indoor Garbage Can	Liberty Torch	Highback Oak Chair	Keg
Large Potted Plant	Mic Stand	Merc Assault Rifle	Newspaper
Metal Garbage Can	Speaker	Motor Oil	Serving Tray
Playing Cards	Spot Light	Newspaper	**Restoratives**
Square Sign	Training Sword	Power Drill	Beer
Stand	**Restoratives**	Propane Tank	Pizza
Velvet Bar	Beer	Small Potted Plant	Vodka
Wheelchair	Snack	Stool	Whiskey
Restoratives	**Clothing**	Water Cooler	**POI**
Beer	Show Girl Head Piece	**Restoratives**	Blender
Pizza	**Special**	Apple	SLOT RANCH CASINO - MAINTENANCE ROOM 4
Vodka	Zombrex (atop stacked boxes)	Coffee	**Weapons**
POI		**Special**	Flashlight
ATMs		Magazine 6 (Bikes)	Gems
Minigame 4 (Cash Me If You Can)			Leaf Blower (right outside)
Minigame 5 (Giant Slot Machine)			Motor Oil
Slot Machines			Training Sword (right outside)

POINTS OF INTEREST

MAINTENANCE ROOM 4

Slot Ranch Casino has just one maintenance room, but it's a good one. It's located in the rear of the performance stage, and there you'll find a flashlight and gems inside—the makings for a limb-severing laser sword. There's a container of motor oil inside the room as well; merge this with the training sword found in the backstage area to assemble some burning infernal arms.

UNEARTHING FORTUNE CITY

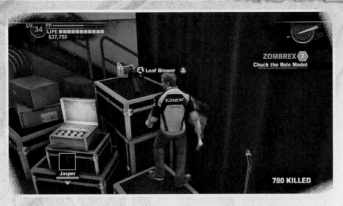

Find another flashlight on the ground to the right of the stage, near the cashier/vault area, and combine this with more gems found on the tables around the stage to build a second laser sword. Swipe another pile of gems off one of the tables and combine these with the leaf blower in the backstage area to craft a long-range gem blower. You can build all four of these lethal combo weapons each time you visit Slot Ranch Casino.

BACKSTAGE ZOMBREX

Climb the boxes near the giant dice in the backstage area. This gives you the elevation you need to leap over and score a hidden dose of Zombrex! Now you don't have to shell out $25,000 clams at a pawnshop to keep Katey from turning.

SUPER SLOTS

You've played plenty of slots around Fortune City, but none can compare to the mega slot machine found along Slot Ranch Casino's northeast wall. Press those big ol' buttons to feed the machine and see if it's your lucky day. Like other slot machines, the price to play is low, but so are the odds of winning.

CASHING IN

Smash up the ATMs outside of the cashier/vault area to pocket some fast funds. Once you advance to Case 3-2, you'll be able to enter this area to find several interesting items, including a deadly assault rifle, along with a drill motor and pitchfork that can be combined at the nearby maintenance room to create a powerful auger.

DRINKS FOR DAYS

Every casino benefits from a well-stocked bar, and at Slot Ranch Casino, you'll find a functional blender behind the counter. Mix up a few juice drinks to give Chuck plenty of healing, along with some special temporary benefits. See the "Appendix" chapter for a complete list of juice drinks and their effects.

CASH ME IF YOU CAN

Grab some fast bucks at the Cash Me If You Can game that stands at the southeast side of the casino floor. Pay the small fee to enter the booth, then mash that onscreen button to snatch up all the moola you can carry before time expires. The faster you are at button mashing, the more you'll benefit from Cash Me If You Can.

DEADRISING 2

SOUTH PLAZA

Coming soon!

NOTE

South Plaza may be unfinished, but it boasts four fully functional maintenance rooms. With so many tools and pieces of hardware lying around, including 2x4s, chain saws, sledge hammers, saw blades, boxes of nails, propane tanks, cement saws, and much more—this is a fantastic place to visit when you really want to put a hurting on those ugly undead.

SOUTH PLAZA - MAIN AREA
Weapons
2x4
Acetylene Tank
Baseball Bat
Box of Nails
Brick
Bucket
Cardboard Box
Cash Register
Cement Saw
Chain Saw
Construction Hat
Crowbar
Dolly
Dynamite
Fire Axe
Folding Chair
Garbage Bag
Gasoline Canister
Green Spray Paint
Green Spray Paint
Large Wrench
Lead Pipe
Mannequin Female
Mining Pick
Paint Can
Pallet
Plastic Bin
Plates
Power Drill
Propane Tank
Push Broom
Pylon
Saw Blade
Serving Tray
Sledge Hammer
Utility Cart
Vacuum Cleaner
Water Gun

Restoratives
Beer
Fries
Hamburger
Large Soda
Orange Juice
Clothing
Underwear
Special
4x4

SOUTH PLAZA - UPPER PLATFORMS
Weapons
2x4
Baseball Bat
Bucket
Cardboard Box
Cement Saw
Chain Saw
Construction Hat
Crowbar
Dynamite
Folding Chair
Green Spray Paint
Handgun
Large Wrench
Lead Pipe
Paint Can
Plates
Power Drill
Pylon
Rocket Fireworks
Water Gun
Restoratives
Beer
Fries
Hamburger
Hot Dog
Large Soda
Orange Juice
Snack

Clothing
Underwear
Special
Magazine 22 (Building)

SOUTH PLAZA - MAINTENANCE ROOM 24
Weapons
Box of Nails
Cement Saw
Plates (right outside)
Propane tank

SOUTH PLAZA - MAINTENANCE ROOM 25
Weapons
Chain Saw (right outside)
Lead Pipe
Paddle
Rocket Fireworks (right outside)

SOUTH PLAZA - MAINTENANCE ROOM 26
Weapons
Pitch Fork
Bucket
Drill Motor

SOUTH PLAZA - MAINTENANCE ROOM 27
Weapons
Green Spray Paint
Pylon (right outside)
Red Spray Paint
Saw Blade (right outside)
Vacuum Cleaner

POINTS OF INTEREST

MAINTENANCE ROOM 24

South Plaza's northwest maintenance room features a cement saw that can be merged with the plates outside to form the fantastic plate launcher. You can also opt to merge the cement saw with any saw blade (they're everywhere in South Plaza) to form a horrific ripper. This maintenance room also contains a box of nails and propane tank that Chuck can splice into a crowd-clearing I.E.D.

UNEARTHING FORTUNE CITY

MAINTENANCE ROOM 25

Find a chain saw just outside of the southwest maintenance room and discover an innocent-looking paddle within. Merge these two items to form an incredibly messy paddlesaw. Combine the room's lead pipe with the rocket fireworks found just outside to form an explosive rocket launcher as well.

MAINTENANCE ROOM 26

The southeast maintenance room contains a pitchfork and drill motor—the ingredients for a killer auger. There's a bucket inside the room as well; combine this with any power drill (they're quite common in South Plaza) to assemble a head-shredding drill bucket.

MAINTENANCE ROOM 27

South Plaza's northeast maintenance room contains a rare vacuum cleaner, and there's a saw blade just outside. This gives Chuck the ingredients for a devious exsanguinator that does anything but suck.

SCAFFOLDING MASTER

Chuck can leap up and climb onto the many elevated stretches of scaffolding that run throughout South Plaza. By climbing the scaffolding near the unfinished Ultimate Playhouse store, you can locate a handy chain saw.

Scale the scaffolding along South Plaza's far-west wall to access a chain saw, handgun, orange juice, and a baseball bat that can be merged with the many boxes of nails around South Plaza to make a lethal spiked bat.

Work your way onto the scaffolding that stretches between the west and central statues to discover, among other things, the *Building* magazine, which triples the durability of construction weapons—very useful here at South Plaza!

Want more chain saw? Climb to the top of the high scaffolding to the south of the central statue to obtain another of these zombie-mauling devices. Find a paddle in the nearby shop that features a passage to Maintenance Room 27 and combine these two items to form a fantastic paddlesaw.

If you're messing around near the entrance to Fortune City Hotel, climb the stacked crates running up the wall near the east statue to reach a long stretch of ventilation. Up here you can acquire two sticks of dynamite, along with the makings for a beer hat.

DEADRISING 2

YUCATAN CASINO

Countless slot machines, blackjack tables and roulette wheels—it must be Yucatan! Come see our signature showpiece, Snowflake the Bengal tiger! Daily feeding shows at 10:00 AM and 10:00 PM.

YUCATAN CASINO - MAIN AREA

Weapons

Stone Statue
Water Gun
Ad Board
Casino Chips
Construction Hat (atop slot machines north of south VIP room)
Croupier Stick
Cushioned Tall Chair
Drink Cart
Flashlight
Handbag
Large Barrel
Large Fern Tree
Lead Pipe
Playing Cards
Rocket Fireworks (atop slot machines southeast of Lucky Marble)
Roulette Wheel
Square Sign
Stand
Tiki Torch
Velvet Bar
Wheelchair
Yellow Tall Chair

Restoratives

Beer
Wine
Drink Cocktail

POI

Slot Machines (require power)
Chopper
Minigame 6 (Lucky Marble)
Minigame 7 (Money to Burn)

YUCATAN CASINO - UPPER PLATFORMS

Weapons

Construction Hat
Flashlight
Gasoline Canister
Handgun
Saw Blades
Sledge Hammer
Stone Statue
Water Gun

Restoratives

Steak
Whiskey

YUCATAN CASINO - SOUTH ENTRY AREA

Weapons

Fancy Painting
Handbag
Indoor Garbage Can
Large Fern Tree
Machete (atop large entry statue)
Small Suitcase
Square Sign
Stand
Stone Statue
Tiki Torch
Velvet Bar

Restoratives

Beer
Snack

YUCATAN CASINO - SOUTH VIP ROOM

Weapons

Cardboard Box
Computer Case (at bar)
Fancy Painting
Fire Extinguisher
Indoor Garbage Can
Keyboard (at bar)
LCD Monitor (at bar)
Plates
Rocket Fireworks

Weapons, cont.

Scissors (at bar)
Small Suitcase (at bar)
Small Vase
Stool (at bar)
Table Lamp
Tennis Racquet
Vacuum Cleaner
Water Cooler

Restoratives

Apple
Beer (at bar)
Coffee
Coffee Creamer
Snack

Clothing

Dealer Outfit

YUCATAN CASINO - WEST FIREPLACE AREA

Weapons

Construction Hat (nearby, to the south)
Flashlight (nearby, to the south)
Hunk of Meat
Lead Pipe (nearby, to the south)
Machete
Pitchfork
Rocket Fireworks (atop stone blocks)
Saw Blade (nearby, to the south)
Tiki Torch

YUCATAN CASINO - NORTH RESTROOM AREA

Weapons

Gasoline Canister
Handbag
Indoor Garbage Can
Metal Garbage Can
Playing Cards
Small Suitcase
Suitcase

Restoratives

Beer

Special

Combo Card 3 (Freedom Bear)

YUCATAN CASINO - EAST CASHIER & VAULT AREA

Weapons

Battery
Casino Chips
Computer Case
Construction Hat
Crowbar
Drill Motor
Keyboard
LCD Monitor
LMG
Merc Assault Rifle
Power Drill
Propane Tank
Small Suitcase
Suitcase

Restoratives

Beer
Cake

Clothing

Dealer Visor

YUCATAN CASINO - MAINTENANCE ROOM 6

Weapons

Box of Nails
Fire Axe
Fire Extinguisher (right outside)
Propane Tank
Push Broom (right outside)
Sledge Hammer (right outside)
Toy Spitball Gun

YUCATAN CASINO - Y101 BARON VON BRATHAUS

Weapons

Large Barrel
Bag of Marbles
Cash Register
Coffee Pot
Cooking Pot
Dolly

UNEARTHING FORTUNE CITY

Weapons, cont.
Fancy Painting
Gasoline Canister
Highback Oak Chair
Keg
Ketchup
Lawn Mower (on grassy ledge)
Machete
Meat Cleaver
Metal Garbage Can
Mustard
Painting
Pan
Plates
Scissors
Servbot Mask
Serving Tray
Small Painting
Stick Pony
Stool
Tennis Racquet (on grassy ledge)
Toy Helicopter
Toy Spitball Gun
Wacky Hammer
Zombie Mask
Restoratives
Beer
Wine
Large Soda
Steak
Special
Magazine (Health 2)
Magazine 7 (Health 2)
POI
Blender
Stove
Blender

YUCATAN CASINO – Y102 SHOAL NIGHTCLUB
Weapons
Beer
Barstool
Cash Register
Chef Knife
Fancy Painting
Fire Axe (near escalator)
Fire Extinguisher
Gift Shop Lamp
Handbag
Handgun
Indoor Garbage Can
Keg
Large Fern Tree
Massager
Nightstick
Serving Tray
Shotgun
Small Vase
Speaker
Square Sign
Stand
Vacuum Cleaner
Velvet Bar
Vinyl Records
Water Gun (near escalator)
Whipped Cream
Restoratives
Vodka
Drink Cocktail
POI
ATMs

POINTS OF INTEREST

MAINTENANCE ROOM 6

Good weapons can be hard to find in Yucatan Casino, but not if you visit its one and only maintenance room. Here you find the components to build an I.E.D. (propane tank + box of nails), along with a toy spitball gun that can be combined with any of the casino's plentiful tiki torches to assemble a searing fire spitter. Don't overlook that fire axe, either; merge it with the nearby sledge hammer to create a lethal defiler.

THE BARON'S BOUNTY

Baron Von Brathaus is your primary source of nourishment at Yucatan Casino. Whenever Chuck's in need of healing, flee to the Baron to find all sorts of food.

There's a blender behind the Baron's bar, along with a never-ending supply of wine that allows Chuck to create countless Quick Steps. Or toss two of the eatery's plentiful beers into the blender to mix up some Pain

The *Health 2* magazine on the counter near the blender doubles the effectiveness of all curatives—make certain to pick this up as Chuck's health increases.

Visit the Baron's kitchen to discover a useful machete, among other sharp pointing things. Place a pan on the stove back here to cook up some PP as well.

LUCKY MARBLE

Explore the center of the casino floor to discover a fun minigame of video roulette. Use the control buttons to place bets in a variety of ways.

You can keep it simple by betting on red or black, or get more involved by betting on specific rows or sections of numbers.

Use the "Choose Category" button to cycle through the various types of bets, such as red/black and high/low. Hit the "Choose Bet" button to cycle through various options within each betting category, shifting from black to red, high to low, etc. You can place up to five separate bets per game.

TIP

Stick with simple bets, such as red/black, even/odd, and high/low for the best odds of winning in Lucky Marble.

When you're all finished gambling, circle around the side of the Lucky Marble and jump onto its wide stone ledges. Keep scaling these until you reach the top.

When you can climb no higher, jump to the high circular platform to land near a powerful LMG and a free dose of Zombrex. Score!

GET TO THE CHOPPER

Chuck can't ride the awesome motorcycle that's prominently displayed atop the slots to the west of the Lucky Marble until he purchases the chopper key. This key is found at the Palisades Mall's second-floor pawnshop, but it'll run you $1,000,000. The thrill of tearing through the Yucatan on this sweet ride is worth the cost—see the previous "Brain Food" chapter for clues on how to amass that kind of wealth.

UNEARTHING FORTUNE CITY

MONEY TO BURN

Examining the unusual fire pit to the east of the Lucky Marble minigame causes Chuck to toss some of his hard-earned cash into the flames. Don't worry, this small sacrifice earns you PP in exchange! Keep heaving dollars into the fire pit to acquire more and more PP—a great way to level Chuck up when you've got lots of money.

FIREPLACE FRIVOLITY

The fireplace along the west wall is largely encased in glass, making it relatively zombie-free. Here you discover several useful weapons, including a machete, pitchfork, and lots of tiki torches that can set the undead ablaze. The steak on the nearby rock is a potent curative, and the rocket fireworks found atop the fireplace can be merged with the lead pipe to the right of this area to form an explosive rocket launcher.

SHOAL SECRETS

On your way to the Shoal Nightclub, vault the small counter to the right to reach a tiny nook where a shotgun and rare vacuum cleaner have been stashed. Merge the shotgun with the pitchfork near the casino's west fireplace to form a boomstick, and combine the vacuum cleaner with the saw blades stashed to the left of the fireplace to assemble an exsanguinator.

The nightclub itself is filled with relatively unspectacular items, but there is plenty of health-restoring booze to be had. You can also find a handgun in the club's northeast corner.

ROBBING THE VAULT

Yucatan's east cashier/vault area remains locked until you advance to Case 3-2. After that point you're able to enter this area, where an assault rifle is always stashed, along with an LMG and other useful items.

CLIMBING HIGH

A series of narrow platforms hang above the Yucatan's floor, and Chuck can climb atop these to locate several interesting items.

Leap from the tops of slot machines and table games to reach these upper platforms, where you'll find construction hats (merge these with beers to form beer hats) and a Servbot mask (combine this with the lawn mower in the grass near Baron Von Brathaus to make a super slicer). There are also gasoline canisters and a water gun up here, which merge to form a flamethrower. Oh, and did we mention there's a broadsword up here as well?

COMBO CARD: FREEDOM BEAR

Head for the Yucatan's restroom and examine the poster on the wall just outside of the men's room to acquire the freedom bear combo card. Grab that LMG off the top of the Lucky Marble minigame and merge it with a robot bear (find one atop the slot machines near the Shoal Nightclub's escalators) to form this cuddly combo.

UNDERGROUND

Authorized personnel only.

> **NOTE**
>
> The Underground is inaccessible until you progress to Case 2-2 in the adventure.

UNDERGROUND - MAIN TUNNEL

Weapons

- Acetylene Tank
- Blast Frequency Gun
- Bow and Arrow
- Brick
- Bucket
- Cardboard Box
- Chain Saw
- Construction Hat
- Dolly
- Folding Chair
- Handgun
- Large Wrench
- Lead Pipe
- Mining Pick
- Pallet
- Pitchfork (on train)
- Plates
- Pylon
- Rocket Fireworks
- Servbot Mask
- Shotgun
- Sledge Hammer
- Tire

Restoratives

- Beer
- Orange Juice (on trains)
- Snack
- Whiskey

Special

- 4x4
- Security 4x4
- Weapon Vending Machine

UNDERGROUND - WAREHOUSE A

Weapons

- 2x4
- Acetylene Tank
- Box of Nails
- Cardboard Box
- Casino Chips
- Cement Saw
- Construction Hat
- Dolly
- Folding Chair
- Garbage Bag
- Large Wrench
- Lead Pipe
- Pallet
- Playing Cards
- Power Drill
- Pylon
- Rocket Fireworks
- Roulette Wheel
- Stool
- Tall Cushioned Chair
- Tire
- Utility Cart
- Wheelchair

Restoratives

- Beer
- Snack

Special

- 4x4
- Magazine 26 (Combat 3)
- Security 4x4
- Slot Machines

UNDERGROUND - WAREHOUSE B

Weapons

- 2x4
- Acetylene Tank
- Assault Rifle
- Box of Nails
- Chain Saw
- Construction Hat
- Dolly
- Fire Axe
- Garbage Bag
- Gasoline Canister
- Large Fern Tree
- Large Wrench
- Lead Pipe
- Mannequin Female
- Mannequin Male
- Motor Oil
- Pallet
- Plates
- Plywood
- Power Drill
- Push Broom
- Saw Blade
- Sledge Hammer
- Steel Shelving
- Utility Cart
- Vacuum Cleaner
- Water Gun

Restoratives

- Hamburger
- Large Soda
- Snack

Special

- 4x4

UNDERGROUND - WAREHOUSE C

Weapons

- Acetylene Tank
- Bow and Arrow
- Cardboard Box
- Dolly
- Fire Axe
- Garbage Bag
- Gasoline Canister
- Metal Barricade
- Pallet
- Parasol
- Plastic Bin
- Push Broom
- Pylon
- Sledge Hammer
- Square Sign
- Steel Shelving
- Utility Cart

Special

- 2x4

UNDERGROUND - WAREHOUSE D

Weapons

- Assault Rifle
- Cardboard Box
- Garbage Bag
- Grenade
- Pallet
- Tire

Special

- Magazine 28 (Blades)

UNEARTHING FORTUNE CITY

UNDERGROUND - WAREHOUSE E
Weapons
2x4
Acetylene Tank
Box of Nails
Cardboard Box
Construction Hat
Dolly
Fire Axe
Gasoline Canister
Pallet
Pitchfork
Plates
Pylon
Sledge Hammer
Tire
Restoratives
Beer
Coffee
Hot Dog
Jellybeans
Orange Juice
Snack
Special
2x4
Motorbike

UNDERGROUND - SECRET LAB
Weapons
LCD Monitor
Keyboard
Computer Case
Blast Frequency Gun
Bowie Knife
Box of Nails
Broadsword (on ceiling vent)
Bucket
Cardboard Box
Chainsaw (on ceiling vent)
Coffee Pot
Construction Hat
Dolly
Fire Axe
Flashlight
Folding Chair
Gas Can
Handgun
Large Wrench
Lead Pipe
Machete
Military Case
Patio Table
Power Drill
Pylon
Queen
Serving Tray
Sledge Hammer
Steel Shelving
Step Ladder

Restoratives
Hamburger
Fries
Large Soda
Coffee Creamer
Pasta
Pizza
Whiskey

UNDERGROUND - MAINTENANCE ROOM 29
Weapons
Battery
Lead Pipe (right outside)
Merc Assault Rifle
Rocket Fireworks
Wheelchair (right outside)

UNDERGROUND - MAINTENANCE ROOM 30
Weapons
Cement Saw
Fire Axe
Saw Blades
Sledge Hammer (right outside)

UNDERGROUND - MAINTENANCE ROOM 31
Weapons
Battery
Construction Hat (right outside)
Dynamite
Leaf Blower
Leaf Rake (right outside)
Parasol (right outside)
Wheelchair (right outside)
Restoratives
Beer (right outside)

UNDERGROUND - MAINTENANCE ROOM 32
Weapons
Amplifier
Baseball Bat
Box of Nails
Propane Tank (right outside)
Special
Zombrex (right outside)

UNDERGROUND - MAINTENANCE ROOM 33
Weapons
Amplifier
Bow and Arrow
Dynamite (right outside)

UNDERGROUND - MAINTENANCE ROOM 34
Weapons
Construction Hat
Fire Extinguisher
Gasoline Canister (right outside)
Lawn Mower (right outside)
Push Broom (right outside)
Servbot Mask (right outside)
Water Gun (right outside)
Restoratives
Beer

UNDERGROUND - MAINTENANCE ROOM 35
Weapons
Cement Saw
Drill Motor
Plates (right outside)
Shotgun (right outside)

DEADRISING 2

POINTS OF INTEREST

MAINTENANCE ROOMS 29-35

The Underground's most interesting items are kept in the warehouses near its many maintenance rooms. Refer to the poster map and tables to see what sorts of lethal devices you can construct at each of these secluded sites.

TUNNEL TRAVEL

Numerous 4x4s are found in the Underground, and we've labeled their locations on the poster map for your convenience. Use these vehicles to navigate this horrible place with less stress, but don't expect them to last long as you plow through the endless army of undead.

The 4x4s are all well and good, but if you truly want to ride in style, hop onto the chopper that's parked at Warehouse E. You don't need the chopper key that's sold at Palisades Mall's pawnshop to ride this bad boy around!

MISPLACED MEDS

Search the elevated rise near Maintenance Room 32 to discover a dose of Zombrex just lying out there in the open. Someone's careless loss becomes Katey's gain.

WALKTHROUGH

TERROR IS REALITY

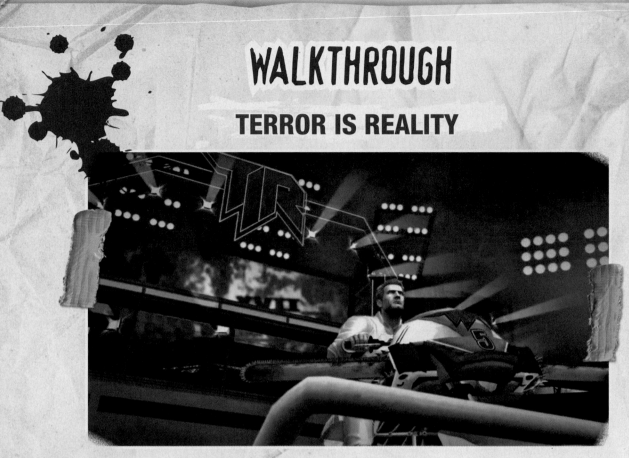

Welcome to Fortune City, where the dead are made to entertain the living. You are Chuck Greene, ex-Motocross wild man and father to darling little Katey. Chuck makes his bucks slaughtering zombies in America's hottest and most dangerous hit reality show: "Terror is Reality." Why risk it all on such gruesome folly? Because poor young Katey Greene is infected, and only the miracle pharmaceutical Zombrex—an extremely pricey prescription—can keep Chuck's beloved little girl from turning.

Each zombie you kill is worth points, and your score is shown at the upper-left corner. Aim for groups of zombies with large pink spheres attached to their heads—these explode when killed, giving you huge bonuses!

It's not long before you're thrown into the action. Seated atop a modified motorbike, an arena filled with the walking dead stretches on before you. Simply hit the gas and start mowing down hapless zombies, aiming to slaughter as many as possible.

NOTE

Don't bother ramming into your rivals; they can't be harmed.

Strive to get the top score—the reward is worth the effort.

FINDING KATEY

If you finished the game show in first place, Chuck earns $10,000 and 5,000 PP (Prestige Points)—a nice way to kick things off here at Fortune City. After pocketing his reward money, Chuck sets off to find his daughter, Katey. She's waiting in one of the arena's green rooms.

NOTE

Money is used to purchase useful items at Fortune City. Collect Prestige Points (PP) by killing enemies and completing various tasks. Chuck "levels up" when he acquires enough PP, becoming more powerful and improving his odds of survival.

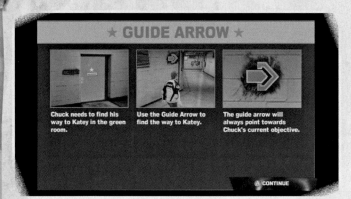

At this point, the "Guide Arrow" tutorial screen is shown. Pause the game and select "Tutorials" to review helpful messages such as this again at any time.

PIT STOP

Follow the guide arrow out of the locker room and toward the green room. You pass a restroom along the way, which is clearly marked by a glowing, green sign.

Chuck is able to save his progress at restrooms. Pop into this one, approach any toilet or stall and press the Interact button to bring up the Save menu. Save your game to mark your progress.

You only get three save slots, so make them count! We recommend you cycle through the slots when saving so you can always go back a bit in case you miss something.

Continue following the guide arrow after visiting the restroom. Speak to Amber in the hall if you feel like being berated by a woman with an attitude. Proceed to the nearby elevator afterward—the green rooms are just upstairs.

Chuck encounters Amber's equally hot and spicy twin sister, Crystal, as she steps off the elevator. After suffering a few more insults, Chuck boards the lift headed for the green rooms.

HELL BREAKS LOOSE

While riding the elevator, a tremendous explosion rocks the arena. Prying open the elevator doors, Chuck sees a terrifying sight: zombies!

Slaughtering zombies on a souped-up motorcycle is one thing; facing a hoard of them on foot is quite another. Hurry and grab a weapon; the nearby baseball bat and fire axe are both ideal.

WALKTHROUGH

NOTE

All weapons are marked by orange gun icons. Food items that replenish Chuck's health are marked by green apple icons. It's a good idea to carry an equal blend of weapons and food.

Don't worry about the people who are dying all around you; there's nothing you can do to save them. Only Katey matters now.

Oodles of weapons are in the hall beyond the elevator, but you'll quickly find that objects that can be swung quickly and with force, such as the aforementioned baseball bat and fire axe, are best suited to wiping out masses of undead. Don't be bashful; take this opportunity to familiarize yourself with the fine art of zombie bashing.

TIP

Storage items, such as trash receptacles and cardboard boxes, can be picked up and thrown to reveal additional items. See the "Getting Started" chapter to learn how to throw objects and other useful controls.

Chuck's health is measured by yellow squares that appear at the upper-left corner, just below the PP gauge. Should the undead start to get the better of him, find something to eat or drink to replenish Chuck's health. All such items are marked by green apple icons so you can easily identify them. Like weapons, some restoratives work better than others.

CAUTION

Any food that is labeled "spoiled" will still restore Chuck's health, but spoiled foods also make him violently ill. While sick, Chuck will periodically vomit (three times, causing him to drop his current weapon each time he hurls and making him easy prey. Consuming three alcoholic beverages in a row promotes a similar effect. Be careful of what Chuck consumes!

Beat back the zombies as you follow the guide arrow toward the green room. In truth there is no urgent rush—Katey won't die suddenly and the clock isn't really ticking just yet—so feel free to spend a bit of time familiarizing yourself with *Dead Rising 2*'s unique brand of carnage during this introductory segment.

TIP

Try freezing zombies with a fire extinguisher, then smashing them with weapons for a few bonus PP. It helps to hold the Aim button when using fire extinguishers and other ranged weapons.

GREAT ESCAPE

Chuck gets a scare when he enters the green room, but finds Katey safe and sound—the clever child was hiding in a wardrobe. Our hero grabs his little girl and prepares to make a life-or-death run through the teeming undead hoard.

Chuck is only able to kick zombies out of his way while carrying Katey, so fighting the undead isn't a sound option anymore. Focus on getting past the cretins while dashing for the arena lobby instead, following the trusty guide arrow.

Unfortunate souls are becoming zombie food all around, but there's still nothing you can do to save them. Just keep moving through gaps in the sea of flesh-eating ghouls as you make for the doors that lead to Fortune City's Platinum Strip.

Bursting out to fresh air, Chuck sees the once-peaceful Fortune City has been transformed into a terrible mess of screams, fire, and the walking dead. Our hero deftly makes his way through the chaos and into the city's emergency shelter just before its outer doors slam shut.

SAFE AT LAST

Chuck, Katey, and a handful of survivors are all that manage to reach the city's bunker, known more properly as the Safe House. On the other side of the massive security door, Chuck has a brief chat with Raymond Sullivan, a military reserve officer. Sullivan notices Katey's scar from when she was bitten during

a previous zombie outbreak, but Chuck assures the man that he's got plenty of Zombrex—the breakthrough drug that's capable of preventing the infected from turning into zombies, provided that it's administered once every 24 hours without fail.

As it turns out, Chuck was lying—he doesn't have any Zombrex at all, just an empty carton. Katey will need some of the drug soon, and Chuck knows he'll have to brave the horrors of Fortune City to find it.

Another survivor, Stacey Forsythe, tells Chuck that he can find some Zombrex in a pharmacy in the mall known as Royal Flush Plaza—all Chuck needs to do is find a way out of the Safe House. Stacey also hands Chuck a transceiver so she can stay in contact as she monitors Fortune City from the Safe House's security room. She promises not to tell Sullivan about Chuck and Katey's plight. It's been a long time since Chuck has seen such a friendly face, but there isn't time to get better acquainted.

FIND KATEY ZOMBREX

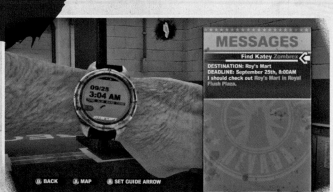

Take a peek at your watch to see that you've only a handful of hours before Katey needs her next Zombrex injection. You've got to find a way out of the Safe House, and fast.

NOTE

Time is a major factor from now on. The military will arrive in just three days to rescue everyone inside the Safe House, and time steadily passes whenever the game is not paused. (Pause the game by looking at the map or any of the Pause menu screens.) Speed is key if you want to see and do everything that Fortune City has to offer, but don't worry; just follow this walkthrough carefully and you won't miss a thing.

TIP

Two heroes are better than one! A co-op buddy can jump into your game at any point, so make things easier on yourself and play with a friend. See the "Brain Food" chapter for more on co-op play.

WALKTHROUGH

LEAVING THE SAFE HOUSE

Grab the milk and orange juice in the security room; these are powerful curatives. Swipe a fresh fire axe from the hall outside as well.

NOTE

At present, the Safe House is full of potent restoratives like milk and orange juice. Supplies dwindle as hungry survivors chow down, however, and you'll soon need to forage for food primarily outside the Safe House. We'll show you the ideal places to gather supplies.

Before moving on, allow Chuck a moment to relieve himself in the Safe House's restroom, which is right outside the security room (and also marked on your map). Save your progress and then return to the hallway.

NOTE

You can also change Chuck's attire by using the lockers inside the restroom. There's no need to do so at present; you haven't unlocked any fresh duds yet. See the "Appendix" chapter of this guide for a complete list of unlockable outfits.

Thanks to the guide arrow, finding the way out of the Safe House couldn't be easier. Simply follow the tool as it leads you down the stairs near the restroom. There's a ventilation shaft in the lower area; interact with its metal door to make Chuck crawl through.

ROYAL FLUSH PLAZA

The vent leads to Royal Flush Plaza's northwest maintenance area. This is the only place where Chuck can enter the Safe House, and it's now marked on your map. Check your map to view the location of Roy's Mart within Royal Flush Plaza—it's marked by a red icon. That's where you need to go, and your guide arrow will lead you there.

Notice that the names of the stores appear as you move your cursor across the map. Handy!

TIP

When you've multiple active tasks, you can tune the guide arrow to any mission through the map screen. You can also set the guide arrow while looking at your watch, but beware: The game does not pause while you're eying Chuck's timepiece, and zombies will assault him if you're not careful!

Pick up the baseball bat near the first set of stairs you encounter in the maintenance area. You should now have a fire axe, baseball bat, milk, and orange juice—a healthy combination for some zombie killin'. The sledgehammer you discover farther down the hall is a sound choice as well.

It's not long before Stacey tests out the transceiver she gave to Chuck. Answer her call by pressing the button shown onscreen. She'll remind you that the Zombrex should be found inside Roy's Mart. You just have to make it there and back in one piece.

NOTE

Ignore the door marked "maintenance" as you trot down the hall. You can't use these special rooms just yet.

DEADRISING 2

Open the double doors at the end of the hall to enter the mall. Beware: Legions of undead lurk just ahead!

Don't waste much time on the zombies in the mall. Kill any that get in your way, but by and large, simply try to avoid them by weaving through, looking for gaps in the throng. Ripping apart zombies is certainly fun but

you'll have plenty of chances to do lots of that as you explore Fortune City. Remember, time is your biggest enemy in *Dead Rising 2*, and you can't waste a second if you want to complete all of those missions.

BOOTING LOOTERS

Upon entering Roy's Mart, Chuck is surprised to find the place being robbed by looters. A hapless woman hides behind the counter, terrified. Time to play the hero!

Looters are faster than zombies, and they attack with actual weapons, making them a bit more dangerous. They're no match for Chuck, however, so waste no time

wiping out this trio of toughs with fast attack combos. Don't relent until all three looters have been beaten to a timely demise.

TIP

If Chuck suffers serious damage, quickly flee and chug some milk or orange juice. You can find more food in the store if you run out.

After the bloodbath, Chuck grabs the Pharmacy Key off of one of the looter's bodies. Jump the counter to speak with Denyce, the store's poor,

terrified employee. Chuck assures the woman that she'll be safe at the Safe House; keep speaking with her until she agrees to follow him.

TIP

Escorting survivors back to the Safe House is a great way to earn PP in *Dead Rising 2*. Chuck scores significant PP whenever he convinces a survivor to join him, and gets even more PP when he successfully escorts survivors back to the Safe House.

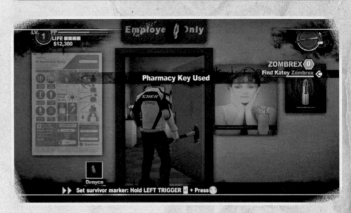

Nice work, but you've still got to find that Zombrex for Katey. Enter the door marked "employees only." Chuck will use the Pharmacy Key to reach the back room of Roy's Mart, where the Zombrex is kept.

The Zombrex sits on a counter next to some orange juice and coffee creamer (an equally potent curative). Grab the Zombrex, along with anything else you might need from the

store, before returning to the Safe House.

CAUTION

All melee weapons deteriorate and shatter after prolonged use. When a weapon's icon begins to blink red in your inventory, it's time to look for a new mauling device.

ESCORT MISSION

Denyce will follow Chuck anywhere he leads, and she's smart enough to avoid zombies on her own. Don't worry too much about her; simply retrace your steps

back to the Safe House, sidestepping the undead as you go. If Denyce screams out in agony, check to see if she's been grabbed by a zombie and do your best to free her without harming the poor woman in the process.

WALKTHROUGH

Make sure Denyce is close by before entering the ventilation shaft leading back to the Safe House. If she's not nearby, she'll be left behind and suffer steady damage until Chuck goes back for her. When you see the little green door icon above her health bar or "out of view" portrait, you know that she's close enough to follow Chuck through.

Denyce is happy to at last be safe from the clutches of looters and the walking dead. You receive additional PP for bringing her back to the Safe House—enough to advance Chuck to level 2! Each time Chuck levels up, he receives random rewards that can include stat bonuses, new skills, and more.

Leveling Chuck up is the secret to survival in Fortune City—see the "Brain Food" chapter for more on this matter.

Sullivan isn't thrilled that Chuck found a way out of the Safe House, but he can't argue with the man's need to save his daughter and other survivors of the outbreak. Run upstairs and save at the restroom after Chuck has his chat with Sullivan.

GREAT EXPLORATIONS

Katey cannot be given a Zombrex shot until after 7:00 AM—it's vital that the drug isn't administered too early. If you've made good time obtaining the drug, you now have several hours of game time to explore Fortune City, leveling Chuck up in preparation for the challenges ahead. Save your game and then venture back out—and don't worry, Stacey will call to remind you about Katey when the clock strikes 7.

TIP

If this isn't your first time through the game and you're playing with a leveled-up Chuck, consider visiting Yucatan Casino at this point to face off against Ted and his beloved tiger, Snowflake. He's the only psycho you can battle at this point, and defeating him right now is an advantage. Ted and Snowflake are a bit too much to handle if this is your first run through the game, however.

Read on to discover some of the fun and profitable things to try out while you wait for the 7 o'clock hour. Don't worry; you won't need to stray too far from the Safe House.

TEST OF STRENGTH

On your way out of the Safe House, grab the sledgehammer from Royal Flush Plaza's northwest maintenance hall and then enter the nearby store called The Man's Sport. Stand before the central display and then hold the Attack button to perform the sledge hammer's heavy attack. This causes Chuck to slam the weapon straight downward onto the pressure plate, rocketing a weight up to ring the bell above. Completing this little test of strength nets Chuck 5,000 PP.

READ ALL ABOUT IT

Near The Man's Sport is a small kiosk called Yesterday, Today and Tomorrow. Chuck finds two magazines here: *Health 1*, which increases the healing benefit of all food items by 50 percent, and *Combat 2*, which gives chuck a 10 percent boost to PP earned from weapon kills. You don't have enough health or inventory slots to make carrying such luxury items worthwhile at the moment, but remember where you saw these mags for future reference.

LUCKY 7

Proceed through the mall until you spy the giant, novelty Flaming Craps table. Vault the fence surrounding the table and dispatch the zombie security guards on the other side, then grab one of those giant dice. Hold the Aim button and then press the Attack button to throw the die, rolling it along the table.

Chuck earns 10,000 PP if the dice come up totaling seven, but don't waste too much time trying for this difficult prize—you can come back to this later.

TIP

The dice show sixes at first, so you can make a seven just by rolling one of them and having it come up a one. Again, don't give it more than a few rolls—there are easier ways to score PP right now.

HOLE IN ONE

Enter the store called SporTrance, which isn't far from the Flaming Craps table, and pay a few thousand bucks to play the Casino Cup minigame against the back wall. Chuck readies a club; press the indicated button to fill the swing meter, then press the same button again when the meter reaches the indicated zone. Success means a hole in one—you only need to sink one ball to walk away a winner!

If you've got the scratch, play the Casino Cup multiple times to win even bigger cash and PP prizes. The difficulty amps up each time—see if you can sink the ball when the meter vanishes to win the ultimate prize!

NOTE

Most minigames that require a fee to play allow you to win multiple times, just like the Casino Cup. Keep paying to play these games—as the cost increases, so do the potential rewards!

GIFTS FOR KATEY

Chuck's little girl means the world to him, and he can show her this—and score some serious PP—by giving her special gifts. Start by entering the nearby store called Ye Olde Toybox and collecting a bag of marbles, a beach ball, and a stick pony. Ensure that Chuck is in good health and drop other items to make room for these special gifts.

Sprint toward the Safe House, making a short detour into Stylin' Toddlers to collect a giant stuffed elephant, or heading into Astonishing Illusions to grab a cute and cuddly robot bear.  Both are ideal gifts for Katey, but Chuck must carry these oversized items with both hands and cannot equip other weapons while transporting them. Don't use these giant stuffed toys as weapons, either—Katey doesn't care for damaged goods.

Bring your four gifts back to the Safe House and hand each one to little Katey, one at a time. Chuck cleans up the PP on this bargain, likely leveling up multiple times. If you still have time to kill, go back for the other giant stuffed animal you couldn't carry before.

WALKTHROUGH

GIVE KATEY ZOMBREX

Between 7:00 AM and 8:00 AM, enter the Safe House's security room and give Katey her Zombrex shot to prevent the world's cutest zombie from emerging. In all seriousness, if you don't give Katey the shot during this brief window of time, you won't be able to enjoy the game's true ending.

Giving Katey Zombrex completes your first Case File task. You're now able to view the entire Case File from the pause menu, helping you keep tabs on upcoming events. (Stacey will regularly remind you about active cases as well.) You're given the option to save your game after you clear a case; go ahead and do so now that you've given Katey her Zombrex for the day.

NOTE

If you happen to fail a Case File task, you can always go back and load a previous save to try again. However, in *Dead Rising 2*, you also have the unique option to restart the game at any point while maintaining all of the PP you've accumulated for Chuck thus far. If the going gets rough, consider restarting with a leveled-up Chuck—there's absolutely no reason not to. It's entirely possible to beat the game on your first playthrough if you're careful about amassing plenty of PP, but restarting certainly makes things easier.

CASE 1-1: BIG NEWS

After giving little Katey a shot of Zombrex, Chuck listens to a TV news report that's actually coming from inside Fortune City.

The reporter, Rebecca Chang, has a tape that proves the zombie outbreak was an intentional act of terrorism, and says she has a source that identifies the perpetrator as Chuck Greene.

Unable to believe his ears, Chuck becomes outraged—he knows he's innocent and must take action to clear his name. He'll

have to work fast; all evidence of the true nature of this horrific tragedy will be lost when the military arrives three days from now. Chuck's next objective: Visit Fortune City Hotel and question the reporter to learn more about her source and the doctored video tape. His only friend in this matter, Stacey, doesn't know what to believe—but she agrees to assist Chuck by keeping an eye on things from the Safe House as best she can.

DEADRISING 2

Watching Rebecca Chang's news story is all it takes to complete Case 1-1. To clear Case 1-2, you'll need to visit Fortune City Hotel, which is now marked on your map. Speak to Sullivan on your way out of the Safe House; he'll give you a special key that allows you to enter and make use of the many maintenance rooms around Fortune City. We'll get to those in a moment.

MORE MESSAGES

Shortly after exiting the Safe House, Chuck receives a call from Stacey, who informs him of a few optional tasks he can explore. As luck would have it, these side missions can be accomplished on the way to Fortune City Hotel. Set your guide arrow to the "Lost…" mission and follow it toward your destination.

Grab the baseball bat inside the maintenance room and place it on the workbench. Do the same with the box of nails on the shelf and Chuck automatically combines the two items into the spiked bat combo weapon. Now you're getting into the swing of things!

HIGH MAINTENANCE

BATTER UP

Exit the maintenance room and put your newfound combo weapon to use against the zombies in the hall. Notice that each zombie you kill with the spiked bat earns you 50 PP— this quickly adds up. Try holding the Attack button to execute the spiked bat's satisfying heavy attack for a guaranteed single-zombie kill that nets you 200 PP. Good stuff!

Before getting very far, Chuck notices a maintenance room and steps inside. Spying a baseball bat and box of nails, Chuck ingeniously decides to combine the two into a powerful combo weapon: the spiked bat! You automatically receive the spiked bat's combo card at this point.

TIP

With its super-fast attacks, lethal power, and respectable durability, the spiked bat is one of the most practical combo weapons in the game. Build one every time you pass by this maintenance room, which you'll do often as you move to and from the Safe House.

TIP

Inspect the storage room across the hall from the maintenance room to acquire another box of nails, which you can combine with the baseball bat at the foot of the stairs you passed a moment ago. This gives you the makings for two spiked bats in one convenient place; make sure Chuck always carries two of these excellent combo weapons.

WALKTHROUGH

SIDE MISSION: HAPPILY EVER AFTER SORT OF

Entering Royal Flush Plaza proper, Chuck sees a woman named LaShawndra standing atop one of The Dark Bean coffee shop's counters. The poor woman is surrounded by zombies and pleading for help; clear out the undead and speak with her until she joins you.

TIP

If you're low on food, The Dark Bean always has a coffee creamer on its outer counter, and two more on its central counter. These are potent curatives and well worth picking up each time you pass by The Dark Bean, which you'll do quite often.

LaShawndra agrees to accompany Chuck to the Safe House, but also hints that her cowardly husband, Gordon, should be somewhere nearby. You can hear Gordon's screams; he's holed up in the nearby Casual Gals clothing store. Check your map to find the store with ease and speak with Gordon to have him join you as well.

NOTE

Most survivors will follow close behind Chuck after they agree to join him. If for some reason they aren't keeping up, press the Call button to yell out to them—they'll rush to Chuck's position. By holding the Aim button before pressing the Call button, you can order survivors to wait at specific locations—this is helpful if you don't want them following Chuck into a dangerous place.

You're right near the Safe House, so go ahead and escort these two survivors back to safety. This earns you a healthy dose of PP that could potentially level Chuck up. Save your progress at the Safe House restroom before exiting to follow the guide arrow toward the "Lost..." mission once more.

TIP

Grab a fresh spiked bat on your way back through Royal Flush Plaza—it helps to have two like-new spiked bats on hand at all times.

SUPER JUICE

As you follow the guide arrow through Americana Casino en route to the "Lost..." side mission, make a quick stop at the casino's central bar, Shots & Awe, where you discover an endless supply of wine, vodka, and whiskey on its spherical shelving. A blender sits on the nearby counter, making this an excellent place to mix up super-nutritional juice drinks!

CAUTION

Shots & Awe is easily accessible by zombies, so be ready to beat back any that shamble near.

You could flip to the "Appendix" chapter of this guide for a complete list of all possible juice drinks, but we'll boil things down for you here. Shots & Awe conveniently allows you to make two very useful juice drinks, and you'd be wise to take full advantage:

Quick Step: Restores six units of health and greatly increases Chuck's movement speed. It's easily made here by combining two wines together, or two coffees or coffee creamers (if you picked them up from The Dark Bean), or any combination of these items (wine + coffee, etc.)

Pain Killer: Restores six units of health and reduces the damage Chuck suffers from enemy attacks. Combine two whiskeys or two vodkas together.

DEADRISING 2

Use the blender to fill Chuck's inventory with Pain Killers, excluding the two slots being occupied by spiked bats. Depending on which of Chuck's stats have improved through leveling up thus far, you may be able to carry two or more Pain Killers. Forgo the Quick Steps for now; although extremely useful, these won't be of much use once survivors begin to follow you.

SIDE MISSION: LOST...

After mixing a few juice drinks at Shots & Awe, follow your guide arrow through Americana Casino and into Platinum Strip. There you find a woman named Doris standing atop a souvenir stand, using firecrackers to lure zombies within range of her handgun.

> **NOTE**
>
> All missions, including cases and side missions, have limited time in which they can be completed. This is shown visually by the bar that runs below the mission's name while viewing your list of messages at the map screen. As the bar shrinks, it changes from white to yellow to red. Keep an eye on your tasks and avoid letting them expire, or you'll miss out on valuable PP and other special extras.

Use your spiked bat to clear zombies away from the rear of the souvenir stand, then jump up onto the stand to speak with Doris. Unfortunately, she won't leave her position of safety until her man Chad finds her. Looks like you'll need to locate this Chad fellow.

> **TIP**
>
> Take a moment to examine the standee that's right near Doris's souvenir stand. Chuck sticks his head in the hole and makes a face, pocketing 1,000 PP for his silly behavior.

Drop down from the stand and sprint north, dodging zombies to make good time. It isn't long before you see Chad letting loose with a shotgun a little farther up Platinum Strip—he's right near Dining at Davey's. Speak with Chad several times until he joins you.

> **TIP**
>
> Want that shotgun? Simply hand Chad any non-combo item and he'll trade it to you.

Lead Chad back to Doris, but be ready for some serious mayhem. Doris's firecrackers have attracted a throng of zombies by now, and you've got to clear out the monsters before Doris will join you. Avoid harming either survivor while you work at clearing away the undead. When the bloodbath subsides, speak with Doris to at last gain her company.

> **TIP**
>
> Use the spiked bat's heavy attack to single out zombies, reducing the odds of whacking nearby survivors. Too many hits from Chuck will cause survivors to defect and turn against our hero!

> **TIP**
>
> If you take heavy damage, climb onto the souvenir stand to catch your breath and consume foods. You can also give healing items to those who have joined you, which they'll immediately consume to replenish their health.

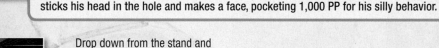

WALKTHROUGH

SIDE MISSION: ONE MAN'S TRASH

With the gun-toting couple following your lead, it's time to get the heck out of here. Set your guide arrow to the "One Man's Trash" mission and sprint north through Platinum Strip, heading for Moe's Maginations. Approach the store's front gate and speak with the looter beyond.

Chuck hates looters, but this one informs him that he can visit pawnshops throughout Fortune City to buy stuff he needs—at an absurd markup, of course. Finish the dialogue to enter the shop and complete this easy side mission. This makes every pawnshop throughout Fortune City accessible to Chuck.

NOTE

The primary item of interest at pawnshops is Zombrex. This is the only reliable source of the drug, which Chuck needs to acquire and administer to Katey everyday between 7:00 AM and 8:00 AM. There are many ways to acquire Zombrex without paying for it, however; follow this walkthrough and you'll never give those filthy looters a penny for Katey's sake.

CASE 1-2: ALIVE ON LOCATION

With Doris and Chad still following your lead, set your guide arrow to Case 1-2 and follow it to reach the lobby of the nearby Fortune City Hotel. Ensure that Chad and Doris are close by before entering the hotel or they won't follow Chuck through. The tiny green door icon that appears near a survivor's onscreen health bar lets you know they're close enough to follow Chuck into the next area.

At the hotel lobby, Chuck encounters the news reporter he recently saw on TV, Rebecca Chang. He wastes no time telling the beautiful woman that she's got her facts mixed up—he had nothing to do with the recent outbreak. Unsure of his story, but nonetheless intrigued, Rebecca suggests they examine the arena's security room to see if they can find any sort of video feed that might clear things up. With no other options, Chuck agrees to accompany her.

NOTE

As long as you're careful not to harm survivors that are following Chuck, you can lead them all around Fortune City if you like. It's therefore best to collect several survivors at once, reducing the number of trips you must make to and from the Safe House and saving precious time. Persuading survivors to follow Chuck is usually enough to complete their associated missions, so you don't need to worry about hurrying them back to the Safe House once they've joined you. If Chuck's charges become badly wounded, simply find a safe place to hole up and hand them food to help them recover.

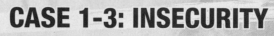

CASE 1-3: INSECURITY

The arena isn't far, but time is short. Speak to Rebecca to have her lead the way to Fortune City Arena's security room.

TIP

If you can't get enough of skateboards, pick up the *Skateboarding* magazine that rests on the coffee table in the hotel lobby—this increases the durability of skateboards and allows Chuck to ollie over obstacles. We prefer Quick Step juice drinks to get us where we're going, but skateboards can certainly help quicken the pace as well. You can find a convenient supply of skateboards at In The Closet, which is right near The Dark Bean in Royal Flush Plaza, and therefore easy to visit as you move to and from the Safe House.

Rebecca cuts through South Plaza, which is still under construction. Before getting very far, she leads Chuck to a nearby restroom— save your game and then speak to Rebecca afterward to get moving again.

TIP

Continue to avoid confrontations with zombies as you rush through South Plaza. In fact, unless otherwise stated by this walkthrough, you should always avoid combat with zombies unless it's absolutely necessary.

The arena is sealed up tight, but the resourceful reporter manages to open the gate. Continue dodging zombies as you follow Rebecca to the security room, then examine the door.

The security room is locked as well, but that won't stop a reporter of Ms. Chang's talents. Rebecca quickly produces a tool and picks the lock.

SPOILER!

Inside, Chuck and Rebecca find the security room torn to shreds, along with the men who were stationed there.

Someone didn't want any evidence of what really happened being left behind, and the absence of any bite marks makes it clear that no zombies did the killing here. Chuck gets a call from Stacey, urging him to return to the Safe House. Looks like this lead has gone cold.

GEARING UP

Before heading back to the Safe House, reenter the security room and collect a magazine from the counter near one of the dead guards. The magazine, *Rescue*, gives Chuck

25 percent more PP from survivor-related activities. By keeping this on hand for the entire adventure, Chuck will level up much faster.

Nab a coffee creamer from a counter near the *Rescue* magazine if you wish, and if you're in need of a good combo weapon, build a pole weapon by merging the machete in the nearby maintenance room with the push broom that stands against the wall just outside the door.

WALKTHROUGH

SIDE MISSION: WORKER'S COMPENSATION

By this point, you've likely received additional missions from Stacey. One of them, "Worker's Compensation," is easy to complete on your way back to the Safe House. Make your way to Americana Casino to find two former employees, Stuart and Brittany, looting the place. Beware: Stuart will attack you!

Strike Stuart until he smartens up and agrees to stop looting the casino. Speak to both looters afterward to get them to join you, thus completing the mission.

PRIZES ON HIGH

Next, head into Bennie Jack's BBQ Shack and take the stairs up to the second floor. Climb onto the counter to the left of the upstairs barbecue pit, and from there, leap to the large hanging light fixture. Your companions can't follow, but don't worry; they'll be OK by themselves for a moment.

Continue hopping along the lights to reach a secret stash of goodies, including a magazine (*Bargaining 1*) and a dose of Zombrex! Leave the mag (you really don't need it) and grab the wonder drug, along with the cash and the giant stuffed rabbit. It's an ideal gift for Katey!

SIDE MISSION: LUSH-IOUS LADY

Before leaving Americana Casino, tune your guide arrow to the "Lush-ious Lady" task and lead your quartet of companions into Americana Casino's north security office, which isn't far. Inside, you discover an incredibly hungover girl named Brittany who's totally oblivious to the recent outbreak. Speak with Brittany to explain the situation and get her to join you, then pick up the poor girl and carry her back to the Safe House, ensuring that your less hapless companions follow you.

COMBO CARD: TENDERIZERS

As you pass through the doors to Royal Flush Plaza, inspect the poster on display in the center of the floor directly ahead. The poster gives Chuck an idea of a new combo weapon: the tenderizers! You can find the MMA gloves required for this weapon inside The Man's Sport, which is right nearby.

NOTE

Although this walkthrough guides you toward each hidden combo card, there's little need to use many combo weapons other than the spiked bat, which is arguably the most efficient. When you have missions to fulfill, avoid going out of your way just to create different combo weapons. A few precious seconds can mean the difference between completing tasks and missing your chance!

Carry the giant stuffed rabbit back to the Safe House, leading your troop of survivors back to the bunker. Set the rabbit down just

outside the security room when you arrive, then enter the room to initiate a dialogue with Stacey, Rebecca, and Sullivan.

CASE 1-4: ALLIANCE

At the Safe House, Chuck finds Sullivan in an uproar. He's seen the footage of what appears to be Chuck causing the outbreak and isn't sure what to believe. Chuck manages to talk Sullivan down, however, and the military reserve man agrees to play things one step at a time for now. After Sullivan departs, Chuck, Stacey, and Rebecca all agree to help one another find out what's really going on in Fortune City.

After forging your alliance with the two beautiful ladies, collect the giant stuffed rabbit you left outside and hand it to Katey to brighten up her day—and pocket some more PP in the process!

KILLING TIME

Case 2-1 doesn't begin until 7:30 PM, so you've got some free time on your hands now. Exit the Safe House after saving, then check your messages to see multiple side missions requiring your attention. Tune your guide arrow to "Welcome to the Family" and head out.

NOTE

Don't worry about the "Short Sighted" mission, which is also running low on time; you'll catch that one on your way back from "Welcome to the Family."

TIP

Remember to grab restoratives at the Safe House or The Dark Bean, and to build a new spiked bat on your way out!

The Palisades Mall is quite a hike, so let's speed things up. Grab all the coffee and coffee creamers you can carry from The Dark Bean, keeping just one spiked bat with

you this time. Bring your caffeinated beverages to Shots & Awe and use them to mix up some Quick Steps—two or three will do the trick. (You can also use the endless supply of wine bottles at Shots & Awe, but grabbing coffee and creamers at The Dark Bean saves a bit of hassle.)

COMBO CARD: LASER SWORD

LASER SWORD: Gems + Flashlight

Immediately down a Quick Step after blending them, then bolt for the doors to Platinum Strip, which isn't far from Shots & Awe. Sprint down the strip and make a quick pit stop into Paradise Platinum Theaters, examining the poster against the far wall to give Chuck the notion for the laser sword combo weapon. We'll show you where to build one of these soon.

WALKTHROUGH

COMBO CARD: HOLY ARMS

Enter Atlantica Casino on your way to Palisades Mall, where the "Welcome to the Family" mission takes place. Make a slight detour and examine the poster on the casino's south wall to acquire the holy arms combo card. You can build this mighty combo weapon right now if you like by entering the nearby magic stage area, also located along Atlantica Casino's south wall—do this only if your spiked bat is wearing out.

To build the holy arms right now, enter the doors to the magic stage area and vault onto the stage. Grab a box of nails that's hidden behind the stage equipment and bring it into the nearby maintenance room, where you find a training sword. Merge these two items to form the awesome holy arms.

Pound another Quick Step and streak into Palisades Mall. Scale the first set of escalators and dart into Chris's Fine Foods. Nab two steaks from the cooler along the store's southwest wall—these will soon come in handy.

If you'd like to trade your current weapon for a laser sword, now's the time. Do this only if you have plenty of time left on the "Short Sighted" side mission. Cross Palisades Mall's second floor, heading for Ned's Knicknackery. Grab gems and a flashlight from within the shop; they are found on top of the various displays. Bring the gems and flashlight to the nearby maintenance room and combine them to form a laser sword.

COMBO CARD: SNOWBALL CANNON

Regardless of whether you wish to build a laser sword, examine the poster between Ned's Knicknackery and the maintenance room to discover the snowball cannon's combo card. Cut back across the second floor afterward and save your game at the nearby restroom—you'll soon be battling a dangerous psycho.

SIDE MISSION: WELCOME TO THE FAMILY

Head downstairs after saving your game and make a dash for Shank's, where the "Welcome to the Family" side mission takes place. Here you find two arguing men—Kenneth and Jack—who are pinned down by zombies. Help them beat back the undead, but be careful not to hit them during the struggle. If you've still got a spiked bat, use its heavy attack as needed to single out pesky zombies.

> **TIP**
>
> Shank's is full of weapons and food, including an awesome broadsword. Smash the display cases and stock up if you're low.

Speak to Kenneth when things settle down, then talk to Jack to get both men to join you. Waste no time exiting Shank's and leading your newfound comrades west into Yucatan Casino.

OPTIONAL PSYCHO: TED AND SNOWFLAKE

The first time you enter Yucatan Casino, you encounter an obese psycho named Ted, who has designs on feeding Chuck to his beloved tiger, Snowflake. Not very friendly!

109

DEADRISING 2

TIP

As the battle begins, hold the Aim button and then press the Call button to order Jack and Kenneth to wait in a nearby corner, out of harm's way.

Ted is one of the easiest psychos, but Snowflake is quite a handful. Ignore the tiger and whale on Ted, who is armed with a lackluster handgun and weak melee attacks. Rush the pudgy psycho and beat him senseless with your spiked bat or weapon of choice. (In a pinch, a fire axe lies on the ground near Ted's starting position.)

Snowflake will pounce on you from time to time as you wallop on her master. If she tackles you to the ground, quickly imitate the onscreen commands to escape and reduce the damage you suffer. Continue to ignore Snowflake until you've dealt with Ted.

If you need to heal up, race for Baron Von Brathaus, where you'll discover all manner of food items, along with the *Health 2* magazine, which doubles the healing effect of all curatives. Use the blender on the counter to mix up juice drinks if you like, or simply down some wine for fast healing. Just don't drink more than three alcoholic beverages or Chuck will get sick!

TAMING THE TIGER

After the fat man finally falls, turn your attention to taming Snowflake. To do this, return to the west fire pit area where the psycho fight first began and grab a third steak off the rock. Stand in the relatively spacious area just outside of the fire pit area and use the Aim button to toss a steak onto the ground in open territory.

You can also find a steak on a table inside of Baron Von Brathaus if you're one short, and there's another atop the casino's overhead platforms, which you can reach by jumping off slot machines and the like. Carrying steaks with you into the casino is the easiest way to go, though.

Position Chuck so that the steak you've thrown is between him and Snowflake. When the vicious kitty charges, she'll catch the steak's scent, slow down, and gobble it up instead.

Lure Snowflake into consuming three steaks to tame her, satisfying an achievement and acquiring a unique breed of survivor.

LOCATING LENNY

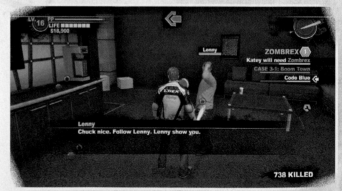

If there's ample time left on the "Short Sighted" mission, call out to gather your survivors—including Snowflake—and make for the casino's south VIP room by entering a door near the bar. Inside you find a man named Lenny, who will only join Chuck if Snowflake has been killed or tamed.

WALKTHROUGH

Speak with Lenny until he joins you, then follow him across the casino floor and into the north maintenance room. Examine the switch that Lenny shows you to turn on all the slot machines within Yucatan Casino. Nice!

COMBO CARD: FREEDOM BEAR

Check your map to find you're right next to the Yucatan Casino's restrooms. Enter them and eye the poster on the wall just outside the men's room to obtain the freedom bear combo card.

COMBO CARD: BLAMBOW

Time is likely running out on the "Short Sighted" mission by now, so don't dally. Lead your gang of survivors back to the Safe House, cutting through the Food Court and Slot Ranch Casino on your way to Royal Flush Plaza. As you move through the Food Court, examine the poster on the southwest wall to acquire the combo card for the awesome blambow.

CAUTION

The clock will likely strike 7:00 PM as you make your way to the "Short Sighted" mission. Day turns to night at this point, and zombies become more aggressive and powerful. Stay sharp and avoid those clusters of brain-eaters!

SIDE MISSION: SHORT SIGHTED

Race back toward Royal Flush Plaza and take an escalator up to its second floor. Bolt into Children's Castle to locate a confused old woman named Esther. Speak with Esther multiple times until she at last comprehends the situation in Fortune City and agrees to join you. This completes the mission, allowing you to relax at last.

Esther is slow and vulnerable, so you'll need to carry her back to the Safe House—this is why we advised you not to visit her until this point. Chuck can only kick while carrying a survivor, so it's a good thing the bunker isn't far. Make sure Chuck's in good health before sweeping Esther off her feet.

NOTE

If you ran out of time trying to save Esther, consider loading a previous save and visiting her first, before going after Kenneth and Jack. Mix your Quick Steps at Shots & Awe as before, but this time, use them to cut through Royal Flush Plaza and rescue Esther. You'll need to carry the poor old woman around for quite a while as you visit Jack and Kenneth and battle Ted and Snowflake. Press the Interact button to set her down as needed, preferably well out of harm's way.

You'll likely get a call from Stacey as you escort your troop back to the Safe House. She asks Chuck to meet her at the security room—this is your clue that you can now begin Case 2, and you're already on your way.

Pat yourself on the back if you manage to bring all five survivors back to the Safe House. Time was against you, but you played it smart and overcame the odds.

Your prize: a metric boatload of PP, and a very exotic gift for Chuck's little girl—Snowflake the tiger!

Save your game at the Safe House restroom, then enter the security office to speak with Stacey. Your next case is about to begin.

DEADRISING 2

CASE 2-1: SIGN OF LIFE

Returning to the Safe House's security office, Chuck notices something on one of the monitors: People are gathered in the underground tunnels beneath Fortune City, and they appear to be shifting some sort of cargo. Desperate for a lead, Chuck wastes no time rushing off to investigate.

SIDE MISSION: MEET THE CONTESTANTS

Chuck may be in a hurry to clear his name, but this also happens to be a perfect time to complete some profitable side missions. Make sure you're carrying two fresh spiked bats, then set your guide arrow to the "Meet the Contestants"

side mission. Cut through Americana Casino on your way to the Platinum Strip, mixing up some Pain Killer juice drinks at your local bar, Shots & Awe.

Follow your guide arrow to Palisades Mall's south end, where Chuck encounters a thrill-seeking psycho named Leon. (You might remember this guy from Chuck's

last "Terror Is Reality" event.) Leon wants revenge and, after slaying an innocent man named Carlos in cold blood, he tosses Chuck the keys to a nearby motorbike and races off.

You can't let a lunatic like that roam free. Climb onto the bike and speed east along the strip, chasing Leon into Fortune Park.

Pursue Leon until you finally catch sight of him—he'll be cruising all around Fortune Park, mowing down zombies. When you finally locate Leon, do the unthinkable

and get off your bike—it's no use trying to ram Leon because he'll always knock you for a loop, and you can't fight him from the bike's seat.

Keep an eye on Leon while moving on foot, doing your best to keep away from tight packs of zombies. Each time Leon zips toward you, run to one side to avoid being hit. It's surprisingly

easy to avoid Leon as long as you see him coming and are quick to react.

Immediately after dodging Leon, round on him and close in to land a few hits with your spiked bat. He'll soon speed away and make another charge, so be ready to dodge to one side and strike again.

WALKTHROUGH

COMBO CARD: PADDLESAW

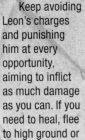

Keep avoiding Leon's charges and punishing him at every opportunity, aiming to inflict as much damage as you can. If you need to heal, flee to high ground or a building—any where Leon isn't likely to reach you. Keep this up until you finally manage to knock Leon off his high horse.

TIP

> If Chuck is near death and you're out of food, hop onto your bike and cruise for the Silver Strip's premier bar, Pub O' Gold. Enter the pub and use the ample food and drink inside, along with the blender, to mix up juice drinks. Two whiskeys, beers, or vodkas mixed together make useful Pain Killers.

Chuck not only earns a huge amount of PP for defeating Leon, but also gains access to the Combo Bay, located at the Silver Strip's far north end. Here, Chuck is free to pursue his favorite hobby: modifying bikes! See the "Unearthing Fortune City" chapter of this guide for complete details on bike modifications, including all the devious devices you can rig up to Chuck's bike for ungodly amounts of mayhem.

Set the "Barn Burner" task as your next objective, then hop onto the motorbike inside the Combo Bay and streak down the strip, heading for Fortune City Arena. This is just a small taste of the epic carnage Chuck can cause from his bike. On your way, pause for a moment and hop off the bike to examine the poster on the standing display at Silver Strip's south end. This gives Chuck the notion to build the delightfully deadly paddlesaw.

DEADRISING 2

SIDE MISSION: BARN BURNER

After pocketing the paddlesaw's combo card, follow the guide arrow to Fortune City Arena's green rooms, where you discover two survivors who are trapped by fire and zombies, and are screaming for help.

Clear away the zombies and then grab a fire extinguisher from the nearby wall. Take aim and spray out the flames that are trapping the people. It's not long before the flames die down.

Enter the green room and speak to the man, Elrod, to get the couple to join you. There are several food items lying around the room that Chuck can munch on if he's wounded.

SIDE MISSION: BRAINS OVER BRAWN

Highlight the "Brains Over Brawn" mission next and make tracks for South Plaza, which isn't far. Ensure that Elrod and Trixie follow you into the area.

TIP

If you're in need of a good weapon, quickly visit South Plaza's southwest maintenance room, where you discover a paddle. A chain saw lies just outside the room; merge these two items to form the paddlesaw that you've just learned how to create. However, don't drop any spiked bats you're carrying in favor of the paddlesaw; we know it's tempting, but spiked bats will serve you better in an upcoming battle.

Follow the guide arrow to locate a quartet of nerdy survivors who are too busy playing a captivating board game to care about the outbreak. Not the sharpest tools in the shed!

Normally, these silly guys would be quite difficult to enlist, requiring Chuck to chat with their "leader," John, for some time. But with a foxy female following you (Trixie), the boys jump at the chance to "be cool" like Chuck. Speak to John with Trixie close by to get all four survivors to join up fast.

WALKTHROUGH

SIDE MISSION: CHUCK THE ROLE MODEL

Fill your inventory with food—there's a bunch near the South Plaza nerds—then set your guide arrow to the "Chuck the Role Model" mission and cut through the arena on your way to Americana Casino. Order your comrades to wait just outside the restroom where it's relatively safe, then head inside to confront a dangerous psychopath named Brandon.

Brandon attacks by darting into close range and slashing at Chuck with a large piece of glass. He can also leap and stab Chuck from a short distance—this is his most dangerous attack. Run circles around the central urinals, attempting to lure Brandon into leaping and missing. Capitalize each time he does with a barrage of bat strikes, landing as many blows as you can before Brandon retaliates with a weak attack and flees.

Brandon commonly leaps over the restroom's stalls, disappearing for a time. The psycho can reappear from any stall—even those on the opposite side of the room—so run away and watch carefully, waiting for him to reappear. Once he does, begin the same game of cat and mouse around the central urinals, aiming to make Brandon miss so you can punish him with your spiked bat.

> **TIP**
>
> Consume food when Brandon flees to the stalls; it's the safest time to do so. If you run out of nourishment, duck out of the restroom and find more at Americana Casino's restaurant, Bennie Jack's BBQ Shack, or mix up some Pain Killers at Shots & Awe. If you need a fresh weapon, the electric guitars and broadswords mounted to the casino's walls will serve you well.

Repeat the process of outmaneuvering and punishing Brandon until the psycho is at last defeated. It isn't easy, but quick reflexes, a sense of timing, and plenty of food will win you the fight.

Slaughter the zombie that emerges after Brandon's passing, then speak with the bound woman, Vikki, to untie her and gain her company. Call out to your other comrades and then save your progress here at the restroom before racing back to the Safe House with your troop.

> **TIP**
>
> Mix up a few Quick Steps at Shots & Awe as you motor back to the Safe House—they'll soon come in handy.

CASE 2-2: TICKET TO RIDE

Case 2-2 is likely running short on time by now, so after escorting your survivors to the Safe House and saving, set your guide arrow and rush off to Palisades Mall. Construct a spiked bat on the way and then down a Quick Step to hasten the trip.

TIP

Cut through Hot Excitorama's rear maintenance hall to reach Palisades Mall more quickly.

Streak to the far end of Palisades Mall and locate a door that leads to Fortune City's Underground. The door is marked with orange signage that reads "service" and the guide arrow leads you directly to it.

After moving through the door, head downstairs and save your game at the restroom at the foot of the stairs. You're about to begin a challenging mission.

Just beyond the stairwell, Chuck spies a group of workers in orange uniforms who are milling about a warehouse. A train soon pulls up, and none other than Tyrone "T.K." King, the obnoxious voice of the "Terror Is Reality" game show, steps off. What could that clown possibly have to do with all of this?

The men notice Chuck, After having a good laugh, T.K. orders his cronies after him. Looks like you'll need to fight your way out of this.

MERCENARY MASH-UP

The men in orange suits are hired mercenaries, and each one carries a rapid-fire assault rifle. Take cover behind the warehouses's tall shelves and

time their firing patterns, popping out to let lose with your spiked bat between bursts.

The mercenaries' gunfire is surprisingly weak, so don't worry about being shot a few times. Be aggressive, using the shelves as cover only when you're not bashing in a

mercenary's brains. Defeat all three orange-clad thugs to advance.

HIGH-SPEED PURSUIT

T.K.'s mercenaries didn't get the job done, and the gutless villain isn't about to hang around. He orders his remaining men to board the train, and quickly departs.

Chuck manages to knock a mercenary straggler off a motorbike. Seeing a golden opportunity, he

WALKTHROUGH

quickly hops onto the bike and races off to catch up to the crooked game show host.

Hit the gas and get after that train. Beware: The mercenaries near the back will open fire and toss debris at you, some of which is dangerously explosive. Do your best to avoid being hit as you race onward.

Your objective is to board the train. To do this, you must race up one of the tunnel's side ramps, using it to catch some air and soar onto the back of the train. You must be very close to the train to make the jump, so avoid falling behind.

TIP

The train slows down as it rounds corners, and there's a ramp on the left side of the tunnel near most of the turns. Keep to the left for the best odds of boarding the train.

Keep speeding toward the train and leaping off ramps until you at last manage to sail aboard. Time for some payback, punks!

TIP

If you waste too much time chasing after the train, consider loading your previous save and trying again. It's possible to board the train very quickly once you get a feel for the event, but it's also easy to burn lots of time fruitlessly looping around the Underground.

TICKETS, PLEASE

You face many more armed mercenaries aboard the train. Dispatch them as you did the previous trio: Hide behind objects, wait for breaks in their firing patterns, then rush out and clobber them with your spiked bat. If all of your bats have broken by now, a handy sledgehammer sits near your starting position on the train, and there are plenty of other weapons to be had as well.

TIP

After killing the first mercenary, grab the assault rifle he was wielding and put it to good use against the rest. Ranged weapons such as these tend to work better if you hold the Aim button while firing.

Make a slow, calculated advance up the train, dispatching each merc you encounter in turn. Don't hesitate to retreat and consume restoratives if Chuck

is gravely wounded—you'll find lots of orange juice and other healing items aboard.

Secure the train, then examine the far door to at last approach the lead car. T.K. applauds Chuck's heroics, but he isn't about to get caught so easily. He suddenly uncouples

his car, then quickly opens fire on Chuck, forcing our hero to duck while the villain makes good his escape.

Chuck wasn't able to stop T.K., but the effort wasn't a total loss: He discovers a key that one of the goons must have dropped. Now you can access Fortune City's Underground

from any service door, not just the one you used at Palisades Mall!

NOTE

All Underground Access service doors now appear on your map.

FIND KATEY ZOMBREX: DAY 2

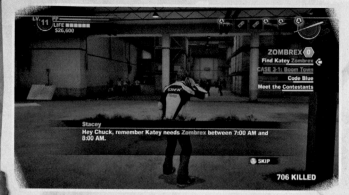

For now, run north along the tunnel, heading for the service door that leads up to Americana Casino. Go upstairs to reach the casino floor.

If you didn't grab the Zombrex from the Americana Casino before, enter Bennie Jack's BBQ Shack and sprint upstairs to its second floor. Hop onto the counter to the left of the upstairs fire pit, then leap along the hanging light fixtures to reach a secret ledge, where a dose of Zombrex awaits.

Case 3 doesn't kick off for a while yet, but Stacey calls Chuck shortly after he pockets the Underground Access Key, reminding him that Katey will need another dose of Zombrex soon. No worries; if you followed this walkthrough carefully, you already found Zombrex on Americana Casino's hidden ledge. Don't worry if you haven't acquired any Zombrex yet; we'll soon show you how to score some.

KILLING TIME, PART 2

Now that you've got Zombrex, it's time to complete some more side missions. Remember, you can't give little Katey her medicine until 7:00 AM, so let's be constructive with the free time you've got. Begin by mixing up a Quick Step at Shots & Awe if you haven't got one.

SIDE MISSION: CODE BLUE

Down your Quick Step and set your guide arrow to the "Code Blue" mission, which is likely running short of time. Enter the Platinum Strip and then make tracks for One Little Duck Bingo, located along the Silver Strip beyond Fortune Park.

Inside, you find a paramedic named Sven who's vainly attempting to resuscitate a goner named Tim Duggan. Poor Tim can't be saved, but Sven certainly can. Speak to Sven until he agrees to join you, then immediately tune your guide arrow to the "Once Bitten" task.

NOTE

If you didn't have time to locate Lenny after defeating Ted and taming Snowflake before, now's the time to do so. Lead Sven to Yucatan Casino and find Lenny inside the south VIP room. Follow Lenny to the casino's control room and turn on the slots, then lead Lenny and Sven through the Food Court and Slot Ranch Casino, heading for the "Once Bitten" side mission.

WALKTHROUGH

SIDE MISSION: ONCE BITTEN

Take an escalator up to the plaza's second floor and follow the guide arrow to locate a man named Jared, who's slumped down on the floor, bleeding profusely from a nasty zombie bite. Give Jared your Zombrex to save his life and get him to join you, then lend him a shoulder and lead your two survivors back to the Safe House.

NOTE

Don't worry about giving your Zombrex to Jared; Sven hands you a free dose after you bring him back to the Safe House!

SIDE MISSION: AN INDUSTRIAL FASHION

You likely still have a bit of time before Katey needs her Zombrex. (If not, go ahead and give her the medicine now.) Exit the Safe House and tune your guide arrow to "An Industrial Fashion," then follow the guide arrow to South Plaza, where you find two female construction workers fighting for their lives against the undead.

Help Terri clear out the undead, then speak with her. She won't come with you until you check on her friend, Willa. Climb onto the nearby crate and scaffolding to speak with Willa, who's badly wounded.

Willa joins after you speak with her. Drop down and talk to Terri once more to get her to join you as well. Carry the wounded Willa and rush back to the Safe House to give Katey her Zombrex if you haven't done so yet.

GIVE KATEY ZOMBREX, DAY 2

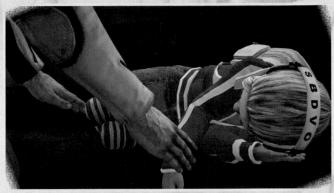

Enter the Safe House after 7:00 AM and give Katey her daily dose of Zombrex. *Someone* deserves a "world's best dad" T-shirt....

KILLING TIME, PART 3

Katey's safe for another 24 hours, and you've got a bit of free time before the next case begins at 10:00 AM. You know what that means....

QUEEN CONTROL

On his way out of the Safe House, Chuck notices a mob of zombies, along with an annoying little bee. Chuck swats the pest from the air, then steps on it. Surprisingly, this causes all of the nearby zombies' heads to explode!

TIP

Keep an eye out for queens from this point forward—you'll periodically find them near clusters of zombies. These special bees have some sort of mysterious control over zombies, and killing a queen wipes out all nearby undead. Chuck can collect any queens he sees, storing them in glass jars for later use.

DEADRISING 2

SIDE MISSION: TASTES LIKE CHICKEN

After the queen scene plays out, duck into the maintenance room and construct a couple of spiked bats. If you're low on food, load up on coffee creamer at The Dark Bean before making your way to the Food Court's Cucina Donnacci.

At the restaurant, Chuck meets a psychotic chef named Antoine, who is apparently making meals out of stray survivors. He has imprisoned a woman in the restaurant's back room and reacts violently when Chuck isn't interested in sampling his cuisine. Time to serve this freak his just deserts.

TIP

Antoine can heal himself, so it's vital that you're able to do the same. If your food stock is lackluster, flee the restaurant after initiating the fight and grab three BBQ chickens from the nearby Wild West Grill House. Bring these to the Rojo Diablo Mexican Restaurant and use the blender there to combine two of the BBQ chickens, creating an Energizer juice drink that restores six units of Chuck's health and makes him invincible for a short time. Splice the third BBQ chicken with the apple near the blender to make a second Energizer. Now you have what you need to shut the chef down.

Antoine is a challenging psycho who can hurl objects at you from afar and whack you with a frying pan up close. He'll also defend against ranged attacks, so you've got to close in to deliver significant damage. Rush Antoine and batter him with your spiked bat until he knocks you for a loop and flees.

CAUTION

Sometimes Antoine leaps onto Chuck after knocking him down, stuffing vile food into Chuck's mouth to inflict damage. Quickly imitate the onscreen commands to shuck off the chef before this attack causes much harm.

After running away, Antoine often moves to one of several food stations around the restaurant and begins gobbling up his sickening cuisine. Antoine recovers health while stuffing his face in this fashion, so it's important not to let him feast. Hurry up and hit him to interrupt his meal, dealing as much damage as possible before Antoine retaliates with a swipe of his pan.

TIP

Try shooting Antoine while he's eating—this is the only ideal time to blast him from range.

Antoine's powerful attacks and ability to recover health can make this a grueling affair. It's best to tackle Antoine with a co-op buddy—this allows one of you to assault him while the other takes a break to heal up. You can always flee the restaurant to seek out recuperative foods in the Food Court, but Antoine will heal himself while you're off doing the same. If you can't seem to beat Antoine and don't have a co-op ally to assist you, flee the scene and save this dangerous psycho for later.

ANTOINE'S CAPTIVE

After dispatching the horrible chef, enter the back room to speak with his prisoner, a terrified woman named Cinda. The traumatized girl won't budge unless

WALKTHROUGH

her trusted friend, Jasper, comes to find her. It looks like you'll need to locate this Jasper fellow.

Exit the restaurant and cross the Food Court, heading for the snack machines near Lombari's. Climb them to reach a secret area along the upper awnings.

Jasper is cowering up here; speak with him to gain his company. Take a moment to explore this area as well. You'll find two bows arrows up here, along with

some dynamite, and a *Bargaining 2* magazine, which lowers the cost of pawnshop items by 10 percent. Grab a bow and arrow and a stick of dynamite if you feel like testing out the blambow, whose combo card you discovered in the Food Court earlier (it's on the wall near the Wild West Grill House).

Bring Jasper to Cinda to gain her confidence and convince her to join you. Case 3 is likely about to begin by this point; hurry back to the Safe House with your survivors, but don't bring them inside if you'd like to complete an Achievement later. Order them to wait near the spiked bat maintenance room instead, then enter the Safe House and speak with Stacey to kick off Case 3.

CASE 3-1

Arriving at the Safe House's security room, Chuck informs Stacey and Rebecca that he believes Tyrone "T.K." King is responsible for the outbreak, and for framing him. Suddenly, an explosion rocks the place—checking her monitors, Stacey discovers men are attempting to break into Fortune City's casino vaults! With no other leads to work with, Chuck vows to stop the criminals.

CASE 3-2: RUN FOR THE MONEY

You may have a few side missions to check on, but Case 3-2 is quite involved, so it's best to get to work on it right away. Head for Americana Casino's vault, grabbing a fresh spiked bat and some restoratives on your way (as usual). If you rescued Jasper and Cinda from the psychotic chef Antoine before, ensure that they follow you.

Shots ring out as you near the vault—armed mercenaries aren't about to let you foil their boss's plans. Say, these guys look familiar—they're T.K.'s hired goons! That greedy villain must be behind these robberies!

Batter T.K.'s men with your bat between bursts of assault rifle fire. Use the environment to your advantage and try not to expose yourself to more than one or two mercs at a time.

> **TIP**
> Run sideways to make it harder for the mercs to hit you.

Slaughter all the mercenaries, then start swinging at the massive drill they're using to crack the vault door. Keep whaling away until the drill becomes inoperable.

Mix some Pain Killers at Shots & Awe and construct a fresh spiked bat on your way to Slot Ranch Casino, where another vault is being robbed. You face a similar task here; wipe out the mercenaries, then destroy their drill.

> **TIP**
> Remember to feed food to your followers, healing them up when they suffer harm.

SIDE MISSION: ROCK HEROES

Before moving on to the third vault at Yucatan Casino, lead Jasper and Cinda to the Silver Strip's giant rock stage, where you discover a trio of metal heads banging out tunes for a crowd of rabid zombies. Climb up on stage to speak to the lead rocker, a righteous chick named Jeanna.

Keep talking to Jeanna until her band, Angel Lust, unleashes their grand finale—a riff so rad that it blows the heads off of the swarming undead. Speak to Jeanna again afterward to get her and her two bandmates, Allen and Floyd, to join you. That's five survivors you've now got following you.

SIDE MISSION: SHOPPING SPREE

"COME ON! FOLLOW ME!" ACHIEVEMENT!

Continue to ignore the Yucatan Casino's vault robbers as you lead your gang into Royal Flush Plaza. Take an escalator up to its second floor and visit Kathy's Space, where three women are having difficulty carrying their giant pile of shopping boxes home. Lend the ladies a hand by offering to carry the shopping boxes for them. You thus acquire three more survivors. That makes eight faithful followers—enough to satisfy the "Come on! Follow me!" Achievement!

WALKTHROUGH

SIDE MISSION: WILTED FLOWER

Lead your eight survivors back to the Safe House for a deluge of PP that is sure to level Chuck up multiple times. Free of followers at last, make your way to Shots & Awe and mix up two or three Quick Steps. Use these to reach Palisades Mall with all speed and enter the Venus Touch Spa to explore the "Wilted Flower" side mission.

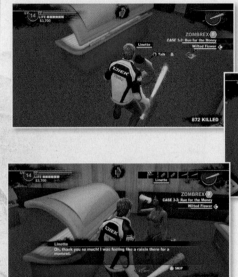

Enter the spa's back room to find a young woman named Linette, who became stuck inside a tanning bed during the outbreak. The poor girl now matches the shop's rosy carpeting and can barely move.

Naturally, Linette is terribly parched from her ordeal. If you don't have any sort of beverage to hand her, exit the back room and locate a cup of coffee on a table inside the store's main area. This does the trick!

Linette feels much better after gulping down her drink and agrees to go to the Safe House. In fact, she even says she knows a shortcut to get you there much faster. Linette asks you to take her upstairs to the Brand New U clothing store, spawning a new side mission.

SIDE MISSION: LINETTE'S PASSAGE

Linette is too sore to move very fast—pick her up and carry her out of Venus Touch Spa, heading for the nearest escalator. Hurry up to the mall's second floor.

Enter the Brand New U clothing store. Linette says the shortcut runs through the rear changing rooms and links to Royal Flush Plaza, which is right near the Safe House. Examine the changing rooms to discover Linette's secret passage!

Bingo! You appear in Royal Flush Plaza's restroom, just as Linette promised. The Safe House is just a short jog away. Funny that Linette knew of a shortcut to the *men's* room, however....

NOTE

The shortcut is a two-way passage, so you can now move quickly between Fortune City's two malls. Excellent!

This shortcut is unavailable until Linette shows it to you. It's also one of the few things that doesn't carry over into subsequent games. Even if you restart the adventure after discovering the shortcut, you must still play through the game to unlock it again by completing the "Wilted Flower" and "Linette's Passage" side missions.

Linette did you a huge favor; the least you could do is hurry the girl back to the Safe House. Rush there without delay to pocket some PP, then return your attention to more urgent matters.

www.primagames.com

BACK TO BUSINESS

Use Linette's shortcut to quickly reach the Yucatan Casino vault, then lay waste to the mercenary thieves you find there. Then destroy the third and final drill to advance the plot.

> **TIP**
>
>
>
> Each time you use Linette's shortcut to reach the Palisades Mall, you emerge right near a blender. Simply vault the second-floor railing to drop to the mall's main floor, then enter the central grotto to find a blender at the bar. Bring coffee and creamers here from The Dark Bean if you plan to mix up Quick Steps, or toss vodka and cocktails into the blender to create Pain Killers. Refer to the "Appendix" chapter of this guide for a complete list of juice drinks.

VAN DAMAGE

You've ruined the thieves' scheme; now you must prevent their getaway. A new Case 3-2 objective marker appears at Fortune Park— exit Yucatan Casino via the south doors to reach the Silver Strip. Load up on food at Luaii Wauii or Pub O' Gold on your way to the case objective.

The remaining mercenaries make a final stand near their getaway van, and there are a lot of them. Kill them all without mercy, using their own assault rifles to gun them down. Be prepared to flee and consume food if Chuck's health drops low. Pub O' Gold is your nearest source of curatives and it also has a useful blender.

After securing the site, turn your ire against the getaway van itself. Punish the vehicle until it is destroyed, at last completing Case 3-2.

> **NOTE**
>
> The next time you visit this area, you'll be able to pass through the gaping hole that remains in the wall where the thieves' van was parked. This serves as a small yet functional shortcut between Fortune Park and the Atlantica Casino vault.

Rebecca was taping the entire battle between Chuck and T.K.'s goons, and the savvy reporter is now starting to believe that Chuck may indeed be innocent. At last she agrees to arrange a meeting between Chuck and her source—the person who gave her the tape that seemingly showed Chuck causing the outbreak. Rebecca tells our hero to meet her at the Shoal Nightclub at 11:00 PM, then departs. Way to go!

KILLING TIME, PART 3

You've loads of time before you must meet Rebecca at the Shoal Nightclub, so let's see how much damage you can cause between now and then.

SIDE MISSION: EVERYONE KNOWS SLAPPY

Now's a good time to take on a dangerous psycho, and for once, the spiked bat is not the ideal weapon to use. Take the maintenance hall shortcut from the Silver Strip's Hot Excitorama shop to quickly enter Palisades Mall, then proceed to the mall's second floor.

> **TIP**
>
> Mix up some Pain Killers at the mall's central grotto in preparation for a challenging battle.

Swing by the High-Noon Shooting Range on the mall's second floor, where a host of firearms is available for the taking. Swipe two shotguns from the

WALKTHROUGH

racks behind the counter, then head for the Severed Ties kiosk at the opposite end of the second floor, closer to your objective.

> **TIP**
>
> Naturally, it's much easier to defeat Slappy with two Chucks instead of one. Have a co-op buddy join you and take down Slappy twice as fast!

Hop onto the top of the Severed Ties kiosk to discover a third shotgun sitting atop the circular sign. With three shotguns and a number of Pain Killers in your inventory, you're ready to fight a psycho.

Move to the nearby Kid's Choice Clothing and examine the gruesome scene of a slumped, lifeless mascot surrounded by corpses. Examining the mascot triggers the Slappy fight.

Slappy is a tough psycho who travels quickly on roller skates. It's pointless trying to keep up with Slappy, so firearms become the ideal tools for the job.

> **TIP**
>
> Use marbles, gumballs, or other items that leave a substance on the floor to cause Slappy to slip while skating, making him an easier target. You can also use Chuck's jump kick move to knock Slappy down, following up with melee blows."

The moment the showdown begins, immediately run away from Slappy, heading for Chris's Fine Foods. It's quite a hike, but Chris's is the ideal place to battle Slappy because it's stocked with nutritional num nums.

Slappy attacks by spewing out jets of fire from his twin flamethrowers—keep out of range to avoid being scorched. Slappy can also switch to a more dangerous fireball spitter that has a far greater range—run to one side to dodge each volley. Whenever you're not skirting Slappy's attacks, unload on him with a shotgun. The best time to damage Slappy is directly after he launches a trio of fireballs.

> **TIP**
>
> If you run out of shotgun ammo, duck into the nearby High-Noon Shooting Range and grab a handgun or two. You'll find an unlimited supply of these basic firearms inside the shop.

Stand your ground in the hallway just outside of Chris's Fine Foods and "joust" with Slappy, blasting away with your shotgun and then fleeing from the psycho's fiery offense. Retreat into Chris's to consume food and gather more healing items. Milk, orange juice, pizza, and steak are among the best foods to grab, and there's an unlimited supply of each inside the store.

> **TIP**
>
> If Slappy's flamethrowers are tanning Chuck's hide, try using a water gun to temporarily douse them!

Continue to avoid Slappy's powerful flamethrower and fireball attacks, and pump the deranged mascot full of lead at every opportunity. Flee to heal as needed, then hurry back for more Slappy blasting. Keep it up until the psycho at last collapses.

> **NOTE**
>
> Beating Slappy not only earns you a load of PP, but also nets you the flamethrower combo card!

SIDE MISSION: PAR FOR THE COURSE

1134 KILLED

With Slappy down for the count, set your guide arrow to the "Par for the Course" mission and take the Brand New U clothing shortcut back to Royal Flush Plaza. (Ignore the "Mail Order Zombrex" and "Here Comes the Groom" missions for the moment.) Go to SporTrance to find a woman named Luz being accosted by zombies.

Lend Luz a hand by wiping out the undead hoard. Speak with Luz afterward to have her join you, then hurry her back to the Safe House.

LUZ HAS JOINED

1167 KILLED

SIDE MISSION: STUART'S SCHEME

1169 KILLED

If you rescued Stuart Holmes earlier in the game (during the "Worker's Compensation" side mission), you'll now find him standing near the Safe House's restroom, all in a huff. Speak with Stuart multiple times to get him to calm him down, thereby preventing a mutiny within the Safe House. You also pocket a tidy sum of PP for completing this easy task. Save your game and build a couple of spiked bats on your way to the Yucatan Casino's Shoal Nightclub—it's time to tackle Case 4.

NOTE

Several survivors will defect if you don't talk Stuart down. If they abandon the Safe House they'll prevent you from saving every survivor. Don't let this happen—you've worked too hard to rescue these poor souls!

CASE 4-1: THE SOURCE

1169 KILLED

1176

A few active side missions await your attention, but time's running short on Case 4-1. Set your guide arrow and build two spiked bats on your way to Royal Flush Plaza's restroom shortcut, saving your progress before traveling through.

TIP

After exiting the shortcut, make a quick stop at Palisades Mall's grotto bar and stock up on Pain Killers—Rebecca's source is not the friendly sort!

Follow the guide arrow through Palisades Mall and into Yucatan Casino. Zombies swarm the tunnel leading to the private nightclub where Rebecca asked you to meet her. Lay into them with a spiked bat to preserve your health as you press toward your objective.

WALKTHROUGH

SOURCE OF EVIL

SPOILER! Arriving at the Shoal Nightclub, Chuck finds Rebecca in a compromising position. She's been bound and is being held captive by none

other than Amber and Crystal Bailey—the gorgeous twins from the Terror Is Reality show! The two women are clearly in cahoots with T.K., and they're determined to put an end to Chuck's meddling in their affairs.

Remain in the center of the club, where you have the most room to move. Spin your view around until you see one or both of the girls rush you with their razor-sharp

swords, then start running to avoid their attacks.

TIP

If you've unlocked the Dodge Roll skill, make liberal use of it to skirt the twins' swift sword strikes. Things unlock at random as Chuck levels up, however, so it's possible you may not have acquired the Dodge Roll skill just yet.

Whether or not you're hit by the twins, quickly counter with a barrage of bat strikes until one of the girls knocks you down and they both flee. As with most psycho fights, focus on pouring on the damage at every opportunity.

TIP

If you're lucky and the twins attack simultaneously, you can hit both of them with each swing of your spiked bat.

You only need to defeat one of the twins to bring this battle to an end, so keep that in mind. Inflict as much pain as you can when they close in, consuming food

when the femmes fatales flee to the shadows.

Seeing her beloved sister murdered before her eyes, the remaining twin spits curses at Chuck before taking her own life. There's two more pointless deaths caused by T.K.'s insatiable greed.

SPOILER! Chuck hurries and unties Rebecca, who lightens the mood with some good news: While she was being held hostage,

Rebecca overheard the twins saying that T.K. has an evac chopper coming in. The villain is planning to flee Fortune City with his ill-gotten wealth—but not if Chuck Greene has anything to say about it.

TIP

Try using one of the swords that the twins leave behind—these are rare and deadly weapons!

FIND KATEY ZOMBREX, DAY 3

It's almost that time again: Katey will need a fresh shot of Zombrex soon. Not to worry; there are several ways to obtain more of the precious drug. Let's take care of some more side missions during your search.

VALUABLE MAGAZINE: *PSYCHOS*

Chuck most likely has a sizable inventory by now. (That's what all the ladies back at the Safe House are saying, anyway.) This is, therefore, a perfect time to collect a very valuable magazine, *Psychos*. Exit the Yucatan Casino via its south doors and enter the Silver Strip.

Visit the Combo Bay at Silver Strip's north end and use Chuck's motorbike to quickly reach Cash Gordon's Casino, located along the Platinum Strip. Get off the bike and climb onto the snack machine outside the casino so you can reach the awning above.

Leap over to the neighboring awning to locate some gems and a flashlight—the makings for a laser sword. Keep going to discover the *Psychos* magazine,

which gives Chuck 25 percent more PP from defeating psychopaths. This one's a keeper!

SIDE MISSION: HERE COMES THE GROOM

Now that you've found the *Pyschos* mag, let's get some use out of it. Get back on Chuck's bike and head for the Swept Away chapel, where yet another dangerous psychopath awaits.

> **TIP**
>
> If your spiked bat supply is low, collect two baseball bats from the Silver Strip's Barrel of Goods kiosk, then go north and enter the easternmost maintenance room at the Silver Strip's dead end, close to the Luaii Wauwii restaurant. Combine your bats with the two boxes of nails found inside the maintenance room.

> **TIP**
>
> Need healing? Use Pub O' Gold's blender to mix up some Pain Killers. Then save your game at Fortune Park's central grotto before carrying on.

Inside the Swept Away Chapel, Chuck witnesses a horrific sight. A deranged lunatic named (appropriately enough) Randy has been capturing women, forcing the

minister (his father) to marry them, and then doing God-knows-what with his newfound "brides." This villain needs to have more than his vows broken, and Chuck's just the man to break stuff.

Randy is much faster than he looks, and his chain saw attacks are vicious. Play cat and mouse around the chapel's pews and pillars, aiming to round on Randy after he charges and misses an attack. Make certain to assail Randy from the side or rear—you don't want to touch that running chain saw!

> **CAUTION**
>
> Randy's rushing attacks are by far the worst. Don't let him charge into Chuck!

Whale on Randy every time he misses, or whenever he pauses to taunt you or catch his breath. These are also ideal times to consume food. If Chuck becomes dangerously low on health, run around the pews with food in hand, waiting for Randy to miss or taunt Chuck before quickly gobbling it down.

> **TIP**
>
> You can always flee the chapel to acquire more curatives—the nearby Pub O' Gold is your best source.

Batter Randy relentlessly at every opportunity until the deviant is at last driven to hell. After Randy meets his timely demise, approach his prisoner, a young bride named Danni, and speak with her to get her to join you.

Try out the giant pink chain saw that Randy leaves behind—it's epically deadly!

SIDE MISSION: JANUS SURVIVOR

With Danni following Chuck's lead, make your way to Fortune Park, heading for the entrance to Atlantica Casino. If you don't have a firearm on hand, climb onto the standing poster

WALKTHROUGH

display at the Silver Strip's south end (the same one that gave you the paddlesaw combo card) and collect a handgun from up top.

A briefcase-toting man named Janus is being harassed by zombies near the entrance to the Atlantica Casino. Wipe out the surrounding ghouls so you may speak with Janus, discovering that his case is full of moola. Janus won't accompany Chuck to the Safe House unless he's packing a firearm—good thing you grabbed that handgun a moment ago.

SIDE MISSION: MAIL ORDER ZOMBREX

With Janus and Danni hot on Chuck's heels, motor into Royal Flush Plaza and save your game in the restroom. Order your followers to wait inside the restroom, then exit and inspect the mail cart that's right outside.

Peeking at the mail cart triggers a showdown against a psychopath named Carl. This guy has gone totally postal, wielding a rapid-fire shotgun and armed with a host of explosive packages. You'd best deliver him some swift justice!

Like Slappy, Carl always fires his shotgun in bursts of three. Circle around Carl to avoid his shots, then quickly close in and deliver as much first-rate punishment as you can.

Eventually, Carl will whack you with his shotgun and flee. When Carl runs, he often hurls an explosive package or two at Chuck, along with a bit of postal humor, like "Special delivery!" Get moving—you don't want to be anywhere nearby when Carl's packages go boom.

Carl's attacks are powerful, but this psycho isn't too difficult to box up. Just stay mobile and circle around Carl to avoid his gunfire before closing in. Flee from those mail bombs, and if you need to heal up, retreat to any store to consume food—there's a carton of orange juice at the nearby Yesterday, Today and Tomorrow newsstand, and you'll find the usual array of coffee creamers at The Dark Bean.

> **TIP**
> You can find additional coffee creamers on the giant Flaming Craps table. If things get really bad, flee to Roy's Mart at the east end of the mall and loot the place for nourishment.

Defeating Carl nets you a healthy dose of PP, and also a much-needed shot of Zombrex. Looks like Katey will be safe from the horrors of undeath for another 24 hours.

> **TIP**
> Collect the shotgun that Carl dropped for some serious firepower!

SIDE MISSION: THE SECRET OF CHARLIE'S GOLD

You've got Katey's Zombrex, but there's still plenty of time between now and 7:00 AM. Bring Danni and Janus back to the Safe House for some PP and a huge amount

of "thank you" cash from Janus, then enter the cafeteria and speak with Lenny, the survivor you rescued from Yucatan Casino's VIP room. Lenny has a story to tell about some hidden loot inside Yucatan Casino's vault; speak with him multiple times to shake loose the vault access code.

Use Linette's shortcut to quickly reach the Palisades Mall, then make tracks to Yucatan Casino. Enter the east cashier area to reach the vault. Examine the control panel near the vault door to open it using Lenny's passcode.

Once inside the vault, examine the lockbox that draws Chuck's eye. This nets you a tidy sum of cash; hurry back into Palisades Mall with your newfound moola.

SIDE MISSION: FETCHING FEMALES

You need a bit of cash for this task—$10,000, to be exact—so it's a good thing you've just come from Yucatan Casino. Make your way to Palisades Mall's central grotto and head up its winding stairs to locate three sassy female survivors.

Speak to the boss-lady, Cora, to find that the women are professional escorts, and that they demand a steep $10,000 fee to accompany you back to the Safe House. Talk about expensive tastes! Pay up to gain the ladies' company, then make your way up to the mall's second floor and take the shortcut back to Royal Flush Plaza.

> **TIP**
> Slide down the grotto's waterslide to give Chuck a rush—and some easy PP!

GIVE KATEY ZOMBREX, DAY 3

Follow your guide arrow to Dining at Davey's, where you find a portly man named Richard who is simply starving. Rich won't budge an inch without food; hand

him whatever goodie you plucked from The Dark Bean to satisfy his craving and convince him to join you.

Katey will be needing Zombrex by now, so give her a shot when you arrive at the Safe House with your three lovely escorts in tow. (Does Chuck know how to make an entrance or does Chuck know how to make an entrance?) Speak with Lenny in the cafeteria afterward to complete the "Legend of Charlie's Gold" side mission, then save your progress and head back into the fray.

> **NOTE**
> If you don't have any food on hand, the nearest source is Juggz Bar & Grill, which is directly across the strip from Dining at Davey's. Again, any solid food item will do the trick.

SIDE MISSION: HUNGER PAINS

Grab a brownie, cake, or any sort of solid food item (no beverages) from The Dark Bean on your way out of the Safe House, then slip through Americana Casino on your way to the Platinum Strip.

SIDE MISSION: TAPE IT OR DIE 1

With Richard following Chuck's lead, run to the far north end of Silver Strip. Enter Luaii Wauwii restaurant and collect some plates from the

WALKTHROUGH

counter, then grab the cement saw that's on the ground right outside the nearby maintenance room. (The one at the Silver Strip's dead end.)

With plates and a cement saw in hand, lead Richard into Palisades Mall, taking the maintenance hall shortcut through Hot Excitorama. Visit KokoNutz Sports Town on the mall's first floor and enter its back door, which is only unlocked between the hours of 6:00 AM and 12:00 PM on Day 3. Here Chuck encounters four survivors that he can't persuade to join him. Instead, one of the survivors, Wallace, asks Chuck to bring him some plates and a cement saw, which you've just acquired. Show these items to Wallace to obtain a secret combo card: the plate launcher!

NOTE

Don't fret over these four survivors; you'll have a chance to recruit them later in the adventure.

SIDE MISSION: ART APPRECIATION

Since you're already kickin' it at the Palisades Mall, head upstairs and visit The Cleroux Collection, a schmancy art shop where you meet a very upset man named Randolph. Speak to the sobbing fellow and agree to buy his funny painting for $3,000—you should easily have this amount on hand. This cheers Randolph up immensely and convinces him to join you. Make sure to collect the funny painting you've just paid for—it's an ideal gift for Katey and this is the only time you can obtain it!

TIP

Pilfer a "peace art" plant from the art store before leaving—you'll need it later and this will save you the trip.

SIDE MISSION: HIGH ROLLERS

With Richard and Randolph in your party, save your game at the nearby restroom on Palisades Mall's second floor, then proceed to Atlantica Casino. Visit the casino's north poker room to encounter three hard-core gamblers who are looking for a fourth player for their high-stakes game of Texas Hold 'Em.

Play against these high rollers by examining the poker table. It costs you $100,000 to buy into the game, and you should easily have this amount if you've followed this walkthrough carefully—saving Janus and completing Lenny's "The Secret of Charlie's Gold" side mission has lined your pockets with loads of paper.

TIP

If you lack the funds to play this poker game, return to Palisades Mall and construct a hacker combo weapon by merging the flashlight and computer case found within the south maintenance room. Use this device on ATMs to zap $10,000 out of each one. Two ATMs stand just south of Palisades Mall's central grotto, and there are a few more along Atlantica Casino's walls. If this still isn't enough cash, seek out additional ATMs along the Silver and Platinum Strips, or simply smash up slot machines.

Luck of the draw plays a role in your success in poker, but it helps to understand the game. Here are the rules: Each player is dealt two "hole" cards, which only they may see. One player automatically posts the big blind (BB), a forced bet meant to stimulate action. The player to the left of the big blind is forced to post the small blind (SB), which is always half of the big blind. The remaining players have the option to review their hole cards before deciding whether to "call" the big blind (bet the same amount and play their hand) or "fold" (bet nothing and sit out the hand). Players may also elect to "raise" on any turn (bet even more than the current wager); once a raise has been made, all other players must call the raise if they wish to continue playing the hand.

After the initial round of blinds and betting, three cards are dealt in the middle of the table. This is known as the "flop." Cards dealt to the center of the table are community cards; all players get to use them. The idea is to combine the central cards with your two secret hole cards to form the best five-card poker hand.

A round of betting follows the flop, in which each player may decide whether to check (take no action) or bet (raise the stakes). If all players check, no additional money is required to see the next community card, called the "turn." If any player bets, all other players must either call the bet to continue playing, or raise the bet, placing even more money into the pot and forcing the initial better to call. The third option is to fold, forfeiting any money you've placed into the pot thus far and giving up on the hand.

A fifth and final card is dealt after the turn; this one's called the "river." A final round of betting follows—afterward, all players who are still in the game must reveal their hole cards, thereby showing their hand. The player whose hole cards help them create the best five-card poker hand wins, collecting all money in the main pot.

NOTE

It's possible to have a "side pot" in poker; this occurs when one player goes "all in," betting their entire stack of chips, while other players with larger stacks carry on betting.

Here are the best Texas Hold 'Em poker hands, from highest (rarest) to lowest (most common):

- Royal Flush (ace, king, queen, jack, 10, all of the same suit)
- Straight Flush (a five-card Straight, all of the same suit)
- Four of a Kind (four of any one card, such as four kings or four 4s)
- Full House (Three of a Kind, plus a Pair)
- Flush (any five cards, all of the same suit)
- Straight (five cards in consecutive order, such as 3, 4, 5, 6, 7.)
- Three of a Kind (three of any one card, such as three jacks or three 3s)
- Two Pair (two separate Pairs of cards, such as two 9s and two 5s)
- One Pair (one Pair of cards, such as two aces or two 2s)
- High Card (If no player has made even one Pair, then the player with the highest hole card wins)

Obviously, the more familiar you are with the game of Texas Hold 'Em, the easier time you'll have of winning this event. Here are some basic tips to keep in mind:

Know When to Fold 'Em: If you're dealt weak hole cards, such as a 4-8 off suit (unsuited), don't hesitate to chuck 'em away. Your rivals can eliminate one another without your help; you don't need to play every hand. The worst starting hand in Hold 'Em is the 7-2 off suit, because you have little chance of making a Flush or Straight, and the value of both cards is low.

Play Your Position: If you've been forced to post the small blind, you might as well call the big blind, even if you aren't sitting on the greatest hole cards. It's usually only a small amount of extra cash to call, and who knows? You might draw a lucky flop and end up winning big.

Read Your Rivals: Consider the community cards, think of all the hands your rivals could potentially have, and then watch how they bet. If you've flopped a pretty good hand, such as Top Pair (the highest possible pair), place a small bet and see how your opponents react. If someone raises you, chances are they may have something even better, such as Two Pair or Three of a Kind—consider folding unless you're certain they're bluffing.

Consider Your Kicker: Being dealt a king is great, but it's less great when your other hole card is weak, like a 3. Even if you pair your king on the flop, a rival may have done the same, and their other hole card (known as the "kicker") would likely be greater in this case. Go ahead and play hands like queen-5 when it's cheap to buy in; fold them immediately otherwise.

Check and Trap: Even if you've made a great hand, such as flopping a Two Pair or Three of a Kind, consider checking instead of betting. This can entice your rivals to bet, assuming that your hand is weak. Call each bet until you reach the river card, then make a bold raise and see if they fall for it. Even if they somehow have you beat, you've risked less money by checking and calling instead of betting and raising.

High Hands Are Rare: It's not very often that someone makes a Straight or Flush in a four-handed poker game—the odds are quite high against it. If you've made Two Pair or Three of a Kind, feel confident that you've drawn the best hand, and play it accordingly. Even Top Pair can be a monster hand in a four-handed event.

WALKTHROUGH

Open Up at the End: Start playing more aggressively as players are eliminated from the game. Lead out and bet with every hand before the flop—this works because players are far more likely to draw weak hole cards than strong ones in Texas Hold 'Em, and betting early will usually entice your rivals to fold. However, if you're bluffing and you're called, expect that your rival has you beat and look for a way out. Pride has no place at the poker table.

Chuck must be the last player standing to win the "High Rollers" poker game, so be prepared to grind it out. The prize pool is well worth the effort: $1,000,000 goes

into Chuck's pocket, and he gains the company of three more survivors!

> **TIP**
>
> Don't shy away from loading your last save if things don't go well at the table. No matter how good you are at poker, sometimes the cards come cold, lending you little chance of winning.

SIDE MISSION: BANK RUN

With a cool mil in your pocket and five faithful followers at your flank, make the short jog across Fortune Park and enter Slot Ranch Casino, looking for a man named Woodrow who's fiddling with an ATM. Beat back the surrounding zombies as you chat with Woodrow, who isn't about to let all of Fortune City's perfectly good money go to waste just because of a little outbreak.

> **CAUTION**
>
>
>
> You'll likely witness a cinematic as you leave Atlantica Casino and enter Fortune Park, in which four psychotic snipers are introduced. Ignore these villains for now; they've taken up elevated positions around the Silver and Platinum Strips. We'll let you know when the time's right to fight them. Until then, just hurry through the strips to avoid being shot.

Follow Woodrow around Slot Ranch Casino and the Food Court as he "liberates" the cash stored in each of its ATMs. Keep the zombies away from Woodrow so he can complete his greedy scheme.

After hitting the final ATM, Woodrow agrees to accompany Chuck to the Safe House. Head back to return all six of your survivors and receive a tidy sum of PP—along with a cool $50,000 from Woodrow and a dose of Zombrex from Richard!

SIDE MISSION: CHEMICAL DEPENDENCY

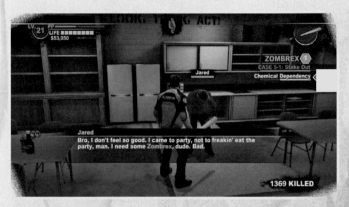

If you rescued Jared Davis during the "Once Bitten" mission, then he's likely in need of Zombrex by now. Fortunately for him, you've just acquired an extra vial. Follow the guide arrow to find Jared in rough shape. Be a pal and give him your spare Zombrex to spare his life and collect a huge PP bonus.

> **TIP**
>
> Don't forget to give little Katey the funny painting you've been carrying around all this time—it'll net you some easy PP.

SIDE MISSIONS: SLAVE TO FASHION AND WWJWD?

These two side missions are best completed simultaneously. Build two spiked bats on your way out of the Safe House and concoct a Quick Step and some Pain Killers at Shots & Awe. Use the Quick Step to hasten your journey to Fortune City Hotel.

Locate a scantily-clad woman named Europa hiding behind some plants near the lobby elevators. She's too embarrassed to follow Chuck back to the Safe House unless Chuck is also nigh-nude. Europa tells Chuck to undress at a shop in the South Plaza. Hey, whatever it takes!

While en route to the shop (which now appears on your map as an objective), you encounter a deranged security guard named Seymour who is taking the law into his own twisted hands by hanging innocent people in the square. You can't allow this psycho to go on killing survivors!

Seymour is armed with a handgun, and he's pretty quick on the draw. He's also packing a club for close-range attacks and can lasso Chuck from medium-range to set up vicious assaults.

There's no science to stopping this lunatic: simply rush Seymour from the start and batter him with relentless blows, interrupting his attack rhythm and keeping him on the defensive. Pound Pain Killers as needed, but otherwise just keep pounding on Seymour.

NOTE

As always, it's best to flee to a safe location before consuming food. There are plenty of nooks and crannies around South Plaza for you to exploit.

After defeating Seymour, listen for the screams of a nearby man named Ray. You'll find him near South Plaza's southeast maintenance room, surrounded by zombies. Kill the fiends and then speak with Ray to get him to join you.

NOTE

Ray will only join you after Seymour has been killed.

Ray's about to get a whole lot more of Chuck Greene than he bargained for. Continue to the clothing store that Europa has pointed out (it's marked as an objective on your

map) and examine the underwear display to undress Chuck, stripping him down to his skivvies. Sorry, Ray—it's either this or death by zombies.

Huff it back to Europa to show her that Chuck's not afraid of running around in his undies. Impressed by our hero's bravado, Europa at last agrees to accompany Chuck back to the Safe House. Don't lead her there just yet, however—time is likely running out on the "Know When to Fold 'Em" task, which is easy to complete and not far away.

WALKTHROUGH

NOTE

The next time you return to the Safe House, you can use the lockers inside the restroom to change back into Chuck's normal attire (if you wish). Or just pop into any clothing store you see to don some fresh duds. Europa won't mind!

SIDE MISSION: KNOW WHEN TO FOLD 'EM

Make tracks to the Silver Strip, moving quickly to avoid being shot by those psychotic snipers. Head into the Shamrock Casino to speak with a real gamblin' man named Bill.

The house always wins, as they say, and poor Bill has lost it all by playing the slots for far too long. But, like any true addict, this guy won't budge until he's recouped his losses. Bail Bill out by handing him $20,000—you should easily have this if you helped Woodrow during the "Bank Run" mission. Incredibly, Bill then demands another $5,000—hand this over as well to finally get him to see reason and join you.

SIDE MISSION: BENT WOOD

With Bill, Ray, and Europa following behind, hurry back to the Safe House, making a quick stop at Royal Flush Plaza's SporTrance store on the way. Grab the golf club on the ground near the Casino Cup minigame—you'll soon find out why you need it.

Once you're back at the Safe House, pop by the lounge and speak with Luz, who's upset because she has no golf club with which to keep her skills sharp. Luz asks you to find her a club—but you're already one stroke ahead. Hand her the one you've just collected to score some easy cash and PP.

NOTE

That's all the side missions you have time for at the moment—Case 5-1 is about to begin. Save your game and then hurry to the Safe House's rooftop to attend your meeting with Rebecca.

CASE 5-1: STAKE OUT

As the clock nears 8:00 PM, Stacey calls Chuck to remind him that Rebecca is waiting for him on the Safe House roof. This is your cue that you may now begin Case 5-1. Tune the guide arrow and follow it to locate the elevator that brings you to the Safe House's rooftop.

Good as her word, Rebecca greets Chuck on the rooftop by handing him a pair of binoculars. T.K.'s chopper should be on its way, and Chuck silently monitors the horizon, scanning for its landing site.

SPOILER!

Sure enough, Chuck spots T.K.'s chopper as it touches down on the roof of the Fortune City Hotel. That scum—there's no way T.K. is going to get away with this. Chuck hurries off to stop the madman once and for all.

SIDE MISSION: SHELL SHOCKED

A side mission is about to expire, so let's quickly tackle it before going after T.K. Head for the Americana Casino to locate a man named Dean, who has taken up position inside the American Historium. Dean's a war veteran and knows his way around a firearm, but he can't stay holed up here forever.

Speak with Dean until he agrees to join you. Unfortunately, Dean's legs were wounded during his service, and he's not about to let Chuck carry him around like some helpless cripple. It's therefore slow going back to the Safe House, but at least it isn't far. Guide Dean back to ensure this hero doesn't meet a tragic end.

TIP

Unless Dean's in a real bind, let him fend for himself and stay a good distance ahead of him. If you hang out too close to Dean, he'll stop walking and begin shooting at zombies, slowing the journey even more.

Grab a bottle of vodka from Shots & Awe on your way back to the Safe House—you'll soon need it.

WALKTHROUGH

SIDE MISSION: DEMAND AND SUPPLY

Deliver Dean to the Safe House for a bit of PP, then visit the cafeteria and speak with Sven, assuming you rescued him during the "Code Blue" side mission a while back. The good doctor has his hands full with treating all of the Safe House survivors and, with dwindling supplies, he asks Chuck to bring him some vodka or whiskey to use as a disinfectant. Hand Sven the bottle of booze you pilfered from Shots & Awe to complete this task in short order, gaining some easy PP. Sven is so thrilled, he also gives Chuck a spare dose of Zombrex in thanks!

SIDE MISSION: MILITIA MEN

PSYCHO SNIPER 1: BIG EARL

As you pass through Fortune Park anytime after 9:00 AM on Day 3, the scene shifts to show a quartet of gun-toting psychopaths picking shots at innocent survivors from an elevated position. You've most likely seen this scene already; the time has come to bring these villains down. Craft two spiked bats on your way out of the Safe House and mix up some Quick Steps at Shots & Awe, downing one on your way to the Platinum Strip.

Don't worry if you don't have a ranged weapon; you'll be confronting these psychos head-on. Hop onto the white cement blocks at the base of Big Earl's perch, using them to climb all the way up to the psycho. Time Earl's gunshots so you aren't hit while vaulting up to him.

Turn left as you enter the Platinum Strip and bolt toward Fortune Park. You catch sight of the first of the four psychos, Big Earl, who has taken position on the scaffolding to the right. Dodge Earl's gunfire as you streak toward his sniper perch; if you've learned the Dodge Roll technique, use it to avoid each shot more easily.

Big Earl is dangerous at close range. He produces a deadly machete when you approach. He prefers to use his powerful rifle though, and will commonly flee to take aim from range. Continue using the Dodge Roll skill to avoid Big Earl's shots, or just circle around the psycho to avoid his bullets.

> **TIP**
>
> Each sniper psycho's rifle gives off a gleam right before they fire. This is your cue to dodge!

Each time Big Earl misses, make him pay dearly with your spiked bat. Pile on the damage to dispatch this psycho fast.

DEADRISING 2

SIDE MISSION: MILITIA MEN, CONTINUED

PSYCHO SNIPER 3: JOHNNY

TIP

Wolf down the food around each sniper's perch to replenish Chuck's health after each showdown. This helps you conserve juice drinks and the like for later use.

Descend the ladder after dispatching Deetz and then sprint through Fortune Park into the Silver Strip. Dash for the maintenance room to the left of the doors leading to Slot Ranch Casino, and scale the ladder you find near the maintenance room's door.

The ladder leads to Royal Flush Plaza's rooftop, where you discover a third sniper named Johnny. You should have the feel for these fights

by now—lay waste to this psycho just as you did to the previous two, then chow down on the rooftop's food before returning to the ground.

PSYCHO SNIPER 2: DEETZ

Deetz is stationed atop the roof of the Paradise Platinum Screens movie theater, which is directly across the strip from Big Earl's perch. Heal after dropping Big Earl, then cut across the strip, sprinting to the alley that runs behind Juggz Bar & Grill, where you discover a ladder.

NOTE

If for some reason Deetz is not visible atop the movie theater, enter the Americana Casino, then turn around and reenter the Platinum Strip to make Deetz appear. (He's a shy one.)

TIP

Use the blender at Juggz Bar & Grill if you need more juice drinks.

Climb the ladder to reach Deetz's rooftop— the coward won't be expecting that. Rush Deetz and bust him up just as you did Big Earl. Keep the pressure on him and don't relent until Deetz goes down.

PYSCHO SNIPER 4: DERRICK

The final rooftop sniper, Derrick, has hunkered down atop the Atlantica Casino. To reach him, cut across the Silver Strip and enter the alley that's just south of Hot

Excitorama. Follow the alley to its end, flinging open a door to locate a ladder.

Climb the ladder to confront Derrick on the roof, using the same tactics to eliminate this final sniper. Excellent work! Fortune City's strips are now much safer thanks to your courage.

TIP

Save your progress at Fortune Park's central grotto— you don't want to fight these four psychos again!

WALKTHROUGH

CASE 5-2: THE GETAWAY

1734 KILLED

That's all the time you have for side missions—you've got to stop T.K.'s getaway. Hurry to Fortune City Hotel to encounter multiple armed mercenaries near the lobby elevators. Take your bat to 'em and wipe out each merc to claim 1,000 PP a pop.

The elevator arrives after you beat down the guards in the lobby, and one last hired gun steps out. Beat him senseless and then board the elevator, using the controls inside to reach the hotel's roof.

1737 KILLED

MAN VERSUS MACHINE

SPOILER!

Chuck arrives just in time to witness T.K. loading untold amounts of ill-gotten cash onto his getaway chopper. The

villain tries to flee, but Chuck manages to hitch a crane winch onto his helicopter at the last second, preventing his escape. Time for some payback, buddy!

To down T.K.'s copter, you must damage it by hurling objects at it. Gunfire and similar ranged attacks won't work; only thrown objects can damage the whirlybird. The

moment the battle begins, quickly turn around and grab one of the spot lights on the helipad, then take aim and hurl it at T.K.'s ride.

TIP

It helps to approach the railing before throwing an object at the helicopter. Aim a little high and target the middle of the chopper for the best odds of scoring a hit.

The winch soon releases, cutting T.K. enough slack to fly around in circles, attempting to clothesline Chuck with the crane. You should have the Dodge Roll skill by

this point—use it to roll under the crane each time it passes by.

NOTE

If you don't have the Dodge Roll skill, you'll need to flee to the far side of the helipad to escape the crane's reach. Stay mobile—the helicopter's gunner will fire on you as well!

A buzzer sounds after a short time (usually after T.K. makes two passes), and the winch controls become active again. Hurry to the control station at the base of the

1736 KILLED

crane and throw the winch to lock down the helicopter once more. Immediately grab another spot light and hurl it at T.K.'s chopper to score more damage. Or, if you're wounded, use the time to consume food instead. Repeat this pattern until T.K.'s chopper comes crashing down.

TIP

You can find more nourishment in the corner to the right of the rooftop elevator.

T.K.'s escape has been foiled, and the cretin is knocked unconscious in the helicopter's crash. Chuck wants answers and decides to bring his nemesis back to

the Safe House for questioning. Sullivan doesn't like it, but he agrees to keep watch over the unconscious mongrel. It won't be long before T.K. awakes....

FIND KATEY ZOMBREX, DAY 4

Only a handful of hours remain until the military arrives, but Katey will need another dose of Zombrex soon. With T.K. in custody, Chuck's only remaining objective is to find more of the precious drug—along with any other survivors he can round up.

NOTE

If you've followed this walkthrough carefully, you should have a spare dose of Zombrex on hand already, which was given to you by Sven. If you don't, you can easily purchase some from any pawnshop with the vast amount of funds you've accumulated thus far.

SIDE MISSION: STRANDED SIREN

Time's running short on this task, so waste no time building a couple of spiked bats on your way out of the Safe House, taking Linette's shortcut to quickly reach the opposite side of the city. Rush to the Atlantica Casino after you emerge.

Follow the guide arrow to locate a woman named Tammy, who is wearing a sweet mermaid outfit. Unfortunately, the getup isn't conducive to fleeing from zombies. Hop onto the giant clamshell and speak with Tammy to get her to join you—but don't carry her off that clamshell stand just yet!

SIDE MISSION: WORLD'S MOST DANGEROUS TRICK

Ready to take on your final side mission psychos? You face two of them at once in this event, so take a moment to mix up some Pain Killers at the Atlantica Casino's central bar, Sipparellos, before entering the doors to the magic stage.

TIP

Even the odds against these psychos and enlist the aid of a co-op buddy for this fight. Each player should choose a psycho and focus on defeating theirs first to avoid accidentally wounding one another.

Approaching the stage, Chuck watches in horror as two would-be magicians attempt to saw a woman in half—and fail miserably. The two men don't enjoy Chuck's criticism and decide to teach him a little "disappearing" act. What a couple of cards!

The talkative psycho, Reed, is the more aggressive and dangerous of the two. He pursues Chuck relentlessly, launching blinding fireworks from his giant cannon that stun, and often following up with a charge or melee blows. Attack Reed relentlessly, fleeing to gobble down food whenever the chance permits.

Roger's sword attacks pack a bit more of a wallop, but he's less aggressive, using hit-and-run tactics. This makes it easy to heal up after you've dealt with Reed. Chase Roger around the casino, assailing him each time he rounds on you to strike.

Defeating these two deviants not only earns you a sizable amount of PP, but also nets you the rocket launcher combo card. Now that's worthy of some applause!

WALKTHROUGH

> ### NOTE
> Feel free to play around with Reed's rocket launcher and Roger's swords after the battle—this is the only chance you'll have to test out these unique weapons!

SIDE MISSION: DEAD OR ALIVE?

Collect Tammy and then sprint into the nearby Palisades Mall. Set Tammy down in the mall's south maintenance room, closing the door behind you to ensure her safety. Then follow the guide arrow to locate a man named Andy, who stands atop a row of slot machines, fending off zombies with a shotgun.

> ### TIP
> If you didn't grab the peace art plant from The Cleroux Collection earlier in the adventure, go upstairs to the mall's second floor and do so now. You'll soon need it!

Climb up to Andy's level and speak with him to initiate a drawn out dialogue. Just keep chatting with Andy until he at last agrees to join you, then drop down and return to the maintenance room to pick up Tammy once more.

SIDE MISSION: TWO'S COMPANY

After grabbing up Tammy, proceed along the maintenance hall to quickly reach the Silver Strip's seediest store, Hot Excitorama. There you find two jokesters who are cracking each other up.

The two men are yearning to know who's funniest and they want Chuck to settle their good-natured argument. Talk to both men to hear each one's latest joke, then collect the prize trophy from the nearby counter. Give the trophy to Royce to make his day and get him to join you; speak to Walter afterward to gain his company as well.

> ### NOTE
> If you hand the trophy to Walter instead, you'll have to pay Royce $5,000 to get him to join. Talk about a sore loser!

SIDE MISSION: ONE HIT WONDER

Carry Tammy and lead the rest of your posse over to Slot Ranch Casino, where you encounter a different sort of psycho who isn't interested in bloodshed. Instead, failing singer Bibi Love is desperate to put on one last show—and she's rigged a few survivors up to explosive tables to ensure that they give her their undivided attention!

> ### TIP
> Set Tammy down out of harm's way before speaking with Bibi. The nearby restroom is a good spot; you can save your progress there as well.

Hop onstage and speak with Ms. Love, who has a few errands for Chuck to run. Her first two demands are a refreshing drink, and that Chuck dress appropriately for the momentous occasion. Hand Bibi any beverage you happen to have on you, then enter Royal Flush Plaza, leaving Tammy behind (you won't be gone long).

If you didn't have a beverage for Bibi before, you can find orange juice in the back room of Roy's Mart, along with a coffee creamer. Enter the

nearby Modern Businessman store afterward and examine the rear dressing rooms to deck Chuck out in a snazzy tuxedo. Make sure to grab the black dress shoes to match!

TIP

Save at Slot Ranch Casino's restroom again on your way back to Bibi, just in case things take a turn for the worse. Leave Tammy there to ensure her safety and order Andy to wait there as well.

Return to Bibi and speak with her again. For her final request, Ms. Love orders you to round up a large audience—her current handful of "fans" just won't

do. Find some fireworks in the backstage area and toss them near the stage to lure zombies toward it. You can also run around a bit, using Chuck as bait to draw in the undead.

Soon enough, Ms. Love declares that she's ready to greet her rabid fans. Speak to Bibi one last time to receive her blessing, then move to the stage controls located

near the bound woman, Allison, and examine them to begin a short rhythm-based minigame.

The goal is simple: Watch the meter at the bottom of the screen, waiting for button icons to scroll by from the right. Press the appropriate button when each

icon passes through the highlighted spot on the left. Timing each press correctly sets off a dramatic pyro display while Bibi belts out her number. The buttons come with greater speed as the show winds to its conclusion; you don't have to hit every button, but try your best!

CAUTION

Don't miss too many buttons or Bibi will become hysterical and her audience will go boom.

Thrilled by her epic comeback performance, Bibi decides to give the crowd what they really want: her! Unfortunately, Ms. Love doesn't realize that her fans only want her because they're mindless zombies starved for human flesh.... But hey, you can't fix crazy.

Bibi might be off her rocker, but she's far from the worst psychopath that Chuck has encountered in Fortune City. Don't let her life end like this; beat back

those zombies to save the would-be star, then speak with Bibi to recruit her as a survivor.

No longer in danger, Bibi's "captive" audience joins Chuck, eager to be away from this awful place. That's eight survivors you've got following you now—quite the posse! Collect Tammy from the restroom, save your game and then lead your crew into Royal Flush Plaza.

WALKTHROUGH

Unfortunately, one of Bibi's captives—Cameron—is injured and can't move very fast. You're already carrying Tammy, so you'll have to wait for Cameron at first. Make sure he makes it into Royal Flush Plaza, then streak for the Safe House, leaving him behind. Drop Tammy off near the Safe House's entrance, then sprint back through the mall to lend Cameron a shoulder. Herd all eight survivors into the Safe House at once for a massive PP injection!

> **NOTE**
>
> If Katey's time is running dangerously low and you haven't located any Zombrex, bring Cameron upstairs to the pawnshop on Royal Flush Plaza's second floor and pick up a dose of the drug before bringing him to the Safe House. It'll cost you some cash, but that shouldn't be a problem by this point.

> **TIP**
>
> Grab a hat from Hat Racks and swipe some shades from Universe of Optics on your way to the Safe House. You'll find out why soon enough!

SIDE MISSION: FORTUNE CITY BOTANY CLUB

Now that you're back at the Safe House, enter the cafeteria and speak with Vikki, the girl you rescued from Brandon Whittaker during the "Chuck the Role Model" mission. Hand Vikki the peace art plant you've been carrying all this time to complete an easy mission worthy of some fast PP.

SIDE MISSION: ANTE UP

Depending on how swift you've been, you may have a few hours to kill before the clock strikes 7:00 AM and Katey needs her medicine. Assuming you've got some Zombrex, spend this free time by playing against fellow survivors in a relaxing game of Texas Hold 'Em within the Safe House.

> **TIP**
>
> Save your game before following the guide arrow to locate the poker room, just in case you lose your shirt.

> **NOTE**
>
> This poker event is only available if you rescued Kristin during "Lush-ious Lady," Trixie-Lynn during "Barn Burner," Cora during "Fetching Females," Jack during "Welcome to the Family," or Woodrow during "Bank Run" (side missions).

The rules and strategies for this game of Hold 'Em mirror those you used to win big against the pros during the "High Rollers" side mission. Flip back a few pages in this walkthrough to refresh your memory on how to play.

The main difference between "Ante Up" and "High Rollers" are the buy-ins: It costs just $25,000 to play against your Safe House pals. In addition, each time a player "busts out" by losing all of their cash, they also lose an article of clothing. That's right—this is a game of strip poker!

Players will automatically buy back into the game as long as they still have some clothes to lose—and the required $25,000 to play. This is why we recommended that you grab a hat and some shades from Royal Flush Plaza's Hat Racks and Universe of Optics clothing stores—these count as clothes, allowing Chuck to buy in a couple of additional times if need be.

Stacey will call to remind you when it's time to give Katey her Zombrex, so just sit back and enjoy yourself until then. See if you can bust out one of your buddies, stripping them down to their humble unmentionables. Eliminating just one player in this fashion is enough to win you this lighthearted side mission.

GIVE KATEY ZOMBREX, DAY 4

It's that time again, Dad. Give little Katey her daily dose of Zombrex at the Safe House security room, just as you've done many times before. This will be the last shot of Zombrex poor Katey has to endure in this hellacious place!

KILLING TIME, PART 5

Katey is safe from turning for another 24 hours, and the military's arrival is imminent. There are still a handful of hours between now and 10:00 AM, however—enough time for you to round up a few more survivors for PP and glory, if you wish.

SIDE MISSIONS: FAMILY FEUD AND TAPE IT OR DIE 2

These two side missions are best completed simultaneously. Save at the Safe House before making the long journey to Fortune City Hotel, using Quick Steps mixed at Shots & Awe to speed your travels (make two of them). Once you arrive at the hotel lobby, take the elevators up to the rooftop—the same ones you used when moving to spoil T.K.'s getaway plan.

Sprint to the far end of the roof to find a young woman named Lillian who's terribly distraught. Apparently, Lillian and her mother had quite an argument about where to hide out, and her mother has stormed off to take shelter in the Atlantica Casino. You've got to go find her!

Pound another Quick Step and bolt back to the lobby, following the guide arrow to the Atlantica Casino. There you find Lillian's mother, Camille, desperately fending off the undead. Clear out the swarm and then speak with Camille to gain her company.

Next, motor to KokoNutz Sports Town and visit the back room, where you encountered Wallace and his three companions before. Help these people defeat the swarming zombies to gain their confidence and at last convince all four to join you.

Rush back to Fortune City Hotel's rooftop and reunite the wayward mother with her sobbing daughter. The two embrace and then Lillian joins you—hurry and lead these final survivors to the Safe House before the clock strikes 10:00 AM!

CAUTION

You receive urgent messages warning you to return to the Safe House throughout the 9 o'clock hour—get back there before 10:00 AM or you'll never discover the truth of what has really happened here in Fortune City.

WALKTHROUGH

CASE 6-1: HELP ARRIVES

Back at the Safe House security room, Chuck, Stacey, Sullivan, and little Katey all watch the monitors with a vested interest as they await the military's imminent arrival. So much time in a dingy bunker tends to make one anxious for rescue, particularly when they're surrounded by the less-than-living.

SPOILER! Mercifully, the military soon comes to the rescue, smashing into the north end of the Silver Strip by way of the city's underground tunnel system. The heavily armed men are more than a match for the mindless zombies and seem to genuinely enjoy slaughtering their way to the Safe House.

SPOILER! Everything seems to be going according to plan—until suddenly, a strange chemical gas begins flooding up from the city's sewer vents. The gas is not the military's doing, and soon the men are surrounded by a thick, green fog.

SPOILER! Not only is the gas a hindrance to vision, it also seems to have some sort of effect on the teeming zombies. Many the undead soon begin to shudder and mutate, becoming far more powerful and aggressive.

SPOILER! Blinded and surrounded by what can only be described as super zombies, the situation quickly deteriorates for the military. Soldiers begin firing on one another in the confusion and chaos, and only the squad leader makes it out alive, fleeing the scene in a humvee.

SPOILER! Back at the Safe House, the survivors watch in shock and horror as the grisly scene plays out. What just happened out there? How could zombies take out a trained military column?

SPOILER! Panic begins to set in, but Sullivan assures his comrades that another rescue attempt will occur in 24 hours. When pressed by Stacey, Sullivan also divulges that, should the second attempt fail, the military's fallback option will be to firebomb the city to ensure the outbreak doesn't spread. Even the Safe House won't be able to withstand a full-scale bombardment like that.

www.primagames.com

DEADRISING 2

Then, more bad news: The gang catches sight of Rebecca running through the green haze and into the underground tunnels. What's she doing out there? Chuck knows he has to go out now and save her.

CASE 6-2: LAST STAND

Chuck gets his first taste of super zombie shortly after leaving the Safe House: Two of the fiends come shambling toward him in the now-hazy maintenance passage. Quickly clobber both zombies with your trusty spiked bat, building two more on your way to Royal Flush Plaza—the spiked bat's fast attacks and widespread knock-back are more valuable now than ever.

CAUTION

Super zombies are much faster and far more aggressive than the sluggish undead you're accustom to. If one grabs Chuck, you'll need to rapidly imitate several button commands to break its grasp. Super zombies can also vomit blood as a ranged attack—this causes Chuck to double over in agony when hit, allowing the undead to swarm him. Don't mess with the walking dead from this point forward; stay mobile and use jumps and the Dodge Roll skill to avoid conflicts.

TIP

Yank the chain saw's ignition cord to start it running—it will then carve into any zombies that get in your way as you dash through the throng.

Streak to Yucatan Casino, hugging the casino's left wall and exiting into Silver Strip via the Yucatan's south doors. When you hit the strip, carry the chain saw over to Chuck's motorbike inside the Combo Bay. Install the weapon onto the bike to create a very deadly set of wheels.

Feel free to motor up and down the strip, sawing through zombies for a constant trickle of PP. Avoid collisions with objects, however, as this harms Chuck. When you're done having fun, speed north toward the Silver Strip's dead end and ride down into the Underground via the wide opening that the military created during their arrival.

GO YOUR OWN WAY

Rather than following the guide arrow to Royal Flush Plaza's southeast service door, exploit the restroom shortcut to emerge at Palisades Mall instead. Vault the fence and visit the grotto bar to mix up some Pain Killers. Grab the chain saw that's stashed behind the counter as well.

TUNNEL OF TERROR

The Underground has been hit hard by the gas—super zombies are everywhere down here. Fortunately, your souped-up motorbike means you've little to fear. Zip over to the nearby restroom, clearing out the undead before hopping off the bike to save your progress. Run toward your objective on foot after saving; it isn't far.

WALKTHROUGH

SERGEANT PSYCHO

SPOILER!

The undead ranks thin out as Chuck nears a crashed humvee. Gunshots ring out from the warehouse beyond; the sergeant is making his final stand here, and he's got Rebecca in custody!

Sgt. Boykin has completely snapped and can no longer tell friend from foe. He opens fire on Chuck—take cover immediately and begin circling around the pillars and cargo crates, aiming to get within striking distance of the militant madman.

In many ways, this fight is similar to the battle against that psychotic mailman, Carl Schiff. Boykin primarily attacks by firing his powerful LMG, but he'll also hurl a grenade at you from time to time—these are most deadly. Listen carefully to what Boykin says and flee from your position whenever he shouts "grenade" or anything to that effect.

Approach Boykin tactfully by circling around pillars and the like. Punish the sergeant with a slew of spiked bat strikes each time you close in. Flee to cover after Boykin responds by knocking you down, shooting you, and heaving you away—then look to repeat the aforementioned approach technique. Recovering health isn't much of an issue here thanks to the plentiful amount of cover.

TIP

Don't forget about Chuck's Dodge Roll skill—it can be a lifesaver should Boykin pin you down with heavy fire!

Continue playing hide and seek with Boykin, bashing his brains in with your bat each time the chance permits. If you like, pick up one of the many military weapons scattered around the ground and cut the sergeant down from afar—grenades are great, and the LMG near Boykin's humvee is particularly nasty. If you came here with enough healing, you should have little trouble handing this fallen hero his discharge papers.

CASE 6-3: LEAN ON ME

Chuck has saved the day once again, but Rebecca didn't escape unscathed this time. Her leg has been badly injured and the shaken reporter is unable to walk. Ensure that Chuck is at full health, then hoist Rebecca and carry her up the access road to the surface. Simply follow the guide arrow toward daylight.

TIP

Save at the restroom you used prior to fighting Sgt. Boykin—it's a long way back to the Safe House.

147

1964 KILLED

Don't worry; the two super zombies near the entrance to the Safe House aren't around anymore. Hurry to the hatch to complete your mission!

1964 KILLED

Running with Rebecca through throngs of super zombies is a suicide mission, but it must be done. As always, look for small pockets of space between the undead masses and just keep moving. Sticking close to the wall is usually a sound plan.

CAUTION

You can't jump or use any skills while carrying Rebecca, so avoiding clusters of zombies is more important than ever.

TIP

Consider moving through Yucatan Casino, into Palisades Mall, and using the second-floor shortcut to return to Royal Flush Plaza more quickly. This allows you to hit the mall's grotto bar if you need more juice drinks.

TIP

Make sure Chuck has plenty of health before entering the Safe House with Rebecca—it's about to become significantly less safe!

REVOLTING REVELATION

SPOILER! Back at the Safe House, Chuck finds that T.K. has finally come to. The guy's as charming as ever and, between needling insults, he lets something slip: He wasn't solely responsible for the Fortune City outbreak. T.K. was acting under orders from someone else—someone with the resources to produce the gas that's now choking out the city.

CASE 6-4: BREACH

SPOILER! Moments later, the gang is startled when zombies begin slamming away at the security office's windows—the Safe House has been breached! Spying a smoking control box, Chuck knows he has to find a way to fix the problem and seal the bunker doors.

TIP

Don't waste time trying to assist the Safe House survivors; they can fend for themselves. Focus on repairing the door.

You must locate three specific objects needed to hot-wire the control box: a generator, a gas barrel, and a spool of wire. All three objects appear on your map, and

★ CLOSE THE GATE ★

Find the Generator, Fuel Barrel and Spool of Wire.

Take each item to the gate panel at the Safe House entrance to hack the gate.

Close the gate and secure the Safe House!

CONTINUE

they're also listed as missions. Simply follow the guide arrow to track down each object in turn.

Spool of Wire Placed

Combine the 3 items to hack the Broken Panel and bring down the Security Gate!

After collecting one of the needed objects, the guide arrow automatically adjusts to point to the sparking control box. Simply carry the object to the box, setting it down nearby when you see the "place item" command. A confirmation message then appears to assure you that the object has been properly seated.

WALKTHROUGH

NOTE

Feel free to use the objects to clobber zombies out of your way if need be, but don't break them.

Set all three objects down at the control box, then interact with it when the "hack" command appears. Begin hammering the indicated button as fast as you can to shut the security gate and stem the tide of undead. Don't worry; the zombies won't interfere while you seal the gate.

UNUSUAL ABSENCE

After shutting the gate and taking care of the lingering zombies, Chuck returns to the security room to check on Stacey and Katey. The two are safe and sound, but Stacey wonders where Sullivan could be—the man was oddly absent during the breach. Chuck decides to look around and find out.

CASE 7-1: BAD TO WORSE

SPOILER!

With the Safe House at last secured, Chuck decides to search around for Sullivan, who was strangely absent during the breach.

Instead, he is surprised to find T.K. free from his handcuffs and being ravaged by a zombie straggler! Acting on instinct, Chuck grabs a fire extinguisher and brains the zombie, saving T.K.'s worthless life. Of course, it's now only a matter of time before the villain turns.

SPOILER!

Back at the clinic, Chuck finds Sullivan nursing a nasty head wound. Apparently T.K. managed to get the better of the

old rascal and may have been responsible for the security breach. T.K. pleads with Chuck to find him some Zombrex—it can't be long before his infection takes hold.

SPOILER!

While deciding his next course of action, Chuck and his comrades catch a news brief that sends shivers up their spines. The news is reporting that the

military found no survivors at Fortune City, so they're proceeding directly with their fallback plan: firebombing the entire quarantine zone! The eradication is set to begin at precisely 7:00 AM.

SPOILER!

Panic takes hold, but cooler heads prevail. Reviewing Rebecca's footage of the military's failed rescue effort, the crew

notices that the mysterious gas had come from beneath the city. Something very strange is going on in those tunnels, and although Sullivan doesn't like the idea, Chuck is determined to investigate.

NOTE

You'll now find queens flying about the Safe House in the wake of the zombie breach. Grab some if you like; they might come in handy.

Don't worry about T.K. for the moment. We'll soon show you a convenient source of Zombrex.

SIDE MISSION: DELTA POINT 1

Scouring the Underground can wait a bit. Drop any firearms you might be carrying, build a couple of fresh spiked bats on your way out of the Safe House, then sprint through Royal Flush Plaza on your way to Fortune Park.

Free of firearms, approach the two soldiers who are making a stand against an onslaught of undead near the park's central grotto. Speak with the men to convince them to accompany Chuck back to the Safe House.

CAUTION

The soldiers will fire on Chuck if he's carrying any sort of firearm. Don't approach the men until you've dropped all of your guns!

One of the soldiers is wounded and can't travel very fast. Lend him a shoulder and speed back to the Safe House, delivering these final two survivors to the bunker.

NOTE

Pat yourself on the back if you've followed the walkthrough flawlessly up to this point—you've just rescued every survivor in Fortune City!

CASE 7-2: THE ONLY LEAD

Construct two new spiked bats on your way out of the Safe House, then take the restroom shortcut to Palisades Mall. Mix up some juice drinks at the grotto and grab the chain saw from behind the bar, carrying it through Yucatan Casino and installing it onto Chuck's motorbike at the Combo Bay as you did before.

Motor into the Underground, following the guide arrow toward your objective. Look for a flashing red light on the tunnel's inside wall near a security gate—this is where you need to go.

TIP

If you wish to save T.K. and need some Zombrex, cruise up the ramp to the west of the security gate and find a dose of the drug just sitting on the high ground.

Park near the control panel to the right of the security gate without fear—the surrounding zombies are more interested in whatever lies beyond the gate than they are in devouring Chuck's flesh. Hop off the bike and examine the panel to open the gate and advance.

WALKTHROUGH

MIND(LESS) CONTROL

SPOILER! After opening the gate, Chuck is surprised when the surrounding zombies calm down and shuffle into the tunnel beyond,

seemingly drawn by some mysterious force. Unhindered by the undead, Chuck cautiously follows suit.

SPOILER! The tunnel leads to a large warehouse with a strange object affixed to the ceiling. The gas seems to be coming from in here!

SPOILER! Chuck isn't the only air-breather down here; he spies a group of armed mercenaries walking along an elevated

catwalk. Just what the heck is going on?

SPOILER! Soon, a horrible, high-pitched noise rings out. The surrounding zombies react badly—within moments, all of their heads

begin to explode in a massive shower of gore, freeing queens that begin madly buzzing about.

Even Chuck is forced to cover his ears at the unnatural sound, but fortunately, his head remains intact. When the noise finally subsides, Chuck watches

in awe as the queens obediently fly into the giant object affixed to the ceiling.

Before Chuck can process what's happening, the mercenaries catch sight of him and open fire. It's fight or flight time, and Chuck Greene never runs from a good fight!

FRANTIC FIREFIGHT

You can't do much against the mercenaries from the low ground. Turn left and sprint for some stairs that lead up to the catwalk.

Dodge Roll your way toward the mercs, beating each one senseless with your trusty spiked bat. Their assault rifle fire is as you've come to expect: rapid but weak. You

should have little trouble securing the warehouse.

> Drop from the catwalk if you need to consume food; it's safer down below.

After neutralizing the mercenaries, chow down on their food to heal up, and feel free to load up on guns and other weapons if you like. (By climbing up to the ceiling

vents, you can obtain a hidden chain saw and broadsword.) When you're ready, follow the guide arrow as it leads you through a circular tunnel, and examine the control panel on the wall beyond to open the nearby door.

DEADRISING 2

LAB RATS

The door leads to a secret lab. Chuck eavesdrops on two lab technicians who are proudly discussing how well things are going with their "tests" in Fortune City. Far from amused, Chuck angrily calls out to the men, who unexpectedly produce handguns and open fire.

You'll likely eat a few bullets at first, as the men have the drop on you. Immediately Dodge Roll toward them, then beat them senseless with your spiked bat. These two pip-squeaks are no match for the wrath of Chuck Greene!

While accessing the men's laptop computer, Chuck discovers the true source of the outbreak: It was the work of the pharmaceutical giant, Phenotrans! Chuck grabs the laptop, along with a nearby transceiver, and also swipes an elevator access card off one of the men. If Rebecca thought she had a story before, she's going to flip when she sees this!

CASE 7-3: WHAT LIES BENEATH

LONG ARM OF THE PHARM'

You've got the evidence you need to blow this conspiracy wide open—you just need to return to the Safe House to put it in Rebecca's capable hands. No need to worry about braving the Underground tunnels again; armed with the Lab Key Card, you can now use the nearby elevator to return to the surface.

You emerge from the elevator in one of the Palisades Mall's maintenance halls. Since you're so close to it, head upstairs and use the shortcut to quickly return to Royal Flush Plaza, then make for the Safe House. Feel free to exploit the grotto bar's blender if you like.

Chuck storms into the security room, eager to show Rebecca his findings. The savvy reporter quickly puts it all together: With fewer and fewer zombie outbreaks, Phenotrans's best-selling drug, Zombrex, isn't in demand like it used to be. Clearly, the pharmaceutical conglomerate has engineered this outbreak to enhance the power of zombies, thereby creating a new crisis designed to stimulate worldwide profits. Diabolical!

Tragically, Rebecca doesn't get the chance to shock the world with her story. As the young reporter begins to phone her radio station, Sullivan puts a bullet through her head. That snake—he's been on Phenotrans's payroll all along!

WALKTHROUGH

SPOILER!

Sullivan has designs on silencing Chuck as well, but Stacey acts fast and knocks his gun from his hand. When Chuck grabs the handgun off the floor, Sullivan takes his opportunity to flee the scene.

THE FACTS

SPOILER!

The awful truth has at last come to light. Pharmaceutical giant Phenotrans, makers of Zombrex, is the true force behind the Fortune City outbreak—and Raymond Sullivan has been working for them all along. Rebecca Chang is dead, killed by Sullivan, who is no doubt trying to escape Fortune City. Little does he realize that Chuck Greene isn't about to let that happen.

> **NOTE**
>
> If you haven't given T.K. his Zombrex yet, go ahead and do so now. Saving T.K.'s life in this fashion allows you to explore the game's special Overtime ending, so swallow your pride and save T.K.

LEVEL UP, CHUCK

With several hours to kill, now is a fantastic time to level up our hero. You need every advantage to beat Sullivan, so use combo weapons against zombies to amass PP, or outfit Chuck's motorbike with a chain saw at the Combo Bay and mow down those ghouls along the strip. Minigames are also good ways to earn PP; see the "Unearthing Fortune City" chapter for a complete breakdown of everything that's available to you in each section of the city.

This is also a perfect time to bring Katey any gifts that you haven't yet given her. You don't have to go far to find these items, and they're each worth significant PP when given to Katey. Only Snowflake and the funny painting that you purchased from Randolph during the "Art Appreciation" side mission were one-time deals—hopefully you were able to give those gifts to Katey when you had the chance. Here's a complete list of the remaining gifts you can give to Chuck's little girl:

GIFTS FOR KATEY		
Got It?	**Gift**	**Location**
☐	Giant stuffed elephant	Stylin' Toddlers on Royal Flush Plaza's first floor.
☐	Robot bear	Astonishing Illusions on Royal Flush Plaza's first floor.
☐	Bag of marbles	Ye Olde Toybox on Royal Flush Plaza's first floor.
☐	Beach ball	Ye Olde Toybox on Royal Flush Plaza's first floor.
☐	Stick Pony	Ye Olde Toybox on Royal Flush Plaza's first floor.
☐	Water gun	The watery areas of Fortune Park; also found in Moe's Maginations on the Platinum Strip.
☐	Giant stuffed bull	Children's Castle on Royal Flush Plaza's second floor.
☐	Giant stuffed donkey	Children's Castle on Royal Flush Plaza's second floor.
☐	Giant stuffed rabbit	The hidden upper platforms of Americana Casino's and Royal Flush Plaza's second floor; also found in Moe's Maginations on the Platinum Strip.

> **NOTE**
>
> If you're not certain which gifts you've given to Katey, simply look around the Safe House's security room to find them all on display.
>
> You no longer need to carry the *Rescue* magazine after you've given all gifts to Katey; there are no other survivor-related activities for you to fulfill.

DEADRISING 2

TO KILL A CRETIN

Sullivan can't be allowed to escape—the blood of countless innocents is on his hands, including poor Rebecca's. The madman must be made to pay for his heinous crimes.

Hurry out of the Safe House and into Royal Flush Plaza. Sullivan is nowhere in sight, and Chuck calls Stacey to ask if she can spot him. She promises to keep watch over the security monitors and let Chuck know if she sees the scoundrel.

GEARING UP

It goes without saying that you'll need lots of powerful curatives on hand for the final battle. Take the shortcut to Palisades Mall, mixing up as many Pain Killers as you can carry at the central grotto.

Long-range weapons are also vital to succeeding in the final encounter, so use this time to track some down. There's an LMG on one of the grotto's lower grassy ledges, and two shotguns can be acquired from the High-Noon Shooting Range on Palisades Mall's second floor. You only need one good melee weapon to help you reach Sullivan, so fill the rest of Chuck's inventory with ranged weapons and curatives.

> **TIP**
>
> Nab the *Health 2* magazine from the bar in Yucatan Casino's Baron Von Brathaus restaurant if you haven't already—it doubles the potency of all healing items.

The fire spitter combo weapon is another fine option against Sullivan. Find two tiki torches inside Palisades Mall's central grotto and an endless supply of toy spitball

guns within the nearby Ultimate Playhouse store. Merge these together at any maintenance room to form a pair of fire spitters.

Stacey eventually pinpoints Sullivan's location: He's awaiting evac on the roof of the Yucatan Casino. Streak off to confront him once you're happy with your array of ranged weapons and curatives.

> **TIP**
>
> Save at Yucatan Casino's restroom in case things go poorly up there on the roof.

Sullivan has hacked the casino's elevator to reach the rooftop. Eliminate the zombies inside the elevator, then use its interior control panel to ride up.

The lift doesn't quite go all the way up to the roof—you need to fight your way through more zombies to get there. Use your lone melee weapon to beat the undead out

of your path as you follow the guide arrow upstairs to a door. Ensure that Chuck is in good health before passing through to reach the final battle.

WALKTHROUGH

SLAYING SULLIVAN

SPOILER!

Up on the Yucatan's roof, Sullivan passionately explains his motives for doing what he's done. The madman believes that the Fortune City outbreak, while tragic, has been for the greater good.

SPOILER!

Chuck isn't buying into Sullivan's pathetic excuses. By assisting Phenotrans in their revolting scheme, the villain has been responsible for countless deaths. He murdered Rebecca Chang in cold blood and would have done the same to Chuck if it hadn't been for Stacey's interference. Raymond Sullivan *will* be made to pay.

The fight against Sullivan is chaotic. Zombies get in your way on the ground, and Sullivan rains down bullets from his elevated central vantage, and he also tosses flares

that cause the overhead gunship to fire devastating blasts. To reduce the odds of being accosted by undead, scamper up onto the scaffolding near Sullivan's perch.

Sullivan has a clear shot at you while you stand on the scaffolding, but he's got a clear shot of you *anywhere*. Do your best to remain on the scaffolding as

you unload your favorite ranged weapon on the villain.

TIP

Leap from the scaffolding to combat Sullivan on his level, but beware his fast melee attacks and counters. Use Chuck's own hand-to-hand special moves to drop Sullivan to one knee, then quickly follow up with additional attacks.

Punish Sullivan as often as you can, holding the Aim button and tracking him as he tucks and rolls to avoid your long-range fire. When you need to heal, fall from your perch and hug Sullivan's—this gives you the best chance of consuming food without being shot.

CAUTION

The overhead gunship will blast holes through the casino's rooftop, revealing masses of undead in the area below. Flee from any targeting flares that Sullivan hurls at you, but be careful not to fall through a hole—you'll have to fight your way back up.

As long as you don't run out of ammo, you shouldn't have much trouble blasting Sullivan to bits. If all of your clips run dry, start throwing things at the villain—even an

empty gun can deal some damage if you score a hit!

NOTE

There are lots of restoratives around the rooftop, but as Sullivan hurls explosives, many will be blown away. Don't miss your chance to grab them while you can!

GAME OVER, RAY

SPOILER!

Having at last defeated the double-crossing dog, Chuck uses the transceiver he stole from the underground lab technicians to call Rebecca Chang's former employer, Channel 6 Action News, with the scoop of a lifetime.

DEADRISING 2

SPOILER!

With new evidence of lingering survivors, the military firebombing of Fortune City is temporarily withheld. It's not long before evac choppers arrive instead, landing on the Safe House's rooftop to whisk away the shaken survivors.

SPOILER!

The rest of the tale depends on you, dear reader. If you failed to give T.K. his dose of Zombrex, then Chuck Greene's fate becomes lost in the pages of history. However, if you took mercy on the ungrateful game show host, turn the page to find out what lies in store for Chuck next....

OVERTIME

No good deed goes unpunished. If you saved T.K.'s miserable life by giving him a shot of Zombrex before defeating Sullivan, then you're treated to a special epilogue ending called Overtime—but it isn't what you might expect.

Having saved the day and proven his innocence, Chuck Greene returns to the Safe House with an evac chopper. Everyone's glad to be getting out of Fortune City—but Stacey and little Katey are nowhere to be found!

Chuck searches the entire Safe House, but finds only Katey's backpack. Distraught, the broken father remains in the city, watching the Safe House's security monitors for any trace of Stacey or his beloved little girl.

Suddenly, an all-too-familiar voice rings out over Chuck's transceiver. It's T.K., and—surprise, surprise—he's not calling to thank his savior. Instead, T.K. has kidnapped Stacey and Katey, and he demands that Chuck retrieve a number of precious valuables scattered all throughout Fortune City before he'll let them go. Scavenger hunt, anyone?

WORKIN' OVERTIME

Fortunately, each of T.K.'s items is very easy to track down. Arm yourself with a couple of spiked bats and plenty of food, then head out in search of T.K.'s loot. Just tune your guide arrow to the first item on the list and work your way down to the last, and you'll collect them all in one swift counterclockwise lap around the city.

> **NOTE**
>
> T.K.'s items are marked by purple icons to help you easily identify them when you approach.

The only tricky item to nab is the case of queens, located in the Underground near the secret lab. To get it, hop over the catwalk's red railing to reach a narrow platform, then leap over to the case of queens' platform and collect the valuable.

After you acquire all of T.K.'s goodies, the villain demands that you bring him the loot in person. Don't worry about stocking up for battle; it won't do you any good. Just head for Fortune City Arena to confront T.K., saving your game at the Americana Casino restroom en route.

WALKTHROUGH

T.K. ambushes Chuck when he reaches the arena, zapping him with a cattle prod until Chuck loses consciousness. This can't be good....

FEAR OF HEIGHTS

When Chuck finally awakes, he finds himself strung upside down, dangling above a mass of zombies inside the arena. Stacey and Katey are in a similar predicament, and it appears that T.K. is running the show.

While T.K. gloats his glorious victory, Chuck acts fast and begins pulling himself up the rope, climbing to the arena's upper catwalks. T.K. hadn't expected Chuck to be so resourceful and rushes to confront his nemesis in an epic finale.

SHOWSTOPPER

At long last, Chuck has a chance to get revenge on T.K.—but he'll need to act fast, or Stacey and his little girl will become zombie food.

First things first: T.K. has relieved Chuck of all of his weapons, so you'll need to find one pronto. Sprint to one side and climb up onto one of the steel walls to locate a lead pipe. This will have to do.

NOTE

A large wrench is another ideal weapon, but you can only find these beyond the steel walls. T.K. unleashes painful pyrotechnics if you venture beyond the walls, so it's best not to risk it.

TIP

Use the Dodge Roll skill to avoid T.K.'s attacks, but don't expect it to save Chuck from those searing pyrotechnics.

Next on the list is food. Drop from the metal wall and make a run around the central crank, grabbing the few cartons of orange juice that lie near piles of cardboard boxes. Jump onto the cardboard boxes as well to quickly bust them open, potentially revealing more curatives.

Once you've got a weapon and some food, stand your ground near the central crank, waiting for T.K. to appear and attack. Dodge T.K.'s vicious blows and retaliate with relentless pipe or wrench strikes before he flees. Strive to land multiple hits during each exchange.

NOTE

Keep an eye on Stacey and Katey's height meter, but don't bother turning the crank to raise them unless it's absolutely necessary. Focus on pounding T.K. to a pulp instead.

TIP

If T.K. is being bashful, start turning the crank to get him to appear—then quickly let go and fight.

157

FORTUNATE ENDING

T.K. has some nasty moves—if he hits Chuck while charging, he'll grab onto Chuck and unleash a series of strong attacks. Use the Dodge Roll to avoid being grabbed. If this doesn't work, counter T.K.'s assaults by quickly imitating the series of onscreen commands, thereby minimizing the damage and breaking free.

Having had his fill of Mr. King's games, Chuck hurls the villain off the high platform—a fall that no one could hope to survive.

With T.K.'s guts decorating the floor below, Chuck hurriedly turns the crank, elevating Stacey and little Katey out of danger. The three have been through quite an ordeal here at Fortune City, but they've managed to survive the countless horrors and to save every possible outbreak survivor along the way. Chuck's good name has been restored, and those who have wronged him have been made to pay the ultimate price. Now that's what we call a happy ending!

Continue to dodge T.K.'s attacks and counter with blows of your own, tuning T.K. up until the brute is at last defeated.

"TERROR IS REALITY"

It's America's hottest game show—the spectacle that's sweeping the nation. It's "Terror Is Reality!" Who needs population control when hopped-up contestants are ready to slaughter zombies by the truckload for fame and prizes? Just remember: You've got to be willing to risk it all if you're ever—really—gonna—*win big*!

GENERAL STRATEGIES

"Terror Is Reality" is a chaotic show, and a certain level of luck plays into your chances of success. Tip the odds in your favor, however, by keeping the following tips in mind:

1. **Play it cool**. Although each event is a messy affair, keeping your wits about you is vital. Stay sharp, be strategic, and don't lose your head out there.

2. **Work fast**. Keeping your cool is key, but so is speed. Don't dally about out there; work quickly and decisively.

3. **Go for multipliers**. Most TIR events allow you to boost your score quickly through multipliers or the killing of special "bonus zombies"—this is vital to success. See each event's section to learn how to score big in each game.

4. **Fight dirty**. It's possible to harass and impede your rivals' progress in many TIR events. Do this whenever the chance permits to upset your opponents' game plans, particularly the current point leader.

5. **Never say die**. Each TIR event is vastly different from the rest, so don't worry if you score poorly in a certain game. The winner of the show will be the player with the highest score at the end of all challenges, so simply strive to remain competitive—you just might come out on top in the end.

TIR EVENTS

In "Terror Is Reality," four players are pitted against each other in a series of frantic, white-knuckle events. You never know what challenges the show's host, Tyrone "T.K." King, is going to feel like putting on for the crowd, so the first four games are always selected for you at random. However, every "Terror Is Reality" episode concludes with a thrilling round of Slicecycles, wherein anyone can jump from zero to hero—provided they're willing to risk it all!

NOTE

The cash you earn at the end of each "Terror Is Reality" contest is deposited into Chuck's savings and made usable in your single-player/co-op adventure. The winnings add up fast, so it pays to play America's hottest game show!

BALL BUSTER

Lock and load—it's time to bust some balls! In Ball Buster, all four players take aim at a wall of doors. Zombies are thrust out of these doors at random, serving as immobile targets. Players must strive to shoot as many zombies as possible, earning points for each kill.

These zombies are worth special rewards to the first player who shoots them! When shot, a bonus zombie either gives the shooter extra points or rapid fire, or it does nothing for the shooter but instead causes all other player's guns to jam.

TIP

Shooting bonus zombies is the key to victory in Ball Buster, so strive to shoot every one.

Don't freak out if your gun ever jams up; just quickly press the series of buttons shown onscreen to get it working again.

It helps to focus on your half of the wall in Ball Buster. Don't aim at zombies across the way; it takes time to aim accurately and your rivals will often be able to fire before you. Simply focus on zombies that are more or less directly ahead of you. This is a particularly effective tactic as the game draws toward its conclusion and lots of zombies are thrust out from the doors.

TERROR IS REALITY

BOUNTY HUNTER

There's a bounty on those filthy zombies' heads, so take aim and get ready to blow 'em clean off! In Bounty Hunter, all four players fire down at a swarm of zombies that emerge from four separate doors. The zombies run blindly toward a central meat grinder—hurry and shoot them before they get there for points!

Make each shot count in Bounty Hunter—firing recklessly causes you to miss more often than not. Make sure to blast those bonus zombies, which have pink balls attached to their heads—they're worth extra points! You don't need to hit the pink balls themselves; just shooting the bonus zombie earns you the points.

TIP

Aim at clusters of zombies whenever possible to potentially score multiple kills with each shot.

Heads up: a special "jackpot" target activates several times over the course of Bounty Hunter, and shooting this target is the key to victory. The moment you're told that the jackpot is active, aim at the top of the central grinder and shoot that rotating target to score big! You can hit the target from any angle, as long as your aim is true.

TIP

Rather than "chasing" the jackpot target, simply rest your crosshairs in its path of travel and shoot the target as it travels past. It may feel like you're wasting a bit of time waiting for the target, but you're far less likely to miss this way.

After one player hits the jackpot target, all other players' vision is impaired by a barricade that rises all around them. The barricades drop after a few seconds, but don't just stand around waiting when you're blocked—move so that you can continue to shoot zombies through the tiny gaps in those steel walls!

HEADACHE

What's better than a fistful of aspirin? Headache, the event that has zombies losing their minds! In this unique challenge, all players must rush to slap special hats atop the heads of the surrounding undead. After placing a number of hats, players must rush to hit a "Trigger" button, causing their hats to activate and grind up those undead heads for points!

The hats are located at the central "pick-up" station, and the Trigger buttons (there are two of them) are found at either end of the arena. Grab your hats at the start of the event, then run around and start placing them onto zombies.

Each hat you place is worth points. Slap on those hats in quick succession to gain a vital score multiplier!

After placing all of your hats, run to the nearest Trigger button and hit it to slaughter your zombies, scoring big points. Or forego pressing the button in favor of grabbing more hats and placing even more of them onto zombies. The more hats you're able to set off at once, the bigger the score multiplier when you hit that button!

NOTE

The multiplier begins after you place your fourth hat and is always shown beneath the scores on the left side of the screen.

Don't go too crazy with those hats, however. All players begin with a stick of dynamite, which they may use at any time to wipe out a cluster of zombies. If you see a lot of hat-wearing zombies that aren't "yours," toss your dynamite into the throng, or run up and shove it into the mouth of a hatless zombie for an even more precise detonation. Obliterating your rivals' hat-wearing zombies with dynamite prevents them from scoring big points!

NOTE

You can carry only one stick of dynamite at a time. If you're out of dynamite, you'll automatically grab another stick when you go back to the center for more hats.

You can't use your dynamite while carrying hats, so it's best to slap on your hats, use your dynamite, then grab more hats and dynamite, and repeat the sequence. Don't risk waiting too long to hit that Trigger button, though—your rivals are certain to catch on and blast your hat-wearing zombies before long!

MASTER SHAFTER

Zombie killing plays a backseat role in Master Shafter, where contestants do battle with one another directly. In Master Shafter, zombies are periodically shot into the arena by surrounding cannons—look for orange targets on the ground, which indicate where the undead will land. Race to those spaces and prepare to impale those falling zombies with your massive shaft!

Once you arrive at a target, press the indicated button to hold your lance-like shaft firmly toward the heavens. It won't be long before a zombie falls on it!

Look out, though—any rival that moves close to you is able to challenge your position, and vice-versa. When such a challenge occurs, a fierce battle takes place: press the onscreen buttons as fast as you can, hammering out the string of commands faster than your rival to seize the advantage!

TIP

Look ahead in the button string to prepare for upcoming buttons, rattling them off as quickly as you can.

TIP

Don't seize up if you make a mistake! Press the proper button to get back on track, then get back in the zone and bash off that combo.

TERROR IS REALITY

The player that's quicker at hitting those buttons ends up the victor, knocking the rival off the target and impaling the inbound zombie for points. Give zombies the shaft without failing in duels against other players to build your score!

Targets only appears two at a time, so you'll often be fighting opponents for each kill. However, it's possible for three players to lock up in a struggle over a single target; when this happens and if you're not involved, take advantage and impale zombies without fear of being challenged!

CAUTION

Avoid joining in a contest between two players. If you get locked in a contest, the remaining player can impale zombies unhindered and gather up points, which isn't good for you!

POUNDS OF FLESH

Ground-up zombies make excellent dog food, and in this unique challenge, contestants are paid by the pound! Players don specialized helmets in Pounds of Flesh, using them to fling zombies onto a central scale. Points are scored for every undead ounce, so go after the fat zombies first!

Charging at those filthy zombies is the key to success in Pounds of Flesh. Don't use the single-zombie flick move; instead, hold the Attack button to rush

the zombies, releasing the button just as you collide with the hoard. Timing your charges properly this way ensures that multiple zombies are flung to the central scale!

TIP

Take a few steps forward to line yourself up before holding the Attack button to charge. This way, you won't have to adjust your approach while charging (which is difficult).

After hoisting some zombies onto the scale, immediately run back to the starting position and charge 'em again! Or, if your herd is thinning, hit the Reload button to receive a fresh load. You can hit the Reload button as often as you like, so don't waste time charging at thin crowds.

TIP

If you're surrounded after a charge, jump to quickly escape from the throng of zombies.

RAMSTERBALL

One of TIR's most beloved events, Ramsterball has all four contestants rocking and rolling inside of giant, indestructible balls. The object: Steal the "power" away from other players, hoarding it for yourself so you may score points!

DEADRISING 2

One player is selected at random to begin the game of Ramsterball with the "power." You can clearly tell who has the power at any given time—their ball glows as if electrically charged.

If you don't have the power, ram the player who does to steal it! You've got to hit them with a bit of force to steal the power away.

TIP

If you don't begin the game with the power, try rolling toward the rival who has it and see if you can steal it away at the very start of the event! It's possible to ram opponents before they even have a chance to roll off the starting platform.

Once you've stolen the power, immediately look to bounce into the many posts around the arena—doing so scores you points. The key to scoring big in Ramsterball lies in bouncing from post to post like a pinball, so after slamming into one post, use your equal and opposite momentum to hit another—and try to keep that combo going!

TIP

Avoid chasing players who have the power—catching them can be tough. Slow down and look to cut them off instead.

You're a prime target after you've stolen the power, so hold the Sprint trigger and put some distance between you and your rivals. Keep to the outside to gain speed, then make a sudden move for the middle to give pursuers the slip. Start bouncing off those posts—it's easiest to hit several when you keep to the center.

Hitting zombies while you've got the power increases the amount of points you'll score when you hit a post, but don't bother aiming for them. You'll likely hit the undead anyway, so simply aim for those posts and try to bounce off as many as you can each time you get the power. Bouncing back and fourth between just two posts can boost your score fast.

STAND UP ZOMEDY

If you're looking for laughs, look no further than Stand Up Zomedy! Players battle to decorate zombies in this lighthearted affair, striving to plant as many comedic "prop" items on the roaming undead as they can. Each prop item you place scores you some points!

There are three different prop items: flowers, dresses, and unicorns. Rush to a prop dispenser to claim some of these items, then quickly start slapping them onto nearby zombies. Decorate those undead quickly as you struggle to keep the lead!

TERROR IS REALITY

NOTE

You receive four of the same prop whenever you claim some from the dispensers. The dispensers are clearly marked with the type of prop they'll give you.

NOTE

If a rival has decorated a zombie with a certain item, you can't counter them with the same item. You can only block a rival from earning the "Pretty Dress" bonus by decorating their zombies with a different sort of decoration.

If you manage to decorate a zombie with all three items, you get a significant "Pretty Dress" bonus. Strive to claim these bonuses—they're the key to victory. Prevent your rivals from achieving this bonus by sticking your decorations on "their" zombies!

Block any rival zombies you're able to (particularly those that the point leader is working on), but focus primarily on decking out zombies with all three props. Earn those "Pretty Dress" bonuses to entertain the crowd and amp up your score!

GRAND FINALE: SLICECYCLES

All TIR shows end with a white-knuckle round of America's favorite event, Slicecycles! In this grueling grande finale, all four contestants ride souped-up motorbikes with chain saws attached to their handles. An arena filled with undead stretches out ahead—gentlemen, start your engines!

Speed back and forth along the arena, aiming to run down as many hapless zombies as possible. Don't worry about collisions with other racers; you can't be harmed in a crash, only knocked off course or slowed down a bit.

Depending on how well you've fared up to this point in the show, you may suffer a slight time penalty before you're able to join in the Slicecycle mayhem. The lower your current score, the longer you have to wait. Don't worry; the penalty is minimal, for it's impossible to score big until the Bonus Round.

The key to succeeding in Slicecycles lies in mastering the art of the turn. After making a run down the arena (lengthwise, of course, to ensure you kill the most zombies with each pass), simultaneously turn and begin feathering the brake. The idea is to gain only a bit of height up the ramped outer edges so that you quickly build speed as you come out of the turn.

DEADRISING 2

Another sound strategy is to turn before you reach the arena's outer ramps, keeping as close to the undead mob as possible. Again, feather the brake as you turn to perform a powerslide instead of coming to a dead stop. If your bike is coming to a complete stop while changing direction, you're wasting precious seconds with each turn, which add up over the course of the game.

Strive to strike as many of those balloon-toting bonus zombies as possible—they're the key to victory. If you see a huge crowd, slow down and try to mow them all down, feathering the brake to make tight turns. Even the slightest contact is enough to kill these poor souls!

The Bonus Round kicks off before long. Many more zombies are deployed to the arena by overhead drop pods. Look for clusters of zombies that carry pink balloons and slaughter them all for huge score bonuses!

Because the zombies are deposited at random, luck plays a role in your Slicecycle success. Sometimes you'll get on a great run. Other times, you'll find you're always out of position while your rivals run away with the victory. Keep your cool and do your best to score as high as you can—a vast amount of points can be won from this final event, and losing the lead is easy if you don't stay competitive!

APPENDIX

If you're looking for fast answers, you've come to the right place. These final tables reveal everything you could possibly want to know about *Dead Rising 2*, including quick info on all Case Files and side missions, tips for attaining all Achievements and Trophies, a complete location list to help you track down all weapons, clothing, food, magazines, and combo cards, and a handy juice drink chart that shows how food items can be blended into potent and beneficial beverages.

CASE FILES

The following table reveals how to complete each Case File, along with their time frames. We've taken steps to avoid revealing any major plot spoilers.

CASE FILES	
Case Name	**Description**
Zombrex 1	"The Zombrex 1 case will automatically start after completing the introductory (tutorial) mission. Chuck must give Katey Zombrex between 7:00 AM and 8:00 AM on Day 1. "
Case 1-1	Case 1-1 will automatically start after completing Zombrex 1. The mission starts at 9:00 AM. This case is completed after watching the cinematic.
Case 1-2	"Case 1-2 starts after completing Case 1-1. Chuck must go to the Fortune City Hotel lobby to Complete Case 1-2. The end time for Case 1-2 is 5:00 PM on Day 1."
Case 1-3	"Case 1-3 starts after completing Case 1-2. Chuck must escort Rebecca to the security office in the arena to complete case 1-3. The end time for Case 1-3 is 5:00 PM on Day 1."
Case 1-4	"Case 1-4 starts after completing Case 1-3. Chuck must go to the security room in the Safe House to complete Case 1-4. The end time for Case 1-4 is 5:00 PM on Day 1."
Case 2-1	Case 2-1 starts at 7:30 PM on Day 1. Chuck must go to the Safe House security room before 8:30 PM on Day 1 to complete the mission.
Case 2-2	"Case 2-2 starts after completing Case 2-1. Chuck must first go to the Underground through an Underground access door in Palisades Mall. Chuck will encounter some mercenaries and will have to defeat them. Chuck must then chase down more mercenaries on a motorbike. Chuck must jump the bike onto the getaway train. After getting on the train, Chuck must fight through the mercenaries to get to the end of the train. Reaching the end of the train will complete Case 2-2. Chuck will receive the Underground Access Key for beating Case 2. The end time for Case 2-2 is 5:30 AM on Day 2."
Zombrex 2	"The Zombrex 2 mission starts at 7:00 AM on Day 2. Chuck must find Katey Zombrex and give it to her between 7:00 AM and 8:00 AM on Day 2. Zombrex can be found through completing side missions. It is also hidden around the city and can be bought at pawnshops."
Case 3-1	Case 3-1 starts at 10:00 AM on Day 2. Chuck must go to the Safe House security room before 11:00 AM on Day 2 to complete the mission.
Case 3-2	"Case 3-2 starts after completing Case 3-1. Chuck's objective is to destroy three drills. The three drills are located in the vaults of the Americana Casino, the Slot Ranch Casino, and the Yucatan Casino. Once all three drills are destroyed, Chuck will need to destroy an armored van outside of the Atlantica Casino in Fortune Park. Destroying the van will complete Case 3-2. The end time for Case 3-2 is 9:00 PM on Day 2."
Case 4-1	"Case 4-1 Starts at 11:00 PM on Day 2. Chuck will need to go to Shoal Night Club in the Yucatan Casino. Chuck will have to fight and defeat a pair of dangerous bosses to complete Case 4-1. Only one of these bosses needs to be defeated to end the battle. The end time for Case 4-1 is 3:00 AM on Day 3."

CASE FILES (CONT.)

Case Name	Description
Zombrex 3	"The Zombrex 3 mission starts at 7:00 AM on Day 3. Chuck must find Katey Zombrex and give it to her between 7:00 AM and 8:00 AM on Day 3. Zombrex can be found through completing side missions. It is also hidden around the city and can be bought at pawnshops."
Case 5-1	Case 5-1 starts at 7:00 PM on Day 3. Chuck must be on the Safe House rooftop before 8:00 PM on Day 3 to complete Case 5-1.
Case 5-2	"Case 5-2 starts after completing Case 5-1. Chuck's first objective is to go to the Fortune City Hotel. Chuck must fight and defeat several mercenary body guards in the lobby. After defeating the guards, Chuck must go to the hotel rooftop and battle a boss that is aboard a helicopter. Destroying the helicopter by throwing objects at it will complete Case 5-2. The end time for Case 5-2 is 4:00 AM on Day 4."
Zombrex 4	"The Zombrex 4 mission starts at 7:00 AM on Day 4. Chuck must find Katey Zombrex and give it to her between 7:00 AM and 8:00 AM on Day 4. Zombrex can be found through completing side missions. It is also hidden around the city and can be bought at pawnshops."
Case 6-1	Case 6-1 starts at 9:00 AM on Day 4. Chuck must go to the Safe House security room before 10:00 AM on Day 4 to complete the mission.
Case 6-2	"Case 6-2 starts after completing Case 6-1. Chuck must go to Warehouse D in the Underground. The entrance is located in the Silver Strip. Once Chuck reached Warehouse D, he must fight a boss. Defeating the boss ends Case 6-2. The end time for Case 6-2 is 5:00 PM on Day 4."
Case 6-3	"Case 6-3 starts after beating Case 6-2. Chuck must escort Rebecca back to the Safe House. Getting Rebecca to the Safe House will complete Case 6-3. The end time for Case 6-3 is 5:00 PM on Day 4."
Case 6-4	"Case 6-4 starts after completing case 6-3. Chuck must gather 3 items and place them next to the broken panel in the Safe House. Chuck must collect a Spool of Wire, Gasoline Barrel and a Generator. Bringing all 3 items back will allow Chuck to complete Case 6-4. The end time for case 6-4 is 5:00 PM on Day 4."
Zombrex 5	Zombrex 5 is an optional mission where Chuck can give a special character Zombrex. The special character is located in the Medical Room in the Safe House. Chuck must give the special character Zombrex to get Overtime mode.
Case 7-1	Case 7-1 start automatically after completing case 6-4. Case 7-1 completes after watching the cinematic.
Case 7-2	"Case 7-2 starts after completing Case 7-1. Chuck must go to the Underground and find the labs. Chuck will enter the labs and must make his way to the upper lab area where he will encounter two easy bosses. Chuck must defeat the two bosses to complete Case 7-2. The end time for Case 7-2 is 12:00 AM on Day 5."
Case 7-3	"Case 7-3 starts after completing Case 7-2. Chuck must go back to the Safe House security room to complete Case 7-3. The end time for Case 7-3 is 12:00 AM on Day 5."
The Facts	"The Facts start after Case 7-3 is completed. Chuck must follow the boss to the Yucatan Casino's rooftop. The elevator is located by the bathrooms in the Yucatan Casino. Chuck must defeat the boss atop the roof to complete the Facts. The end time for the Facts is 7:00 AM on Day 5."
Overtime	"Overtime will start if the Facts have been completed and Zombrex has been given to the aforementioned special character. Chuck will need to find items for the special character. Once all the items are collected, Chuck must go to the arena and interact with the west entrance doors. This will start a special boss fight that Chuck cannot bring any food or weapons into. Chuck must defeat the boss to complete Overtime."

APPENDIX

SIDE MISSIONS

The following table lists all the side missions, along with their availability time frames. Complete every side mission to encounter all characters, defeat each psycho, and rescue all survivors, thereby filling Chuck's notebook while attaining a number of Achievements and Trophies.

SIDE MISSIONS		
Scoop Name	**Type**	**Description**
Snowflake Boss Battle	Psycho Fight	"Snowflake and Ted are found in the Yucatan Casino. A survivor named Lenny is hiding in the Yucatan Casino's VIP room. Lenny will not join until Snowflake has been killed or tamed. To tame Snowflake you must feed her three steaks. Snowflake then becomes a follower and can be given to Katey as a gift. This Psycho is available from 7:00 AM on Day 1 through 10:00 AM on Day 2. "
Happily Ever After Sort Of	Stranded Survivors	"LaShawndra and Gordon are found in Royal Flush Plaza. LaShawndra can be found in the Dark Bean Coffee Shop and Gordon is in Casual Gals. Talk to both of them to get them to join. This side mission is available from 6:45 AM to 3:45 PM on Day 1."
Pawnshop Scoop	Special	"A non-hostile looter is found in Moe's Maginations in Platinum Strip. Talk to the looter to unlock all the pawnshops. This side mission is available from 9:00 AM on Day 1 through 12:00PM on Day 5. "
Lost	Stranded Survivors	"Chad and Doris can be found on the Platinum Strip. Chad will be roaming near Dining at Davey's and Doris can be found near the arena entrance. Doris will not join until Chad has been brought to her. This side mission is available from 9:10 AM to 10:10 PM on Day 1."
Short Sighted	Stranded Survivors	"Esther can be found in the Children's Castle store in Royal Flush Plaza. Talk to her to get her to join. Esther will move slowly but Chuck can carry her. This side mission is available from 10:00 AM to 7:30 PM on Day 1."
Welcome to the Family	Stranded Survivors	"Jack and Kenneth are found in Shank's in the Palisades Mall. Help Kenneth kill all the zombies, then talk to Jack to get the two survivors to join. This side mission is available from 11:00 AM to 7:00 PM on Day 1."
Workers Compensation	Stranded Survivors	"Brittany and Stuart are found in the Americana Casino. Stuart will attack Chuck; fight back until Stuart surrenders to get the two survivors to join. This side mission is available from 1:00 PM to 10:00 PM on Day 1."
Lush-ious Lady	Stranded Survivors	"Kristin is located in the security office in Americana Casino. Talk to her to get her to join. Kristin will move slowly but Chuck can carry her. This side mission is available from 2:00 PM on Day 1 through 2:30 AM on Day 2. "
Meet the Contestants	Psycho Fight	"Leon's boss battle can be triggered by walking to the bike display in front of the arena in the Platinum Strip. This gives Chuck the Bike Key. The fight with Leon will take place in Fortune Park. Killing him will unlock the Combo Bay in the Silver Strip near the Yucatan Casino entrance. This psycho is available from 2:30 PM on Day 1 through 8:30 AM on Day 2."
Brains Over Brawn	Stranded Survivors	"John, Kevin, Curtis, and Brian can be found in South Plaza. Talk to John to get them to join. They will join instantly if there is a female survivor already with Chuck. This side mission is available from 3:30 PM on Day 1 through 2:00 AM on Day 2."
Chuck the Role Model	Psycho Fight	"Brandon's boss battle will start by entering the bathroom in the Americana Casino. Talk to Vikki after killing Brandon to get her to join. This psycho is available from 5:00 PM on Day 1 through 12:00 PM on Day 2."
Barn Burner	Stranded Survivors	"Elrod and Trixie-Lyn are found in the back hallways of the Arena. There is a wall of fire that must be put out with a fire extinguisher to get to them. Talk to Elrod after the fire is out for them to join. This side mission is available from 5:00 PM on Day 1 through 2:00 AM on Day 2."

www.primagames.com

DEADRISING 2

Scoop Name	Type	Description
Once Bitten	Stranded Survivors	"Jared can be found in Wily Travels in Royal Flush Plaza (second floor). Chuck needs to give him a dose of Zombrex before Jared will join. Jared will be wounded but Chuck can carry him. This side mission is available from 7:35 PM on Day 1 through 8:35 AM on Day 2."
Code Blue	Stranded Survivors	"Sven is located in One Little Duck Bingo on the Silver Strip. Talk to Sven to get him to join. Sven will give Chuck some Zombrex when returned to the Safe House. This side mission is available from 10:00 PM on Day 1 through 7:00 AM on Day 2."
Tastes Like Chicken	Psycho Fight	"Chef Antoine's boss battle starts by entering the Cucina Donnacci restaurant in the Food Court. Defeat him to open the freezer door where Cinda can be found. She will not leave until Jasper is brought to her. He is located on the Food Court's upper platforms above Burger Fiefdom. This psycho is available from 10:30 PM on Day 1 through 8:30 PM on Day 2. "
An Industrial Fashion	Stranded Survivors	"Terri and Willa are found in South Plaza. Terri will not join until Willa is brought to her. Willa will be wounded but Chuck can carry her. This side mission is available from 3:00 AM to 3:30 PM on Day 2."
Rock Heroes	Stranded Survivors	"Jeanna, Allen, and Floyd are found on the stage in the Silver Strip. Talk to Jeanna to get them to join. Floyd will give Chuck the power guitar combo card when returned to the Safe House. This side mission is available from 4:00 AM to 3:00 PM on Day 2. "
Shopping Spree	Stranded Survivors	"Bessie, Rosa, and Erica are located in Kathy's Space in Royal Flush Plaza. Chuck must carry the girls' shopping boxes for them to follow. This side mission is available from 8:00 AM to 4:00 PM on Day 2. "
Everyone Knows Slappy	Psycho Fight	"Slappy's boss battle starts by interacting with the dead female mascot next to Kid's Choice Clothing in Palisades Mall. Chuck receives the flamethrower combo card after defeating Slappy. This psycho is available from 12:00 PM on Day 2 through 3:00 AM on Day 3. "
Wilted Flower	Stranded Survivors	"Linette is located in Venus Touch Spa in Palisades Mall. She will not join until she is brought a drink. After she joins, a new mission will trigger (""Linette's Passage"") that will show a shortcut to Royal Flush Plaza. Bring Linette to the Brand New U store in Palisades to unlock the shortcut. This side mission is available from 12:30 to 5:30 on Day 2. "
Here Comes the Groom	Psycho Fight	"Randy's boss battle will start by interacting with the doors of the Swept Away Wedding Chapel in the Silver Strip. Talk to the Danni (the bride) after killing Randy to get her to join. This psycho is available from 5:00 PM on Day 2 through 9:00 AM on Day 3. "
Janus Survivor	Stranded Survivors	"Janus is located outside the entrance to the Atlantica Casino in Fortune Park. He will not join unless Chuck has a gun in his inventory. Chuck will receive bonus money for bringing Janus to the Safe House. This side mission is available from 7:00 PM on Day 2 through 9:00 AM on Day 3."
Par For the Course	Stranded Survivors	"Luz is located in SporTrance in Royal Flush Plaza. Help her kill all the zombies around her to get her to join. This side mission is available from 8:00 PM on Day 2 through 3:00 AM on Day 3."
Stuart's Scheme	Special	"This side mission will occur only if Stuart was rescued. Stuart is located in the Safe House. Chuck will need to talk to him or else there will be a mutiny in which several survivors will leave the Safe House for good. This side mission is available from 9:30 PM on Day 2 through 2:30 PM on Day 3."
Mail Order Zombrex	Psycho Fight	"Carl's boss battle will start by interacting with the mail cart in Royal Flush Plaza. Defeating Carl will get you a dose of Zombrex. This psycho is available from 11:00 PM on Day 2 through 2:00 PM on Day 3."
High Rollers	Stranded Survivors	"Jessica, Jacob, and Nevada are located in the poker room in the Atlantica Casino. Chuck must beat all three players in Texas Hold 'Em to get them to join. Chuck will also be awarded $1,000,000 for beating them. This side mission is available from 1:00 AM to 1:00 PM on Day 3."

APPENDIX

	SIDE MISSIONS (CONT.)	
Scoop Name	**Type**	**Description**
Hunger Pains	Stranded Survivors	"Richard is found in Dining at Davey's in the Platinum Strip. He will not join until he is given a food item. Richard will give Chuck some Zombrex when he returns to the Safe House. This side mission is available from 2:00 AM to 10:00 AM on Day 3."
Fetching Females	Stranded Survivors	"Cora, Nina, and Summer are located on the top of the Grotto in Palisades Mall. Chuck will have to pay them $10,000 to get the girls to join. Keep talking to Nina and Chuck might get a discount. This side mission is available from 3:00 AM to 9:00 AM on Day 3."
Secret of Charlie's Gold	Special	"This side mission will occur only if Lenny was rescued. Lenny is located in the Safe House cafeteria. Talk to him and he'll direct Chuck to the vault in the Yucatan Casino. Go to the vault and interact with the lockbox to get a cash reward. This side mission is available from 4:00 AM to 10:00 AM on Day 3."
WWJWD	Psycho Fight	"Seymour's boss battle starts by getting close to the hanging bodies outside the hotel in South Plaza. After killing Seymour, talk to Ray, who is hiding near a maintenance room, to get him to join. This psycho is available from 4:00 AM to 7:00 PM on Day 3."
Bank Run	Stranded Survivors	"Woodrow is located next to the bar in Slot Ranch Casino Protect him as he runs to the different ATMs throughout Slot Ranch Casino and the Food Court. Woodrow will give Chuck bonus money when he is returned to the Safe House. This side mission is available from 6:00 AM to 5:00 PM on Day 3. "
Tape It or Die 1	Stranded Survivors	"Left Hand Lance, Wallace, Gretchen, and Johnny are located underneath KokoNutz Sports Town in Palisades Mall. The door leading to them will only be unlocked during the duration of this side mission. To complete the first quest, Chuck will need to bring Wallace two items, a cement saw and plates. Once both items have been brought to Wallace, he will give Chuck the plate launcher combo card and the side mission will be complete. This side mission is available from 6:00 AM to 12:00 PM on Day 3. "
Ante Up	Special	"This side mission will only be available if one of the following survivors have been rescued: Kristin, Trixie-Lynn, Cora, Jack, or Woodrow. Defeating one of the survivors in Texas Hold 'Em will complete the side mission. Chuck will be able to go back later and play the survivors that have not been beaten. Completing this side mission unlocks the knight helmet, which is stored in Chuck's locker at the Safe House. This side mission is available from 9:00 AM on Day 3 through 9:00 AM on Day 4."
Militia Men	Psycho Fight	"This psycho battle will start by entering Fortune Park. Big Earl is located on the construction platform next to the hotel in the Platinum Strip. Johnny is located on the roof of the Royal Flush Plaza, which can be accessed via a ladder in the Silver Strip. Derrick is located on the roof of the Atlantica Casino, which can be accessed via a ladder in the Silver Strip. Deetz is located on the roof of Paradise Platinum Screens, which can be access via a ladder behind Juggz Bar & Grill in the Platinum Strip. These psychos are available from 9:00 AM on Day 3 through 9:00 AM on Day 4."
Slave to Fashion	Stranded Survivors	"Europa is located next to the elevators in the lobby of Fortune City Hotel. She will not join until Chuck has undressed. Chuck will need to go to the underwear display located at South Plaza's west end to undress. This side mission is available from 9:15 AM to 6:15 PM on Day 3."
Chemical Dependency	Special	"This side mission will occur only if Jared has been rescued. Jared is located in the Safe House. Chuck will need to get Jared another dose of Zombrex to complete this side mission. This side mission is available from 11:00 AM to 3:00 PM on Day 3."
Art Appreciation	Stranded Survivors	"Randolph is located in The Cleroux Collection in Palisades Mall (second floor). Chuck must buy his painting for $3,000 for him to join. This side mission is available from 11:10 AM to 7:10 PM on Day 3."
Know When to Fold 'Em	Stranded Survivors	"Bill is located in the Shamrock Casino in the Silver Strip. He will not join until Chuck gives him $25,000. This side mission is available from 1:00 PM to 9:00 PM on Day 3."
Shell Shocked	Stranded Survivors	"Dean is located in the American Historium gift shop in the Americana Casino. Talk to Dean to get him to join. Dean will move slowly but Chuck cannot carry him. This side mission is available from 1:15 PM to 10:15 PM on Day 3."

SIDE MISSIONS (CONT.)

Scoop Name	Type	Description
One Hit Wonder	Psycho/Survivor	"Bibi is located on the stage in the Slot Ranch Casino. Walk up to the stage to start the event. She will ask Chuck to do three tasks. Chuck will need to get Bibi a drink, change into a tuxedo, and attract enough zombies to make a crowd. Once the three tasks are complete, Chuck will need to start the show by interacting with a switch backstage. Complete the minigame and Allison, Cameron, and Juan will join afterward. To get Bibi to join, Chuck will need to clear the zombies around her, then speak with Bibi. This side mission is available from 3:00PM on Day 3 through 12:00 PM on Day 4. "
Bent Wood	Special	"This side mission will occur only if Luz has been rescued. Luz is located in the Safe House. Bring her a golf club to complete the side mission. Luz will give Chuck bonus money when the mission is complete. This side mission is available from 4:00 PM to 8:00 PM on Day 3."
Stranded Siren	Stranded Survivors	"Tammy is located on the large shell in the Atlantica Casino. Talk to Tammy to get her to join. This side mission is available from 6:00 PM on Day 3 through 3:00 AM on Day 4."
Dead or Alive	Stranded Survivors	"Andy is located on top of some slot machines in the Palisades Mall. Talk to Andy to get him to join. If you don't listen to all of Andy's conversation he will kill himself. This side mission is available from 8:00 PM on Day 3 through 7:00 AM on Day 4."
Demand and Supply	Special	"This side mission will occur only if Sven has been rescued. Sven is located in the Safe House. Bring Sven either whiskey or vodka to complete the side mission. Sven will give Chuck some Zombrex as a bonus reward. This side mission is available from 9:00 PM on Day 3 through 1:00 AM on Day 4."
Two's Company	Stranded Survivors	"Walter and Royce are located in Hot Excitorama in the Silver Strip. Chuck will need to talk to both survivors to hear their jokes, then give one of them the trophy on the counter. If the trophy is given to Walter, Chuck will need to pay Royce $5,000 to get him to join. This side mission is available from 11:00 PM on Day 3 through 7:00 AM on Day 4. "
Deadliest Trick	Psycho Fight	"Reed and Roger are located at the magic stage in the Atlantica Casino. Approach the stage to start the boss battle. Chuck will receive the rocket launcher combo card as a bonus after the battle. These psychos are available from 12:00 AM to 9:00 AM on Day 4."
Family Feud	Stranded Survivors	"Lillian is located on the roof of the Fortune City Hotel. Chuck must talk to her for Camille to become available. After talking to Lillian, Chuck must find Camille, who is located inside the Atlantica Casino. Bring Camille back to Lillian to get them to join. This side mission is available from 2:00 AM to 11:00 AM on Day 4."
Fortune City Botany Club	Special	"This side mission will occur only if Vikki has been rescued. Vikki is located in the Safe House. Bring Vikki a peace art item from The Cleroux Collection in the Palisades Mall (second floor) to complete the side mission. This side mission is available from 4:00 AM to 12:00 PM on Day 4."
Delta Point 1	Stranded Survivors	"Michael and Matthew are located in Fortune Park. Chuck must not have a gun to get these survivors to join him. Matthew will be injured and will move slowly, but Chuck can carry him. This side mission is available from 9:00 AM to 6:00 PM on Day 4."
Tape It or Die 2	Stranded Survivors	"This side mission will occur only if the first ""Tape It or Die"" side mission was completed. Left Hand Lance, Wallace, Gretchen, and Johnny are located in KokoNutz Sports Town in the Palisades Mall. Help them kill the zombies to get them to join Chuck. This side mission is available from 9:15 AM to 5:15 PM on Day 4. "

APPENDIX

ACHIEVEMENTS AND TROPHIES

There are plenty of Achievements and Trophies for you to attain in *Dead Rising 2*, and the following table lists them all. Many of these are based on your progression through the game, and you'll attain them as you follow our detailed walkthrough. Check the sections that follow after the table for tips on how to complete the more involved challenges.

> **NOTE**
>
> Chuck's customized motorbike helps him attain several Achievements and Trophies with less hassle. Defeat the psychopath Leon Bell during the "Meet the Contestants" side mission to unlock the Combo Bay, where Chuck's bike can be customized. Refer to the following "Combo Bay Bike Modifications" table to discover all the deadly weapons you can graft onto Chuck's bike to make it an even more effective killing machine.

ACHIEVEMENTS AND TROPHIES				
Achievement Title	**Gamerscore**	**Trophy Type**	**Description Text**	**Tips**
Zombie Slaughter	20	Bronze	Kill 500 zombies	You'll do this easily.
Zombie Destruction	20	Bronze	Kill 5,000 zombies	Exploit the Combo Bay and slaughter zombies along the strips with a modified motorbike.
Z-Genocider 2: Genocide Harder	20	Silver	Kill 53,596 zombies	Exploit the Combo Bay and slaughter zombies along the strips with a modified motorbike.
Zombie Genocide Master	20	Gold	Kill 72,000 zombies	Exploit the Combo Bay and slaughter zombies along the strips with a modified motorbike.
Vigilante Justice	20	Bronze	Defeat five psychopaths	Refer to the walkthrough or the previous "Side Missions" table to learn where to find and how to kill each psycho.
Judge, Jury and Executioner	20	Bronze	Defeat 10 psychopaths	Refer to the walkthrough or the previous "Side Missions" table to learn where to find and how to kill each psycho.
Zombie Fu	20	Bronze	Kill 1,000 zombies bare-handed	Collect the Hand-to-Hand magazine from Ragazines on Royal Flush Plaza's second floor to aid you.
Wrong kind of "Chopper"	20	Bronze	Kill 1,000 zombies while riding a motorcycle	Exploit the Combo Bay and slaughter zombies along the strips with a modified motorbike.
He hasn't covered wars...	20	Bronze	Use every type of firearm to kill a zombie	See the "Skills, Weapons, and Combos" chapter to discover each weapon's category.
Head Trauma	20	Bronze	Use every type of melee weapon to kill a zombie	See the "Skills, Weapons, and Combos" chapter to discover each weapon's category.
Death From Afar	20	Bronze	Use every type of ranged weapon to kill a zombie	See the "Skills, Weapons, and Combos" chapter to discover each weapon's category.

DEADRISING 2

Achievement Title	Gamerscore	Trophy Type	Description Text	Tips
Explosive Temper	20	Bronze	Use every type of explosive to kill a zombie	See the "Skills, Weapons, and Combos" chapter to discover each weapon's category.
Slaughter - S = Laughter!	20	Bronze	Use every type of novelty weapon on a zombie	See the "Skills, Weapons, and Combos" chapter to discover each weapon's category.
Come on! Follow me!	20	Bronze	Escort eight survivors at once	Order survivors to wait (Aim trigger + Call button) a short distance away from the Safe House whenever you need to enter. Keep this up until you have eight survivors following you.
Saving the Day	20	Bronze	Save 10 survivors	Refer to the walkthrough or the previous "Side Missions" table to learn where to find and how to save each survivor.
Hero of Fortune City	20	Bronze	Save 50 survivors	Refer to the walkthrough or the previous "Side Missions" table to learn where to find and how to save each survivor.
Needs more chainsaw	20	Bronze	Create a combo weapon	You'll do this easily.
Duct Tape FTW	20	Bronze	Create all combo weapons	See the following "Weapon Locations" and "Combo Cards" tables to learn how to create every combo weapon and where to find their components.
Apprentice Rising	20	Bronze	Reach level 25	Follow the walkthrough carefully, collecting the Rescue and Psychos magazines early in the adventure and completing all side missions, and you'll have little trouble leveling Chuck all the way up.
Professional Rising	20	Bronze	Reach level 50	Follow the walkthrough carefully, collecting the Rescue and Psychos magazines early in the adventure and completing all side missions, and you'll have little trouble leveling Chuck all the way up.
Fashion Efficienato	20	Bronze	Change into 10 different pieces of clothing	See the following "Clothing Locations" table to learn where to find every piece of clothing.
Chuck Greene: Cross Dresser?	20	Bronze	Changes into all pieces of clothing in the game	See the following "Clothing Locations" table to learn where to find every piece of clothing.
Clean Record	20	Silver	Complete the Facts	Refer to the walkthrough or the previous "Case Files" table to learn how to complete this case.
Bartender	20	Bronze	Mix a drink	Check the poster map to discover the locations of all blenders and place any two food items into one to complete this.
Look at all that juice!	20	Bronze	Create and consume all mixed drinks in the game	Refer to the following "Juice Drinks" table to learn how to mix every type of drink using food items and a blender.
Finally Full	20	Bronze	Eat all types of food in the game	Refer to the following "Food Locations" table to learn the locations of each type of food.

APPENDIX

ACHIEVEMENTS AND TROPHIES (CONT.)

Achievement Title	Gamerscore	Trophy Type	Description Text	Tips
Having a gas	20	Bronze	Kill 1,000 "special" zombies	After reaching Case 6-2, modify Chuck's motorbike at the Combo Bay and use it to slaughter "special" zombies along the strip.
Custom Finish	20	Bronze	Give your bike a custom paint job	Bring any can of spray paint to the Combo Bay and combine it with Chuck's motorbike.
Curiously Inventive	20	Bronze	Collect all world-hint combo cards	See the following "Combo Cards" table to discover how to acquire every combo card.
Life Saver	20	Bronze	Collect all survivor combo cards	See the following "Combo Cards" table to discover how to acquire every combo card.
Tough Guy	20	Bronze	Collect all psycho combo cards	See the following "Combo Cards" table to discover how to acquire every combo card.
Half Deck	20	Bronze	Collect 25 combo cards	See the following "Combo Cards" table to discover how to acquire every combo card.
Full Deck	20	Gold	Collect all combo cards	See the following "Combo Cards" table to discover how to acquire every combo card.
Tape it or DIE!	Secret - 20	Hidden Silver	Discover the secret combo card	See the following "Combo Cards" table to discover how to acquire every combo card.
Data Miner	20	Gold	Fill all entries in the notebook	Follow the walkthrough carefully, or refer to the previous "Side Missions" table, to discover every survivor and fill the notebook.
Smashy	20	Bronze	Smash 100 zombies into environmental objects	Level Chuck up to unlock the Smash skill move, then use it to knock zombies into environmental objects, such as slot machines.
Stick 'em up	20	Bronze	Cover a zombie in objects	See the following "Stick 'Em Up" section for details.
Father of the Month	20	Bronze	Give Katey a gift	See the following "Katey's Gifts" table to learn which items can be given to Chuck's daughter as gifts.
Father of the Year	20	Bronze	Give Katey all possible gifts	See the following "Katey's Gifts" table to learn which items can be given to Chuck's daughter as gifts.
Justice Served	20	Silver	Complete Overtime mode	Give a special character some Zombrex before completing the Facts case to unlock Overtime mode, then refer to the walkthrough for tips on how to complete it.
Better with a friend	20	Bronze	Solve all case files in Co-op mode	Connect with a buddy, then refer to the walkthrough or previous "Case Files" table for tips on completing every case.
Don't you die on me!	20	Bronze	Revive another player in Co-op mode	Give a fallen co-op partner some food when they're dying to revive them.
Big Spender	20	Bronze	Spend $10,000,000 total	See the "Brain Food" chapter for tips on how to earn lots of cash, then spend it all at pawnshops to unlock cool stuff and reach this goal.

www.primagames.com

ACHIEVEMENTS AND TROPHIES (CONT.)

Achievement Title	Gamerscore	Trophy Type	Description Text	Tips
Window Shopper	20	Bronze	Enter all the stores in the game	Simply visit every store in the city, including kiosks. Reference the map to find them all. You must complete the "One Man's Trash" side mission to unlock the pawnshops and visit them as well.
The Skill To Survive	20	Bronze	Tame Snowflake	After killing Ted during the "Ted and Snowflake" side mission psycho battle, feed Snowflake the tiger three steaks by tossing them to the ground, then luring her toward them. Find unlimited steaks at Chris's Fine Foods on the Palisades Mall's second floor.
Masquerade	20	Bronze	Have 10 zombies with masks	Collect masks such as the Lizard Mask and Goblin Mask from toy stores and the like, placing 10 of them on zombies' heads. See the following "Item Locations" tables to learn where to find masks.
Improper Behavior	20	Bronze	Spray-paint all Zombrex posters	Collect spray paint, using it to spray Zombrex posters around the city. See the following map to discover the locations of every Zombrex poster you need to spray.
TK's Favorite	20	Bronze	Play and win in all nine online events	See the "Terror Is Reality" chapter for tips on how to succeed in each online TIR event.
Rising Star	20	Bronze	Come in first place in a single online event	See the "Terror Is Reality" chapter for tips on how to succeed in each online TIR event.
Win Big!	20	Bronze	Come in first place in an online match	See the "Terror Is Reality" chapter for tips on how to succeed in each online TIR event.

STICK 'EM UP

This Achievement/Trophy requires you to stick four unique objects into or onto a single zombie. Many objects can be used to satisfy this challenge, as detailed in the lists below. To complete this challenge without killing the zombie, it's generally best to first put an object on the zombie's body (painting, tire, etc.), then the head (mask, bucket, etc), as these won't do much harm. Afterward, impale the zombie with two other objects (stick pony, protestor sign, bow and arrow, etc.) to finish the job.

APPENDIX

ZOMBREX POSTER LOCATIONS

Use the following map to help you discover the locations of all Zombrex posters you need to spray paint in order to attain the "Improper Behavior" Achievement/Trophy.

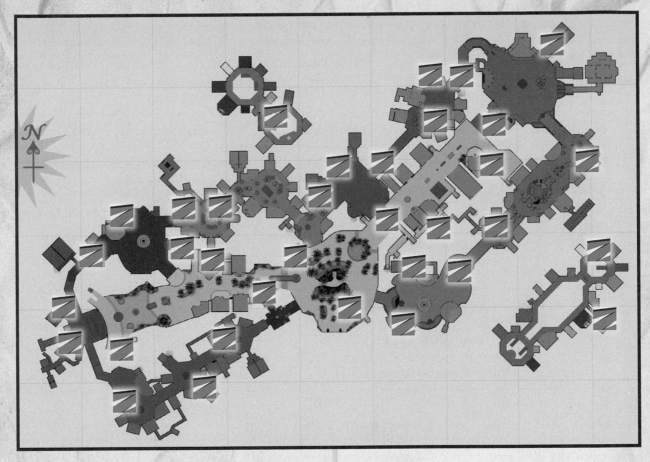

GIFTS FOR KATEY

Bring the following gifts to Katey at any point during the adventure to cheer her up and score some easy PP for Chuck.

GIFTS FOR KATEY	
Gift	**Location**
Giant stuffed elephant	Stylin' Toddlers on Royal Flush Plaza's first floor.
Robot bear	Astonishing Illusions on Royal Flush Plaza's first floor.
Bag of marbles	Ye Olde Toybox on Royal Flush Plaza's first floor.
Beach ball	Ye Olde Toybox on Royal Flush Plaza's first floor.
Stick pony	Ye Olde Toybox on Royal Flush Plaza's first floor.
Water gun	The watery areas of Fortune Park; also found in Moe's Maginations on the Platinum Strip.
Giant stuffed bull	Children's Castle on Royal Flush Plaza's second floor.
Giant stuffed donkey	Children's Castle on Royal Flush Plaza's second floor.
Giant stuffed rabbit	The hidden upper platforms of the Americana Casino's and the Royal Flush Plaza's second floors; also found in Moe's Maginations on the Platinum Strip.
Snowflake	Tame this ferocious tiger by feeding her three steaks after dispatching her master, Ted, at the Yucatan Casino.
Funny painting	Can only be obtained at The Cleroux Collection in Palisades Mall during the "Art Appreciation" side mission. Costs $3,000.

TIP

If you're not sure which gifts you've already given to Katey, simply look around the Safe House's security room to find them all on display.

DEADRISING 2

BIKE MODIFICATIONS

Defeat the psychopath Leon Bell during the "Meet the Contestants" side mission to gain access to the Combo Bay, which is located at the Silver Strip's north end. Then modify Chuck's motorbike with the following items to make it even more lethal.

COMBO BAY BIKE MODIFICATIONS

Bike Name	Item Required	Best Source	Notes
Bazooka Bike	Rocket launcher (combo weapon)	Unlimited rocket fireworks at Rockets Red Glare (Silver Strip); lead pipes in alley south of Hot Excitorama (Silver Strip)	Bike with fireworks rocket launcher attached. Beware of splash damage! Ammo: 150.
Chain Saw Bike	Chain saw	Atop "Angel Lust" stage's steel girders (Silver Strip)	Bike with chain saws mounted to the sides.
Machine Gun Bike	LMG	Atop the Yucatan Casino's Lucky Marble minigame.	Bike with twin machine guns attached. Ammo: 250.
Rabbit Bike	Giant stuffed rabbit	Moe's Maginations (Platinum Strip)	Bike with a stuffed rabbit attached. Zombies bounce off.
Wheelchair Bike	Wheelchair	Slot Ranch Casino or south end of Platinum Strip	Bike with an attached wheelchair. Survivors and co-op partners can ride in it!
Red Rocket	Red spray paint	American Historium (Americana Casino)	Paints the bike red.
Blue Thunder	Blue spray paint	American Historium (Americana Casino)	Paints the bike blue.
Green Machine	Green spray paint	American Historium (Americana Casino)	Paints the bike green.
Purple Punisher	Purple spray paint	Food Court (near central platform)	Paints the bike purple.
Great American	USA spray paint	American Historium (Americana Casino)	Paints the bike with a USA theme (red, white, and blue).

COMBO CARDS

Combo cards increase the effectiveness of combo weapons by causing them to give Chuck double the normal PP bonus with each kill. In addition, owning a combo card allows Chuck to use that combo weapon's heavy attack if it has one. The following table reveals how to acquire all combo cards in the game.

NOTE

Combo cards that are acquired through leveling are always gained in the order listed in the table.

COMBO CARDS

Combo Card	How to Get
Drill Bucket	Acquired by leveling.
I.E.D.	Acquired by leveling.
Molotov	Acquired by leveling.
Pole Weapon	Acquired by leveling.
Air Horn	Acquired by leveling.
Gem Blower	Acquired by leveling.
Fountain Lizard	Acquired by leveling.
Hacker	Acquired by leveling.
Ripper	Acquired by leveling.
Electric Chair	Acquired by leveling.

COMBO CARDS (CONT.)

Combo Card	How to Get
Flaming Gloves	Acquired by leveling.
Heliblade	Acquired by leveling.
Fire Spitter	Acquired by leveling.
Beer Hat	Acquired by leveling.
Sticky Bomb	Acquired by leveling.
Driller	Acquired by leveling.
Defiler	Acquired by leveling.
Hail Mary	Acquired by leveling.
Freezer Bomb	Acquired by leveling.
Knife Gloves	Acquired by leveling.

APPENDIX

COMBO CARDS (CONT.)

Combo Card	How to Get
Roaring Thunder	Acquired by leveling.
Super Slicer	Acquired by leveling.
Handy Chipper	Acquired by leveling.
Dynameat	Acquired by leveling.
Electric Rake	Acquired by leveling.
Parablower	Acquired by leveling.
Boomstick	Acquired by leveling.
Auger	Acquired by leveling.
Infernal Arms	Acquired by leveling.
Porta-Mower	Acquired by leveling.
Super B.F.G.	Acquired by leveling.
Tesla Ball	Acquired by leveling.
Spear Launcher	Acquired by leveling.
Blitzkrieg	Acquired by leveling.
Flamethrower	Acquired by defeating the psychopath Slappy (Brent Ernst).
Rocket Launcher	Acquired by defeating the magician psychopaths (Reed Wallbeck and Roger Withers).

COMBO CARDS (CONT.)

Combo Card	How to Get
Plate Launcher	Reward from the side mission "Tape It Or Die 1."
Blazing Aces	Reward for rescuing Left Hand Lance during the side mission "Tape It Or Die 2."
Exsanguinator	Reward for rescuing Wallace Hertzog during the side mission "Tape It Or Die 2."
Power Guitar	Reward for rescuing Floyd Stone during the side mission "Rock Heroes."
Burning Skull	Hidden in Fortune City (see poster map).
Laser Sword	Hidden in Fortune City (see poster map).
Blambow	Hidden in Fortune City (see poster map).
Holy Arms	Hidden in Fortune City (see poster map).
Freedom Bear	Hidden in Fortune City (see poster map).
Paddlesaw	Hidden in Fortune City (see poster map).
Snowball Cannon	Hidden in Fortune City (see poster map).
Tenderizers	Hidden in Fortune City (see poster map).
Spiked Bat	Hidden in Fortune City (see poster map).

ITEM LOCATIONS

WEAPON LOCATIONS

The following table reveals the best sources for every weapon in the game.

WEAPON LOCATIONS

Name	Primary Location(s)
2x4	South Plaza; Underground; various maintenance halls/areas; back alleys; rooftops.
Acetylene Tank	Underground; South Plaza.
Acoustic Guitar	Tunemakers (Royal Flush Plaza 1F); Entertainment Isle (Palisades Mall 1F); Silver Strip (stage area).
Ad Board	Outside various stores around the city.
Amplifier	Tunemakers (Royal Flush Plaza 1F); Entertainment Isle (Palisades Mall 1F).
Assault Rifle	Casino security offices and cashier/vault areas.
Bag of Marbles	Ye Olde Toybox (Royal Flush Plaza 1F); Children's Castle (Royal Flush Plaza 2F); Ultimate Playhouse (Palisades Mall 1F).
Barstool	Bars, restaurants, and casinos.

WEAPON LOCATIONS (CONT.)

Name	Primary Location(s)
Baseball Bat	Royal Flush Plaza 1F (NW maintenance hall); SporTrance (Royal Flush Plaza 1F); Barrel of Goods (Silver Strip).
Basketball	SporTrance (Royal Flush Plaza 1F); KokoNutz Sports Town (Palisades Mall 1F).
Bass Guitar	Tunemakers (Royal Flush Plaza 1F); Entertainment Isle (Palisades Mall 1F); Silver Strip (stage area).
Battery	Various maintenance rooms (see poster map).
Battleaxe	Ned's Knicknackery (Palisades Mall 2F).
Beach Ball	Ye Olde Toybox (Royal Flush Plaza 1F); Palisades Mall (several shops).
Bench	Found all over.
Bingo Ball Cage	One Little Duck Bingo (Silver Strip).

WEAPON LOCATIONS (CONT.)

Name	Primary Location(s)
Blast Frequency Gun	Secret lab (Underground).
Bow and Arrow	The Chieftain's Hut (Royal Flush Plaza 1F); Shank's (Palisades Mall 1F); Food Court (Upper Platforms).
Bowie Knife	Shank's (Palisades Mall 1F); various kitchens and eateries.
Bowling Ball	SporTrance (Royal Flush Plaza 1F).
Box of Nails	South Plaza; Underground; various maintenance halls/areas; back alleys; rooftops.
Boxing Gloves	The Man's Sport (Royal Flush Plaza 1F); Flexin' (Palisades Mall 1F).
Brick	South Plaza; Underground; various maintenance halls/areas; back alleys; rooftops.
Broadsword	Americana Casino (hung on walls); Shank's (Palisades Mall 1F); Ned's Knicknackery (Palisades Mall 2F).
Broom Handle	Break push brooms to acquire. (See "push broom.")
Bucket	South Plaza; Underground; various maintenance halls/areas; back alleys; rooftops.
Bull Skull	Wild West Grill House (Food Court).
Cactus Plant	Food Court.
Cardboard Box	Found all over.
Cardboard Cutout	Found inside various shops, including Paradise Platinum Screens (Platinum Strip).
Cash Register	Found inside many shops.
Casino Chips	Found near table games in various casinos.
Cement Saw	South Plaza; Underground; various maintenance halls/areas.
Centurion Bust	Found atop slot machines in Yucatan Casino and Palisades Mall.
Chainsaw	South Plaza; Underground; various maintenance halls/areas.
Chef Knife	Antoine's (Royal Flush Plaza 2F); various kitchens and eateries.
Coffee Pot	Various kitchens and eateries.
Comedy Trophy	Unique item found only in Hot Excitorama (Silver Strip) during the "Two's Company" side mission.
Computer Case	Found in many modern stores, security offices, and also found in casino cashier/vault areas.

WEAPON LOCATIONS (CONT.)

Name	Primary Location(s)
Construction Hat	South Plaza; Underground; various maintenance halls/areas.
Cooking Oil	Found inside various kitchens and eateries.
Cooking Pot	Found inside various kitchens and eateries.
Croupier Stick	Found near table games in various casinos.
Crowbar	South Plaza; Underground; various maintenance halls/areas; back alleys; rooftops.
Cushioned Tall Chair	Found in many casinos near slot machines.
Dolly	South Plaza; Underground; various maintenance halls/areas.
Donkey Lamp	Rare item found only in the Arena's green rooms and the Rojo Diablo Mexican Restaurant (Food Court).
Drill Motor	South Plaza; Underground; Food Court (upper platforms).
Drink Cart	Found in many casinos around the main floors.
Drum	Tunemakers (Royal Flush Plaza 1F); Silver Strip (stage area).
Dumbbell	The Man's Sport (Royal Flush Plaza 1F); Flexin' (Palisades Mall 1F).
Dynamite	Hidden in many areas, including the grass around Fortune Park; the potted plants at the south end of Palisades Mall's second floor; the upper platforms in South Plaza and the Food Court; and also in or near various maintenance rooms (see the poster map).
Electric Guitar	Americana Casino (hung on walls); Tunemakers (Royal Flush Plaza 1F); Entertainment Isle (Palisades Mall 1F); Silver Strip (stage area).
Fancy Bench	Found all over.
Fancy Painting	The Cleroux Collection (Palisades Mall 2F); also found in many fine shops.
Fancy Small Chair	Found in fine stores.
Fancy Tall Chair	Found in fine stores.
Fire Axe	South Plaza; Underground; various maintenance halls/areas.
Fire Extinguisher	Found in many shops and various maintenance halls/areas.
Firecrackers	Astonishing Illusions (Royal Flush Plaza 1F); Rockets Red Glare (Silver Strip)

APPENDIX

WEAPON LOCATIONS (CONT.)

Name	Primary Location(s)
Flashlight	Found in various offices and various maintenance halls/areas; also carried by looters.
Flower Pot	Decoratively sprinkled in several feminine boutiques, such as The Venus Touch (Palisades Mall 1F).
Foam Hand	Found on the ground in and around the arena.
Folding Chair	South Plaza; Underground; various maintenance halls/areas; back alleys; rooftops.
Football	SporTrance (Royal Flush Plaza 1F); Fortune Park (grassy areas).
Fountain Firework	The American Historium (Americana Casino); Astonishing Illusions (Royal Flush Plaza 1F); Rockets Red Glare (Silver Strip).
Funny Painting	Unique item found only in The Cleroux Collection (Palisades Mall 2F) during the "Art Appreciation" side mission.
Garbage Bag	South Plaza; Underground; various maintenance halls/areas; back alleys; rooftops.
Garbage Can	Found all over.
Gas Barrel	Unique item found only in the Safe House during Case 6-4.
Gas Can	Secret lab (Underground).
Gasoline Canister	South Plaza; Underground; Yucatan Casino (upper platforms); Atlantica Casino (upper platforms); various maintenance halls/areas; back alleys.
Gems	Marriage Makers (Royal Flush Plaza 1F); Eternal Timepieces (Royal Flush Plaza 2F); Everything Diamond (Palisades Mall 2F); Ned's Knicknackery (Palisades Mall 2F); Slot Ranch Casino (stage area).
Generator	Unique item found only in the Safe House during Case 6-4.
Giant Die	Royal Flush Plaza 1F "Flaming Craps" table.
Giant Pink Chainsaw	Unique item found only after defeating the psychopath Randy during the "Here Comes the Groom" side mission.
Giant Stuffed Bull	Children's Castle (Royal Flush Plaza 2F); Food Court (upper platforms).
Giant Stuffed Donkey	Small Fry Duds (Royal Flush Plaza 2F).
Giant Stuffed Elephant	Stylin' Toddlers (Royal Flush Plaza 1F); Children's Castle (Royal Flush Plaza 2F).
Giant Stuffed Rabbit	Americana Casino (upper platforms); Royal Flush Plaza 2F (upper platforms); Moe's Maginations (Platinum Strip); Kid's Choice Clothing (Palisades Mall 2F).

WEAPON LOCATIONS (CONT.)

Name	Primary Location(s)
Gift Shop Lamp	Found at various toy/hobby stores, such as Astonishing Illusions (Royal Flush Plaza 1F).
Goblin Mask	Children's Castle (Royal Flush Plaza 2F); near a maintenance room along the Silver Strip (see poster map).
Golf Club	SporTrance (Royal Flush Plaza 1F and 2F).
Grenade	High-Noon Shooting Range (Palisades Mall 2F); Fortune Park (various grassy areas to the south).
Gumball Machine	Children's Castle (Royal Flush Plaza 2F); Chocolate Confession (Palisades Mall 1F); Lombardi's (Food Court); Paradise Platinum Screens (Platinum Strip).
Handbag	Found all over.
Handgun	High-Noon Shooting Range (Palisades Mall 2F); also found in many security offices and casino cashier/vault areas.
Hanger	Found all over, particularly in clothing stores.
Highback Oak Chair	Found all over.
Hockey Stick	KokoNutz Sports Town (Palisades Mall 2F).
Hunk of Meat	Found by slaying zombies; can also be found outside certain maintenance rooms (see the poster map).
Indoor Garbage Can	Found all over.
Katana Sword	Unique item found only after defeating the psychopaths during Case 4-1.
Keg	Found near various bars.
Ketchup	Found at various eateries.
Keyboard	Found in many modern stores, security offices, and also found in casino cashier/vault areas.
Lamp	Found all over.
Lance	Hamburger Fiefdom (Food Court); Ned's Knicknackery (Palisades Mall 2F).
Large Barrel	Found outside the Wild West Grill House (Food Court) and Baron Von Brathaus (Yucatan Casino).
Large Fern Tree	Found all over.
Large Planter	Found all over.
Large Potted Plant	Found all over

WEAPON LOCATIONS (CONT.)	
Name	**Primary Location(s)**
Large Vase	Found in fine arts and craft stores, such as The Cleroux Collection and Ned's Knicknackery (both on Palisades Mall 2F).
Large Wrench	South Plaza; Underground; various maintenance halls/areas; back alleys; rooftops.
Lawn Dart	Found in various grassy areas around Royal Flush Plaza, Palisades Mall, and Fortune Park.
Lawnmower	Found in various grassy areas around the city.
LCD Monitor	Found in many modern stores, security offices, and also found in casino cashier/vault areas.
Lead Pipe	South Plaza; Underground; various maintenance halls/areas; back alleys; rooftops.
Leaf Blower	Slot Ranch Casino (backstage area); Fortune Park (north of the central grotto); Palisades Mall 1F (atop the central grotto).
Leaf Rake	Found in various grassy areas around the city, including Royal Flush Plaza and Fortune Park.
Liberty Torch	Unique item found only near the Slot Ranch Casino's stage.
Lizard Mask	Americana Casino (Bennie Jack's BBQ Shack and near the maintenance room); Moe's Maginations (Platinum Strip).
LMG	Yucatan Casino (atop "Luck Marble" minigame); Palisades Mall (on a low grassy ledge of the central grotto); Platinum Strip (atop the north upper platforms).
Long Stick	Fortune City Hotel (vases of bamboo in the lobby).
Machete	Shank's (Palisades Mall 1F); Albert's Apparel (Royal Flush Plaza 2F); various kitchens and eateries.
Magician Sword	Unique item found only after defeating the psychopaths Reed and Roger during the "Deadliest Trick" side mission.
Mailbox	Found at various places along the Silver and Platinum strips.
Mannequin Female	Found at various clothing stores.
Mannequin Male	Found at various clothing stores.
Massager	Hot Excitorama (Silver Strip).
Mayonnaise	Chris's Fine Foods (Palisades Mall 2F); various kitchens and eateries.
Meat Cleaver	Shank's (Palisades Mall 1F); various kitchens and eateries.

WEAPON LOCATIONS (CONT.)	
Name	**Primary Location(s)**
Medicine Ball	Flexin' (Palisades Mall 1F).
Merc Assault Rifle	Found at casino security offices and cashier/vault areas; also dropped by enemy mercenaries when killed.
Metal Barricade	Found all over.
Metal Baseball Bat	The Man's Sport (Royal Flush Plaza 1F); KokoNutz Sports Town (Palisades Mall 2F).
Metal Garbage Can	Found all over.
Mic Stand	Silver Strip (stage area); Atlantica Casino (magic stage).
Military Case	Underground (secret lab); Fortune City Hotel (rooftop).
Mining Pick	South Plaza; Underground; Wild West Grill House (Food Court).
MMA Gloves	The Man's Sport (Royal Flush Plaza 1F)
Money Case	Fortune City Hotel (rooftop).
Moosehead	Food Court (atop information booth); High-Noon Shooting Range (Palisades Mall 2F)
Motor Oil	Underground; various maintenance halls/areas.
Music Discs	Found at music stores, such as Players (Royal Flush Plaza 2F) and Entertainment Isle (Palisades Mall 1F).
Mustard	Found at various eateries.
Newspaper Box	Found all over in malls and strips outside shops.
Nightstick	Found in security offices; also dropped by zombie security guards.
Novelty Beer Mug	Juggz Bar & Grill (Platinum Strip); Juggz Bar & Grill Kiosk (Silver Strip).
Novelty Cell Phone	Rush Wireless (Royal Flush Plaza 2F); Robsaka Mobile (Palisades Mall 2F).
Novelty Liquor Bottle	Leigh's Fine Liquor (Palisades Mall 2F).
Novelty Perfume Bottle	Roy's Mart (Royal Flush Plaza 1F); Estelle's Fine-Lady Cosmetics (Royal Flush Plaza 2F); FairMoans (Palisades Mall 1F).
Novelty Poker Chip	Barrel of Goods (Silver Strip); also found at various casinos.
Padded Blue Chair	Atlantica Casino (magic stage area).

APPENDIX

WEAPON LOCATIONS (CONT.)	
Name	**Primary Location(s)**
Paddle	South Plaza (various areas); Palisades Mall (central grotto); Under the Sea Travels (Palisades Mall 2F); Luaii Wauwii (Silver Strip); Silver Strip (south alley).
Paint Can	South Plaza; Underground; various maintenance halls/areas; back alleys; rooftops.
Painting	The Cleroux Collection (Palisades Mall 2F); also found in fine shops.
Pallet	South Plaza; Underground; various maintenance halls/areas; back alleys; rooftops.
Pan	Found in various kitchens and eateries.
Parasol	Found at various restaurant patios; also found atop the Palisades Mall's central grotto.
Patio Chair	Found at various restaurant patios.
Patio Table	Found at various restaurant patios.
Peace Art	Unique item that's only found at The Cleroux Collection (Palisades Mall 2F).
Pitchfork	Underground; Wild West Grill House (Food Court); Palisades Mall (near tall trees between the escalators).
Plastic Bin	Found all over, particularly in maintenance areas and back alleys.
Plastic Garbage Can	Found all over, particularly in maintenance areas and back alleys.
Plates	Found in various eateries and kitchens.
Playing Cards	Found in various casinos near table games.
Plywood	Underground; various maintenance halls/areas; back alleys; rooftops.
Power Drill	South Plaza; Underground; various maintenance halls/areas; back alleys; rooftops.
Propane Tank	South Plaza; Underground; various maintenance halls/areas; back alleys; rooftops.
Protestor Sign	Platinum Strip (near TIR souvenir kiosks and Fortune City Arena entrance).
Push Broom	Found in various maintenance halls/areas; can also be attached to utility carts.
Pylon	Found all over, particularly in South Plaza, the Underground, various maintenance halls/areas, and rooftops.
Queen	Found near clusters of zombies; can emerge when zombies are killed.

WEAPON LOCATIONS (CONT.)	
Name	**Primary Location(s)**
Robot Bear	Astonishing Illusions (Royal Flush Plaza 1F); Chocolate Confessions (Palisades Mall 1F); Brand New U (Palisades Mall 2F); Yucatan Casino (atop slot machines near Shoal Nightclub escalators).
Rocket Fireworks	Rockets Red Glare (Silver Strip); also found near several maintenance rooms (see poster map).
Rocket Launcher	Unique item found only after defeating the psychopaths Reed and Roger during the "Deadliest Trick" side mission.
Rotating Display	Found near various shops such as Royal Flush Plaza's Roy's Mart and Universe of Optics.
Roulette Wheel	Found in various casinos near table games.
Round Potted Plant	Found all over.
Sandwich Board	Found all over, usually just outside shops.
Saw Blade	South Plaza; Underground; various maintenance halls/areas; back alleys; rooftops.
Scissors	Safe House (security room); Wave of Style (Royal Flush Plaza).
Servbot Mask	Ultimate Playhouse (Palisades Mall 1F); Silver Strip (north alley).
Serving Tray	Found in various eateries and kitchens.
Shampoo	Found in various salons such as Wave of Style (Royal Flush Plaza 2F).
Shopping Boxes	Found in fine stores such as Kathy's Space (Royal Flush Plaza 2F).
Shopping Valuables	Unique item found only in Kathy's Space (Royal Flush Plaza 2F) during the "Shopping Spree" side mission.
Shotgun	High-Noon Shooting Range (Palisades Mall 2F); Severed Ties (Palisades Mall 2F, on top of kiosk); Platinum Strip (along south upper platforms); also dropped by zombie security guards.
Shower Head	Safe House (near restroom).
Six Shooter	Unique item found only after defeating the psychopath Seymour during the "WWJWD?" side mission.
Skateboard	In the Closet (Royal Flush Plaza 1F); SporTrance (Royal Flush Plaza 2F); KokoNutz Sports Town (Palisades Mall 2F).
Sledge Hammer	South Plaza; Underground; various maintenance halls/areas; back alleys.
Small Fern Tree	Found all over.

WEAPON LOCATIONS (CONT.)

Name	Primary Location(s)
Small Painting	The Cleroux Collection (Palisades Mall 2F); various fine shops.
Small Potted Plant	Found all over.
Small Suitcase	The Sturdy Package (Royal Flush Plaza 1F); Bagged! (Palisades Mall 1F).
Small Vase	Found in fine arts and craft stores, such as The Cleroux Collection and Ned's Knicknackery (both on Palisades Mall 2F).
Sniper Rifle	High-Noon Shooting Range (Palisades Mall 2F); Royal Flush Plaza 2F (upper platforms).
Soccer Ball	KokoNutz Sports Town (Palisades Mall 2F).
Speaker	Found near sources of loud noise, such as performance stages and music shops.
Spear	Ned's Knicknackery (Palisades Mall 2F).
Spool of Wire	Unique item found only in the Safe House during Case 6-4.
Spot Light	Found in grassy areas along the Platinum Strip; also found on various rooftops.
Spray Paint	In the Closet (Royal Flush Plaza 1F); The American Historium (Americana Casino); various maintenance halls/areas.
Square Sign	Found all over.
Stand	Found in many casinos; also found in the Fortune City Hotel lobby.
Steel Shelving	Underground; South Plaza; various maintenance halls/areas.
Step Ladder	Underground; South Plaza; various maintenance halls/areas.
Stick Pony	Ye Olde Toybox (Royal Flush Plaza 1F); Children's Castle (Royal Flush Plaza 2F).
Stone Statue	Found all over Yucatan Casino.
Stool	Common around bars and places with high counters.
Suitcase	The Sturdy Package (Royal Flush Plaza 1F); Bagged! (Palisades Mall 1F).
Swordfish	Luaii Wauwii (Silver Strip); Atlantica Casino (affixed to wall).
Table Lamp	Found all over.

WEAPON LOCATIONS (CONT.)

Name	Primary Location(s)
Tennis Racquet	KokoNutz Sports Town (Palisades Mall 1F).
Tiki Mask	Luaii Wauwii (Silver Strip).
Tiki Torch	Found all over Yucatan Casino; also found in Palisades Mall's central grotto.
Tire	Underground; various maintenance halls/areas.
Tomahawk	The Chieftain's Hut (Royal Flush Plaza 1F); also carried by looters.
Toy Helicopter	Ye Olde Toybox (Royal Flush Plaza 1F); Children's Castle (Royal Flush Plaza 2F); Ultimate Playhouse (Palisades Mall 1F).
Toy Spitball Gun	Ye Olde Toybox (Royal Flush Plaza 1F); Ultimate Playhouse (Palisades Mall 1F).
Training Sword	Slot Ranch Casino (backstage area); Atlantica Casino (maintenance room and upper platforms); Hamburger Fiefdom (Food Court).
Treasure Chest	Atlantica Casino (all over the main floor, atop slot machines, etc.)
Utility Cart	Various locations, usually found in maintenance halls but can be in main floors of malls/casinos, too.
Vacuum Cleaner	Somewhat rare item found in Yucatan Casino's south VIP room and also near the Shoal Nightclub's cash register. Also found in several maintenance rooms (see the poster map.)
Velvet Bar	Found in many casinos; also found in the Fortune City Hotel lobby.
Vinyl Records	Entertainment Isle (Palisades Mall 1F).
Wacky Hammer	Moe's Maginations (Platinum Strip).
Water Bottle	Found by destroying water coolers.
Water Cooler	Found in various offices and maintenance halls/areas.
Water Gun	Ultimate Playhouse (Palisades Mall 1F); Kid's Choice Clothing (Palisades Mall 2F); also found in various watery areas around Fortune Park and the Atlantica Casino.
Wheelchair	Found in various areas, usually near transition points between two sections of the city.
Whipped Cream	Found near bars, including Palisades Mall's central grotto bar and the Yucatan Casino's Shoal Nightclub.
Yellow Tall Chair	Found in various casinos near slot machines.
Zombie Mask	Stylin' Toddlers (Royal Flush Plaza 1F).

APPENDIX

FOOD LOCATIONS

The following table reveals the best sources for every food item in the game.

Name	Health Boost	Primary Location(s)
Apple	2	Food Court; Chris's Fine Foods (Palisades Mall).
Bacon	2	Food Court.
Baked Potato	2	Bennie Jack's BBQ Shack (Americana Casino).
BBQ Chicken	3	Food Court.
BBQ Ribs	3	Food Court; Bennie Jack's BBQ Shack (Americana Casino).
Beans	1	Food Court.
Beer	2	Food Court; Bennie Jack's BBQ Shack (Americana Casino); Baron Von Brathaus (Yucatan Casino); Pub O' Gold (Silver Strip).
Brownie	1	Food Court; The Dark Bean (Royal Flush Plaza); Chocolate Confession (Palisades Mall 1F).
Burrito	2	Food Court.
Cake	2	Food Court; The Dark Bean (Royal Flush Plaza).
Chili	3	Food Court.
Coffee	1	Food Court; The Dark Bean (Royal Flush Plaza).
Coffee Creamer	4	Food Court; The Dark Bean (Royal Flush Plaza).
Cookies	1	Food Court; Chocolate Confession (Palisades Mall 1F).
Donut	1	Food Court; The Dark Bean (Royal Flush Plaza).
Drink Cocktail	2	Shoal Nightclub (Yucatan Casino); Palisades Mall (grotto bar).
Fish	3	Chris's Fine Foods (Palisades Mall); Luaii Wauwii (Silver Strip); Atlantica Casino (in watery areas).
Fries	1	Food Court; various shops.
Hamburger	3	Food Court; Chris's Fine Foods (Palisades Mall); Bennie Jack's BBQ Shack (Americana Casino).
Hot Dog	2	Fortune City Arena (various places); Platinum Strip (various places).
Ice Cream	2	Food Court.
Jellybeans	1	Food Court; Chris's Fine Foods (Palisades Mall); Chocolate Confession (Palisades Mall 1F).
Large Soda	1	Food Court; Baron Von Brathaus (Yucatan Casino).

FOOD LOCATIONS (CONT.)

Name	Health Boost	Primary Location(s)
Lobster	6	Atlantica Casino (watery areas).
Melon	2	Chris's Fine Foods (Palisades Mall).
Milk	4	Food Court; Chris's Fine Foods (Palisades Mall).
Onion Rings	1	Food Court.
Orange Juice	4	Chris's Fine Foods (Palisades Mall); Roy's Mart (Royal Flush Plaza).
Pasta	4	Food Court.
Pie	1	Food Court; Dining at Davey's (Platinum Strip).
Pineapple	2	Chris's Fine Foods (Palisades Mall).
Pizza	4	Food Court; Chris's Fine Foods (Palisades Mall).
Snack	1	Found all over; can purchase from snack machines as well.
Spoiled Bacon	2	May pop out of trash receptacles.
Spoiled BBQ Chicken	3	May pop out of trash receptacles.
Spoiled BBQ Ribs	3	May pop out of trash receptacles.
Spoiled Fish	3	May pop out of trash receptacles.
Spoiled Hamburger	3	May pop out of trash receptacles.
Spoiled Hot Dog	2	May pop out of trash receptacles.
Spoiled Lobster	6	May pop out of trash receptacles.
Spoiled Steak	6	May pop out of trash receptacles.
Spoiled Sushi	4	May pop out of trash receptacles.
Steak	6	Chris's Fine Foods (Palisades Mall); Baron Von Brathaus (Yucatan Casino).
Sushi	4	Luaii Wauwii (Silver Strip).
Taco	2	Food Court.
Vodka	3	Food Court; Shots & Awe (Americana Casino); Palisades Mall (grotto bar); Pub O' Gold (Silver Strip); Leigh's Fine Liquor (Palisades Mall 2F).

DEADRISING 2

FOOD LOCATIONS (CONT.)

Name	Health Boost	Primary Location(s)
Whiskey	3	Food Court; Bennie Jack's BBQ Shack (Americana Casino); Pub O' Gold (Silver Strip); Leigh's Fine Liquor (Palisades Mall 2F).
Wine	5	Chris's Fine Foods (Palisades Mall); Shots & Awe (Americana Casino); Baron Von Brathaus (Yucatan Casino); Leigh's Fine Liquor (Palisades Mall 2F).

CLOTHING LOCATIONS

The following table reveals the locations of every article of clothing in the game.

Name	Body Part	Primary Location(s)
American Showman Helmet	Headwear	The American Historium (Americana Casino).
American Showman Jumpsuit	Body	The American Historium (Americana Casino).
Army Jacket Pants	Body	High-Noon Shooting Range (Palisades Mall 2F).
Aviator Glasses	Facewear	Universe of Optics (Royal Flush Plaza 1F).
Banana Hammock	Body	Beach Body Swim House (Palisades Mall 1F).
Bare Feet	Feet	Chuck's locker (Safe House).
Baseball Cap Sport	Headwear	SporTrance (Royal Flush Plaza 2F); KokoNutz Sports Town (Palisades Mall 2F).
Baseball Cap TIR	Headwear	Souvenir Kiosk (Platinum Strip); Hostile Zone (Fortune City Arena).
Baseball Uniform	Body	SporTrance (Royal Flush Plaza 2F); KokoNutz Sports Town (Palisades Mall 2F).
Basketball High Tops	Feet	SporTrance (Royal Flush Plaza 2F); KokoNutz Sports Town (Palisades Mall 2F).
Basketball Uniform	Body	KokoNutz Sports Town (Palisades Mall 1F).
Black Canvas Sneakers	Feet	The Shoehorn (Royal Flush Plaza 1F).
Black Cowboy Boots	Feet	Earmark Leather (Royal Flush Plaza 2F).
Black Cowboy Hat	Headwear	Earmark Leather (Royal Flush Plaza 2F).

CLOTHING LOCATIONS (CONT.)

Name	Body Part	Primary Location(s)
Black Cowboy Outfit	Body	Earmark Leather (Royal Flush Plaza 2F).
Black Dress Shoes	Feet	Three Club Monte, Modern Business Man (both on Royal Flush Plaza 1F); Albert's Apparel (Royal Flush Plaza 2F); Bagged! (Palisades Mall 1F).
Black Military Boots	Feet	High-Noon Shooting Range (Palisades Mall 2F).
Black Rimmed Glasses	Facewear	Finders Peepers (Palisades Mall 1F).
Blue Grey Work Overalls	Body	South Plaza (maintenance room).
Blue Hair	Headwear	Wave of Style (Royal Flush Plaza 1F); FairMoans (Palisades Mall 1F).
Blue Oyster Biker Outfit	Body	Hot Excitorama (Silver Strip).
Boardwalk Apparel	Body	Space (Palisades Mall 2F).
Bowling Shirt	Body	*Case Zero* exclusive.
Bunny Slippers	Feet	Kicks for Her (Palisades Mall 2F).
Business Casual	Body	Modern Businessman (Royal Flush Plaza 1F); For Your Leisure (Palisades Mall 1F).
Casual Beachwear	Body	Shots & Awe (Americana Casino).
Champion Jacket	Body	Unlockable—win a match of TIR online.

APPENDIX

Name	Body Part	Primary Location(s)
CLOTHING LOCATIONS (CONT.)		
Cleats	Feet	KokoNutz Sports Town (Palisades Mall 2F)
Collegiate Ensemble	Body	Modern Businessman (Royal Flush Plaza 1F); Albert's Apparel (Royal Flush Plaza 2F).
Dealer Outfit	Body	Unlockable—attain the "Chuck Greene: Cross Dresser?" Achievement/Trophy
Dealer Visor	Headwear	Americana Casino (north security office); Yucatan Casino (cashier/vault area).
Diner Waitress	Body	*Case Zero* exclusive.
Fedora	Headwear	Three Club Monte (Royal Flush Plaza 1F); Que's Hats (Palisades Mall 2F).
Flip Flops	Feet	Hot Excitorama (Silver Strip); From Fortune with Love (Platinum Strip).
Flower Head Piece	Headwear	Fortune Park (bush near central grotto, west side).
Football Helmet	Headwear	SporTrance (Royal Flush Plaza 1F).
Football Uniform	Body	SporTrance (Royal Flush Plaza 1F).
Fortune City Grey Shirt	Body	From Fortune with Love (Platinum Strip).
Fortune City Red Shirt	Body	The American Historium (Americana Casino).
Full Beard Moustache	Facewear	Wave of Style (Royal Flush Plaza 1F).
Funny Goblin Mask	Headwear	Children's Castle (Royal Flush Plaza 2F).
Funny Lizard Mask	Headwear	Ye Olde Toybox (Royal Flush Plaza 1F).
Funny Servbot Mask	Headwear	Ultimate Playhouse (Palisades Mall 1F).
Funny Zombie Mask	Headwear	Kid's Choice Clothing (Palisades Mall 2F).
Go-go Boots	Feet	Hot Excitorama (Silver Strip).
Grey Hair	Headwear	Estelle's Fine-Lady Cosmetics (Royal Flush Plaza 2F); The Venus Touch (Palisades Mall 1F).
Hawaiian Holiday Gear	Body	From Fortune with Love (Platinum Strip).
Highbrow Ensemble	Body	Wallington's (Palisades Mall 1F).

Name	Body Part	Primary Location(s)
CLOTHING LOCATIONS (CONT.)		
Hip Hop Outfit	Body	In the Closet (Royal Flush Plaza 1F).
Hockey Mask	Facewear	Unlockable—attain the "Head Trauma" Achievement/Trophy.
Hula Dress	Body	Under the Sea Travels (Palisades Mall 2F).
Hunting Jacket	Body	*Case Zero* exclusive.
Hygiene Mask	Facewear	Roy's Mart (Royal Flush Plaza 1F).
Kid's Super Hero Boots	Feet	Stylin' Toddlers (Royal Flush Plaza 1F); Kid's Choice Clothing (Palisades Mall 2F).
Kid's Super Hero Costume	Body	Ultimate Playhouse (Palisades Mall 1F).
Kid's Super Hero Eye Mask	Facewear	Children's Castle (Royal Flush Plaza 2F).
Knight Armor	Body	Unlockable—attain the "Justice Served" Achievement/Trophy.
Knight Boots	Feet	Moe's Maginations (purchase for $2,000,000).
Knight Helmet	Headwear	Unlockable—win at strip poker during the "Ante Up" side mission.
Knit Cap	Headwear	Small Fry Duds (Royal Flush Plaza 2F); Que's Hats (Palisades Mall 2F).
Knotted Top Cutoffs	Body	Casual Gals (Royal Flush Plaza 1F); Kathy's Space (Royal Flush Plaza 2F); Trendy City (Palisades Mall 1F).
Ladies Hat	Headwear	Casual Gals (Royal Flush Plaza 1F); Que's Hats (Palisades Mall 2F).
Loud Summer Special	Body	Space (Palisades Mall 2F).
Mesh Party Wear	Body	Hot Excitorama (Silver Strip).
Mid-Length T-shirt Jeans	Body	KokoNutz Sports Town back room/basement area (only available during the "Tape It or Die" side mission.)
Mohawk Hair	Headwear	Shank's (Palisades Mall 1F).
Novelty Glasses	Facewear	Astonishing Illusions (Royal Flush Plaza 1F).
One-Piece Pajama	Body	Stylin' Toddlers (Royal Flush Plaza 1F); Small Fry Duds (Royal Flush Plaza 2F).
Orange Prison Outfit	Body	Unlockable - Attain the "Judge, Jury and Executioner" Achievement/Trophy.

DEADRISING 2

CLOTHING LOCATIONS (CONT.)

Name	Body Part	Primary Location(s)
Overalls	Body	*Case Zero* exclusive.
Pink Hair	Headwear	Estelle's Fine-Lady Cosmetics (Royal Flush Plaza 2F); FairMoans (Palisades Mall 1F).
Plaid Suit	Body	Albert's Apparel (Royal Flush Plaza 2F).
Polo Shirt Blue Jeans	Body	Three Club Monte (Royal Flush Plaza 1F); For Your Leisure (Palisades Mall 1F).
Rocker Glasses	Facewear	Finders Peepers (Palisades Mall 1F).
Russian Hat	Headwear	Que's Hats (Palisades Mall 2F).
Sandals	Feet	For Your Leisure (Palisades Mall 1F).
Shaved Head	Headwear	Shank's (Palisades Mall 1F).
Show Girl Head Piece	Headwear	Slot Ranch Casino (backstage area).
Skater Outfit	Body	In the Closet (Royal Flush Plaza 1F).
Sport Glasses	Facewear	Universe of Optics (Royal Flush Plaza 1F).
Sporty Track Suit	Body	SporTrance (Royal Flush Plaza 1F); KokoNutz Sports Town (Palisades Mall 1F).
Summer Dress	Body	Trendy City (Palisades Mall 1F); Brand New U (Palisades Mall 2F).
Surf Wetsuit	Body	Beach Body Swim House (Palisades Mall 1F).
Swat Helmet	Headwear	High-Noon Shooting Range (Palisades Mall 2F).
Swat Outfit	Body	High-Noon Shooting Range (Palisades Mall 2F).
Tattered Clothes	Body	Unlockable—attain the "Zombie Fu" Achievement/Trophy.
Tennis Head Band	Headwear	KokoNutz Sports Town (Palisades Mall 1F).
Tennis Outfit	Body	KokoNutz Sports Town (Palisades Mall 1F).
TIR Helmet	Headwear	Unlockable—win a total of $1,000,000 or more from playing TIR online.
TIR Uniform	Body	Unlockable—win a total of $5,000,000 or more from playing TIR online.
Toddler Outfit	Body	Kid's Choice Clothing (Palisades Mall 2F).
Tourist Boat Hat	Headwear	Hat Racks (Royal Flush Plaza 1F); Beach Body Swim House (Palisades Mall 1F); Space (Palisades Mall 2F).
Tube Top Mini Skirt	Body	Kathy's Space (Royal Flush Plaza 2F); Brand New U (Palisades Mall 2F).

CLOTHING LOCATIONS (CONT.)

Name	Body Part	Primary Location(s)
Tuxedo	Body	Modern Businessman (Royal Flush Plaza 1F); Wallington's (Palisades Mall 1F).
Underwear	Body	Chuck's locker (Safe House); South Plaza (underwear display near SW unfinished store).
White Cowboy Boots	Feet	Earmark Leather (Royal Flush Plaza 2F).
White Cowboy Hat	Headwear	Earmark Leather (Royal Flush Plaza 2F).
White Cowboy Outfit	Body	Earmark Leather (Royal Flush Plaza 2F).
White Leisure Suit	Body	The American Historium (Americana Casino).
White Low heels	Feet	Brand New U, Kicks for Her (both on Palisades Mall 2F).
White Tennis Shoes	Feet	KokoNutz Sports Town (Palisades Mall 1F).
Wild Frontier Hat	Headwear	Hat Racks (Royal Flush Plaza 1F); Space (Palisades Mall 2F).
Willamette Mall Security Uniform	Body	Unlockable—attain the "Hero of Fortune City" Achievement/Trophy.
Yellow Sneakers	Feet	In the Closet, The Shoehorn, SporTrance (all on Royal Flush Plaza 1F); Bagged! (Palisades Mall 1F); Space (Palisades Mall 2F).
Yellow Tinted Glasses	Facewear	Universe of Optics (Royal Flush Plaza 1F).
Yellow Track Suit	Body	Space (Palisades Mall 2F).

MAGAZINE LOCATIONS

The following table reveals the locations of every magazine, along with their effects.

MAGAZINE LOCATIONS

Magazine	Description	Location
Bikes	Bikes have three times the durability.	Slot Ranch Casino (vault area).
Amusement	Novelty items have three times the durability.	Ultimate Playhouse (Palisades Mall 1F).
Bargaining 1	Will lower the cost of items in the pawnshop by 10%.	Americana Casino (Upper Platforms).

APPENDIX

MAGAZINE LOCATIONS, CONT.

Magazine	Description	Location
Bargaining 2	Will lower the cost of items in the pawnshop by 10%.	Food Court (Upper Platforms).
Blades	Edged weapons have three times the durability.	Underground (Warehouse D).
Building	Construction items have three times the durability.	South Plaza (Upper Platforms).
Combat 1	Get a 10% boost to PP earned from weapon kills.	Stan's Large Print Books & Magazines (Palisades Mall 2F).
Combat 2	Get a 10% boost to PPs earned from weapon kills.	Yesterday, Today and Tomorrow (Royal Flush Plaza).
Combat 3	Get a 10% boost to PP earned from weapon kills.	Underground (Warehouse A).
Domestic	Furniture items have three times the durability.	Maintenance Room 12 (Fortune Park).
Drinking	Drinking alcoholic drinks will not make Chuck sick.	Atlantica Casino (Upper Platforms).
Driving	4-wheel vehicle durability will last three times longer.	Bennie Jack's BBQ Shack (Americana Casino).
Gambling 1	Significant increases when playing gambling games.	Ragazines (Royal Flush Plaza 2F).
Gambling 2	Significant increases when playing gambling games.	Stan's Large Print Books & Magazines (Palisades Mall 2F).
Gambling 3	Significant increases when playing gambling games.	Shamrock Casino (Silver Strip).
Games	Entertainment items have three times the durability.	Atlantica Casino (north poker room).
Hand-to-Hand	Significant boost in power to bare-handed attacks.	Ragazines (Royal Flush Plaza 2F).
Health 1	Food items' health restoration boosted by 50%.	Yesterday, Today and Tomorrow (Royal Flush Plaza).
Health 2	Food items' health restoration boosted by 100%.	Baron Von Brathaus (Yucatan Casino).
Horror 1	Get a 10% boost to PP from killing zombies.	Ragazines (Royal Flush Plaza 2F).
Horror 2	Get a 10% boost to PP from killing zombies.	Stan's Large Print Books & Magazines (Palisades Mall 2F).
Juice Boost	Consumed juices' effects last twice as long.	Luaii Wauwii (Silver Strip).
Leadership	Survivors are more effective while in Chuck's party.	One Little Duck Bingo (Silver Strip).

MAGAZINE LOCATIONS, CONT.

Magazine	Description	Location
Playboy	Get a 10% boost to PP from female survivor-related activities.	Palisades Mall 1F (atop the central grotto).
Psychos	Get a 25% boost from defeating psychos.	Platinum Strip (north upper platforms).
Rescue	Get a 25% boost to PP from survivor-related activities.	Fortune City Arena (security room).
Skateboarding	Gain the ability to do a new trick while on the skateboard. Skateboard durability lasts three times longer.	Fortune City Hotel.
Sports	Sports items have three times the durability.	Stan's Large Print Books & Magazines (Palisades Mall 2F).

ZOMBREX LOCATIONS

The following table reveals the locations of all hidden doses of Zombrex in the city.

WEAPON LOCATIONS

Location	How to Get
Roy's Mart (Royal Flush Plaza)	Acquired during the normal progression of the story.
Americana Casino	Go to the second floor of Bennie Jack's BBQ Shack, then leap along the casino's light fixtures.
Slot Ranch Casino	Climb onto the crates behind the north stage, then leap to the Zombrex.
Yucatan Casino	Climb to the top of the Lucky Marble minigame, then leap to the Zombrex.
Underground	Search the rise in the tunnel near Maintenance Room 32.

NOTE

Zombrex can also be obtained for no charge by completing the "Code Blue," "Mail Order Zombrex," "Hunger Pains," and "Demand and Supply" side missions. See the walkthrough for details.

BLENDER LOCATIONS

Blenders are used to combine two food items into potent juice drinks with valuable benefits. Here's where you'll find each blender:

- Shots & Awe (Americana Casino)
- Slot Ranch Casino (at the bar)
- Rojo Diablo Mexican Restaurant (Food Court)
- Baron Von Brathaus (Yucatan Casino)
- Palisades Mall (first-floor grotto bar)
- Sipparellos (Atlantica Casino)
- Pub O' Gold (Silver Strip)
- Juggz Bar & Grill (Platinum Strip)

DEADRISING 2

JUICE DRINKS

By combining two food items together in a blender, Chuck can mix up valuable juice drinks that give him temporary benefits. Here are the different juice drinks that can be made:

Energizer: Chuck takes no damage.
Nectar: Attracts a queen to Chuck.
Pain Killer: Reduced damage.
Quick Step: Gives Chuck super speed.

	Apple	Bacon	Baked Potato	BBQ Chicken	BBQ Ribs	Beans	Beer	Brownie	Burrito	Cake	Jellybeans	Chili	Cocktail	Coffee	Ketchup / Mustard	Cookies	Cooking Oil	Coffee Creamer	Donuts	Fish	Fries	Hamburger	Large Soda	Lobster	Hotdog	Ice Cream	Onion Ring	Orange Juice	Mayonnaise	Melon
Apple	N	Z	N	E	U	R	N	Z	S	Z	Z	S	E	Q	N	N	D	Q	N	N	Z	Z	N	E	Z	N	Z	N	Z	E
Bacon		U	U	U	R	P	U	Z	U	Z	R	U	Q	U	U	D	Q	D	S	U	U	N	N	S	Q	S	S	R	N	N
Baked Potato			E	U	U	R	S	S	S	Z	Z	R	S	Q	S	Z	D	Q	D	S	U	U	N	N	S	Q	S	S	E	N
BBQ Chicken				E	P	U	S	U	U	Z	R	U	Q	U	S	U	D	U	D	S	U	U	N	P	S	Q	S	S	E	N
BBQ Ribs					U	U	S	U	U	U	Z	R	U	Q	U	S	U	D	D	S	U	P	N	P	S	Q	S	S	E	N
Beans						R	R	U	R	Z	Z	S	R	S	R	D	D	R	Z	D	U	U	N	E	Z	R	S	N	R	N
Beer							P	Z	R	U	N	R	D	Q	P	Z	D	D	D	D	S	S	D	E	Z	Q	Z	N	D	N
Brownie								S	S	Z	R	N	Q	Z	Z	Z	D	Q	Z	U	U	U	U	Z	R	D	Q	U	N	N
Burrito									S	S	Z	R	R	S	R	S	D	D	S	U	S	S	D	R	S	D	R	S	R	S
Cake										Z	Z	Z	N	Q	Z	Z	D	Z	Z	Z	Z	Z	Z	Z	Z	Z	Z	N	Z	N
Jellybeans											Z	Z	N	Q	Z	Z	D	Z	Z	Z	Z	Z	Z	Z	Z	Z	Q	Z	N	N
Chili												E	S	R	R	R	D	R	R	R	R	R	R	R	R	R	R	R	S	S
Cocktail													P	Q	P	N	D	Q	Q	Z	N	Z	N	D	Q	D	N	P	S	N
Coffee														P	Q	Q	D	Q	S	U	Z	S	Z	Q	Q	Q	Q	Q	S	N
Ketchup / Mustard															S	S	S	S	Z	Z	U	U	Z	U	S	U	S	U	N	U
Cookies																U	D	Q	Z	Q	Z	U	N	Z	U	U	Q	Z	N	N
Cooking Oil																	S	D	Z	Z	Z	S	D	U	D	D	D	D	D	D
Coffee Creamer																		Q	Q	D	U	U	U	Q	P	U	Q	U	Q	Q
Donuts																			S	S	S	N	Z	Z	Q	Z	Q	N	U	N
Fish																				Z	U	Z	N	E	U	D	S	N	Z	N
Fries																					S	U	N	S	Z	S	U	N	U	N
Hamburger																						U	N	P	U	S	S	N	U	N
Large Soda																							S	N	R	Q	U	Q	Z	N
Lobster																								E	S	D	U	D	N	N
Hot Dog																									U	S	S	N	S	N
Ice Cream																										S	P	Q	Q	N
Onion Ring																											S	N	Z	N
Orange Juice																												N	R	E
Mayonnaise																													Z	Z
Melon																														E
Milk																														
Pasta																														
Pie																														
Pineapple																														
Pizza																														
Steak																														
Snack																														
Sushi																														
Taco																														
Vodka																														
Whiskey																														
Wine																														
Spoiled Bacon																														
Spoiled BBQ Chicken																														
Spoiled BBQ Ribs																														
Spoiled Fish																														
Spoiled Lobster																														
Spoiled Hamburger																														
Spoiled Hot Dog																														
Spoiled Steak																														
Spoiled Sushi																														
Energizer Juice																														
Nectar Juice																														
Quick Step Juice																														
Randomizer Juice																														
Spitfire Juice																														
Untouchable Juice																														
Zombait Juice																														
Pain Killer Juice																														
Repulse Juice																														

	LEGEND
E	Energizer
R	Repulse
P	Pain Killer
Z	Zombait
U	Untouchable
S	Spitfire
N	Nectar
Q	Quick Step
D	Randomizer

APPENDIX

Randomizer: Randomly grants another drink's ability, or just makes Chuck sick.

Repulse: Zombies are not attracted to Chuck at all.

Spitfire: Turns Chuck's spit into a fireball (to spit, hold the Aim trigger and attack with no weapon equipped).

Untouchable: Zombies cannot grab Chuck.

Zombait: Zombies are attracted to Chuck (not good!).

The following chart tells you what sorts of juice drinks you'll make by combining various food items in blenders. Use juice drinks as often as possible to gain an advantage.

	Milk	Pasta	Pie	Pineapple	Pizza	Steak	Snack	Sushi	Taco	Vodka	Whiskey	Wine	Spoiled Bacon	Spoiled BBQ Chicken	Spoiled BBQ Ribs	Spoiled Fish	Spoiled Lobster	Spoiled Hamburger	Spoiled Hot Dog	Spoiled Steak	Spoiled Sushi	Energizer Juice	Nectar Juice	Quick Step Juice	Randomizer Juice	Spitfire Juice	Untouchable Juice	Zombait Juice	Pain Killer Juice	Repulse Juice
Apple	N	U	U	E	Z	U	N	N	Z	N	E	Q	D	D	D	D	D	D	D	D	D	S	N	N	S	N	N	D	E	R
Bacon	U	Z	Q	N	U	D	U	U	R	D	D	Q	D	D	D	D	D	D	D	D	D	E	N	Q	D	S	U	Z	P	R
Baked Potato	U	Z	Q	E	U	D	U	U	R	P	D	Q	D	D	D	D	D	D	D	D	D	E	N	Q	D	S	U	Z	P	R
BBQ Chicken	U	Z	Q	E	U	D	U	U	R	R	P	D	D	D	D	D	D	D	D	D	D	E	N	Q	D	S	U	Z	P	R
BBQ Ribs	D	Z	Q	E	U	D	U	U	R	R	D	Q	D	D	D	D	D	D	D	D	D	E	N	Q	D	S	U	Z	P	R
Beans	R	Z	U	R	Z	Z	Z	Z	D	U	R	R	D	D	D	D	D	D	D	D	D	E	N	Q	D	S	U	Z	P	R
Beer	D	U	N	N	E	E	Z	Q	S	D	N	N	D	D	D	D	D	D	D	D	D	E	N	Q	D	S	U	Z	P	R
Brownie	Z	Z	Z	Z	Z	Z	Z	Z	Z	D	N	N	D	D	D	D	D	D	D	D	D	E	N	Q	D	S	U	Z	P	R
Burrito	R	S	Z	S	S	S	S	S	S	R	R	Q	D	D	D	D	D	D	D	D	D	E	N	Q	D	S	U	Z	P	R
Cake	Z	Z	Z	Z	D	Z	Z	Z	N	N	N	Q	D	D	D	D	D	D	D	D	D	E	N	Q	D	S	U	Z	P	R
Jellybeans	Q	U	N	E	S	S	Z	Z	S	P	P	Q	D	D	D	D	D	D	D	D	D	E	N	Q	D	S	U	Z	P	R
Chili	U	R	R	E	R	R	R	R	R	S	S	Q	D	D	D	D	D	D	D	D	D	E	N	Q	D	S	U	Z	P	R
Cocktail	Q	Z	Q	N	S	U	N	U	S	P	P	Q	D	D	D	D	D	D	D	D	D	E	N	Q	D	S	U	Z	P	R
Coffee	Q	S	Z	E	Q	U	S	S	S	P	P	Q	D	D	D	D	D	D	D	D	D	E	N	Q	D	S	U	Z	P	R
Ketchup / Mustard	Z	S	S	N	Z	U	S	Z	S	P	P	Q	D	D	D	D	D	D	D	D	D	D	U	S	U	S	S	S	S	Z
Cookies	Q	Z	Z	E	Z	Q	Z	S	S	N	S	Q	D	D	D	D	D	D	D	D	D	E	N	Q	D	S	U	Z	P	R
Cooking Oil	D	D	D	D	D	U	P	U	R	D	D	Q	D	D	D	D	D	D	D	D	D	D	U	S	U	S	S	S	S	Z
Coffee Creamer	Q	Z	Z	Q	D	D	Q	S	S	S	P	Q	D	D	D	D	D	D	D	D	D	E	N	Q	D	S	U	Z	P	R
Donuts	Q	Q	Q	E	Q	Q	Z	U	U	U	U	Q	D	D	D	D	D	D	D	D	D	E	N	Q	D	S	U	Z	P	R
Fish	D	U	S	E	U	U	Z	S	S	P	S	Q	D	D	D	D	D	D	D	D	D	Z	U	Z	E	D	E	Z	Z	R
Fries	U	U	U	E	U	U	U	S	S	S	U	Q	D	D	D	D	D	D	D	D	D	E	N	Q	D	S	U	Z	P	R
Hamburger	U	U	U	E	E	E	U	E	E	E	U	Q	D	D	D	D	D	D	D	D	D	E	N	Q	D	S	U	Z	P	R
Large Soda	Q	Z	Z	E	U	U	U	U	U	P	P	Q	D	D	D	D	D	D	D	D	D	E	N	Q	D	S	U	Z	P	R
Lobster	D	E	Z	E	E	E	U	E	E	E	S	Q	D	D	D	D	D	D	D	D	D	E	N	Q	D	S	U	Z	P	R
Hot Dog	S	S	S	E	S	S	U	S	S	S	S	Q	D	D	D	D	D	D	D	D	D	E	N	Q	D	S	U	Z	P	R
Ice Cream	Q	Q	Q	E	Q	Q	D	D	D	Q	D	S	D	D	D	D	D	D	D	D	D	E	N	Q	D	S	U	Z	P	R
Onion Ring	U	U	U	E	U	U	U	E	U	U	S	Q	D	D	D	D	D	D	D	D	D	E	N	Q	D	S	U	Z	P	R
Orange Juice	N	U	U	N	Z	Z	N	Z	U	E	N	Q	D	D	D	D	D	D	D	D	D	S	N	N	N	N	N	D	R	E
Mayonnaise	Q	U	U	Z	U	S	U	R	U	S	U	Q	D	D	D	D	D	D	D	D	D	E	Z	Q	D	S	U	Z	P	R
Melon	N	N	N	N	N	N	E	N	P	P	Q	Q	D	D	D	D	D	D	D	D	D	E	N	Q	D	S	U	Z	P	R
Milk	Q	U	Z	E	D	D	Q	D	D	N	D	Q	D	D	D	D	D	D	D	D	D	Q	Q	Q	D	Q	Q	Q	Q	Q
Pasta		N	D	E	E	E	Z	E	E	E	E	Q	D	D	D	D	D	D	D	D	D	E	N	Q	D	S	U	Z	P	R
Pie			U	E	Z	S	Z	U	U	U	U	Q	D	D	D	D	D	D	D	D	D	E	U	U	Z	Z	U	D	R	R
Pineapple				E	N	U	N	N	S	E	N	Q	D	D	D	D	D	D	D	D	D	E	N	Q	D	S	U	Z	P	R
Pizza					Z	Z	Z	U	U	U	U	Q	D	D	D	D	D	D	D	D	D	E	N	Q	D	S	U	Z	P	R
Steak						U	U	U	U	U	U	Q	D	D	D	D	D	D	D	D	D	E	U	U	Z	Z	U	D	R	R
Snack							S	U	U	S	S	Q	D	D	D	D	D	D	D	D	D	E	N	Q	D	S	U	Z	P	R
Sushi								U	U	U	Z	Q	D	D	D	D	D	D	D	D	D	Z	U	Z	E	D	E	Z	Z	R
Taco									N	R	R	Q	D	D	D	D	D	D	D	D	D	E	N	Q	D	S	U	Z	P	R
Vodka										P	D	D	D	D	D	D	D	D	D	D	D	E	N	Q	D	S	U	Z	P	R
Whiskey											P	D	D	D	D	D	D	D	D	D	D	E	N	Q	D	S	U	Z	P	R
Wine												Q	D	D	D	D	D	D	D	D	D	Q	Q	Q	D	Q	Q	Q	Q	Q
Spoiled Bacon													D	D	D	D	D	D	D	D	D	D	D	D	D	D	D	D	D	D
Spoiled BBQ Chicken														D	D	D	D	D	D	D	D	D	D	D	D	D	D	D	D	D
Spoiled BBQ Ribs															D	D	D	D	D	D	D	D	D	D	D	D	D	D	D	D
Spoiled Fish																D	D	D	D	D	D	D	D	D	D	D	D	D	D	D
Spoiled Lobster																	D	D	D	D	D	D	D	D	D	D	D	D	D	D
Spoiled Hamburger																		D	D	D	D	D	D	D	D	D	D	D	D	D
Spoiled Hot Dog																			D	D	D	D	D	D	D	D	D	D	D	D
Spoiled Steak																				D	D	D	D	D	D	D	D	D	D	D
Spoiled Sushi																					D	D	D	D	D	D	D	D	D	D
Energizer Juice																						E	S	E	N	Z	U	N	R	P
Nectar Juice																							N	Q	S	E	S	N	E	R
Quick Step Juice																								Q	D	S	U	Z	Z	R
Randomizer Juice																									Q	U	Z	E	S	D
Spitfire Juice																										S	S	Z	R	R
Untouchable Juice																											U	U	P	R
Zombait Juice																												Z	P	R
Pain Killer Juice																													P	P
Repulse Juice																														R

PRIMA GAMES
AN IMPRINT OF RANDOM HOUSE, INC.
3000 LAVA RIDGE COURT, SUITE 100
ROSEVILLE, CA 95661

WWW.PRIMAGAMES.COM

DEADRISING 2

WRITTEN BY:
STEPHEN STRATTON

PRIMA OFFICIAL
GAME GUIDE

Product Marketing Manager: Todd Manning
Design: In Color Design
Layout: In Color Design
Copyedit: Sara Wilson
Manufacturing: Stephanie Sanchez & Suzanne Goodwin

Stephen Stratton has authored over 40 guides in his seven years with Prima. His personal favorites include *Lost Planet 2, Resident Evil 4: Wii Edition, Mercenaries: Playground of Destruction, Mass Effect*, and pretty much every guide he's written that has either "Mario" or "Zelda" in its title.

Steve is a lifelong video gamer who attended the Rochester Institute of Technology in Rochester, NY. In addition to his Prima Games guides, he also held a staff position with Computec Media and managed the strategy section of their incite.com video game website.

We want to hear from you! E-mail comments and feedback to **sstratton@primagames.com**.

ISBN: 978-0-307-46734-8
Library of Congress Catalog Card Number: 2010913192
Printed in the United States of America

10 11 12 13 LL 10 9 8 7 6 5 4 3 2 1